WANNABE
A WRITER?

JANE WENHAM-JONES

ACCENT PRESS LTD

Published by Accent Press Ltd – 2007

ISBN 1905170815 / 9781905170814

Printed and bound in the UK

Cover Design by Compound Eye
Cover Photo: Bill Harris L.R.P.S.

With thanks to the family gene pool and in memory of Miss Dorothy Morris – the sort of primary-school teacher who understood the concept of being so engrossed in a book that one missed maths.

ACKNOWLEDGEMENTS

I will not even attempt to list everyone who helped with this book but I am hugely grateful to each author, agent, publisher, journalist and all the other contributors who appear in it and so generously shared their wisdom. Thank you very much indeed; I couldn't have done it without you – literally. Others too, who may not make the index, deserve a mention. Thank you to my sister Judith for life-saving admin help when time was running short and my mother, Felicity, for checking my commas when I could no longer see straight. Also Catherine Merriman, Bill Harris and Julia Goddard for their expertise; and everyone on the 'mewriters' email list for their friendship and support and providing such great displacement activity. My thanks to Teresa Chris for her shopping know-how (!) and everyone at Accent Press - especially Hazel, for her enthusiasm, and Bob, who deals so calmly with my neuroses. Finally, and in the hope of covering all bases, my apologies to whoever I've forgotten, and my love and appreciation to my family and all that keeps me sane: wonderful friends, the cast of *Eastenders* and any vineyard producing Macon Blanc Villages. Thank you.

FOREWORD

People often say you can't teach people to write. Maybe you can't. But you can teach them the craft and business of writing. There are so many easily-avoided pitfalls which I wish I'd known about when I started out. (My first attempt at a Mills and Boon didn't have the hero enter until chapter three – the beginning of chapter three, but still two chapters too late!)

I don't regret the years spent learning my craft (there were rather a lot of them) but I don't think I'd have taken quite so long to write a publishable novel if I'd had this book to hand! And it would have helped with all the work after acceptance, too. There's so much to learn about editing, copy editing, proof reading, publicity – things you never thought you'd have to master, embarking on a solitary profession like writing. This book is the best friend you could have to support you through the ordeal. With its wealth of distinguished contributors, *Wannabe a Writer?* is like having lots of best-selling writers at your side to keep you at it when the going gets hard. It doesn't actually provide you with their mobile numbers, but you do get their accumulated wisdom in an easily digested form.

Wannabe a Writer? is light-hearted, fun, tremendously informative, and a really good present for yourself (if you Wannabe a Writer), your friend, your partner or your mother – even if they don't want to write, but just want to be entertained and informed. I wish it had been on the shelves when I started out.

Katie Fforde

CONTENTS

...I'LL FINISH

NOVELS ARE NOT THE ONLY FRUIT

INTRODUCTION

I have heard many authors tell the story – with varying degrees of truth or accuracy – of how they first got into print. I have listened as certain of them have stood up in a room of writers, all of whom desperately want to be published, and have made it sound as though, when they very first tried their hand at the writing game, it all fell into their laps.

Typically, they woke up one morning with this little idea that they might write a novel. So they dashed one off over the course of a few rainy weekends, found an agent on the Monday, were in a frenzied auction with ten top publishers by the Tuesday and banked their six- figure cheque on Friday just before they flew off to the States to discuss the screen-play.

They seem touchingly bewildered by their overnight success.

But not as bewildered as I am when I have known for a fact that the author in question had written three previous novels before the one that made it and had burst into tears at the Writers' Circle Christmas Party when the twenty-seventh agent had written to suggest she stuck to crossword puzzles instead.

I have looked at the audience at these talks, their faces crossed with a mixture of envy and despair, and thought how unfair it seems.

I vowed, when I was a much-rejected wannabe, that when I was published I would tell the truth about how long it took and how difficult it was.

Nobody fought over my manuscript. Rather, they unplugged their phones, switched email addresses, took long sabbaticals on the other side of the world and instructed their assistants to tell me they'd died of a rare and sudden tropical disease.

My file marked "AGENTS – those who've said sod off" bulged and broke its seams. Publishers cowed from my offers of sexual favours, and remained unmoved when I chained myself to their railings.

I wept, wailed, got horribly drunk and spent £156.98 on postage. I did strange spells, took up chanting, consulted psychics, threatened to hang myself from the shower-rail if I didn't get a book-deal and took to stalking.

What I didn't do was give up. I was determined to get that novel published, even if it meant rolling up to my launch party with no teeth and a colostomy bag. I think we can safely say I was obsessed.

And published it was. I did sell my book in the end, on a gloriously ecstatic, champagne-soaked day in August 2000 but it was by a long, circuitous and torturous route.

I kept going because after all the joy, elation, tears and liver damage I'd suffered writing an entire manuscript – don't believe anyone who says it's easy – I didn't want it wasted. Many have seen this attitude as a strength but it is also one of my failings. Sometimes you do have to waste things. As a writer you need a built-in crap-o-meter and an iron nerve to discard all the stuff that doesn't work.

But first and foremost you need determination. If faint heart never won fair lady it certainly didn't get a book deal either. If you, too, are on the point of cutting your throat because nobody wants to publish you, hold off until you've read this book. It might change your life.

Or if you've always wanted to write, but have never quite got round to it, this could be just the spur you need.

And if you've no interest in writing at all and have only read this far because it's raining outside the bookshop and you've got twenty minutes to kill before the bus comes, don't be such a skinflint.

Buy it anyway and give it to someone for Christmas.

I could do with the sales.

IN THE BEGINNING…

Becoming a Writer Part One

How it was for me…

The other things writers always tell you is that they could read before they could walk and spent their childhoods devouring the classics, scribbling out sagas, playing libraries and flogging their own hand-printed literary magazine to the neighbours.

The author Daniel Blythe says: "I don't believe you become a writer – you simply ARE one." He spent his formative years "writing sci-fi epics with a blunt pencil in spare exercise books" and his teenage ones sitting at a typewriter instead of drinking or chasing girls. Do not worry if you weren't as strange as this. I wasn't either.

I didn't hanker to be a writer. When I was seven I wanted to be a show-jumper. In my teens I fancied being an actress and for a brief period in my twenties I toyed with the vision of being Business Woman of the Year with a large desk, two telephones and a young male secretary I could send out on errands of a personal nature.

But mostly I didn't want to be anything very much and by the time I was twenty-five, my main regret was that I hadn't been born with a private income so I could stay in bed all day. This may make me rather odd after all, as I come from A Writing Family.

Back in the Dark Ages, my father wrote textbooks, such as *English with Animals* and the imaginatively-titled sequel: *More English with Animals*, together with my Uncle John who has published books of poetry about dogs (not the most poetic creatures on the planet) and who is an expert on palindromes and the author of a book called *Lid off a Daffodil* – which is one, in case you hadn't noticed. His daughter, my cousin Helen, is a journalist.

On my mother's side, my aunt Shelagh has published three children's novels, one of which won the Whitbread Children's Book of the Year award back in 1977. Her brother, Uncle Peter, has written books on everything from How to Love Your Horse to the History of Assassins, my other Uncle John (there are three of them) is another poet, as is my mother, who has popped up in antholgies and published several collections of Haiku.

Even bad old Grandad Frank had his memoir *I Remember the Tall Ships* (Seafarer Books) published when he was in his eighties (Foyles put on a very nice window display). I wasn't that interested in sea-faring tales at the time but I heard one of the Uncles John say that the rude bits were on page 94 so I just read those (very tame).

So writing was always seen as A Good Thing, and I did think that it might be a nice thing to do – write a book one day – and I carried on thinking this for three decades but only in the way you think it might be nice to go on a really strict diet and end up being the envy of all your friends by weighing 7 ½ stone. I didn't believe I ever actually would or could.

I'd quite liked writing stories at school (it beat the hell out of maths) and I did once make a tiny replica of *Jackie* magazine in the days when agony aunts Cathy and Claire gave advice on things like blushing, and how to persuade your mum to give you more pocket money, instead of how to pull Darren in year eleven and whether or not, now you're twelve, you should get your nipples pierced, but that was more to do with my fascination for all things miniature (something I grew out of once I'd discovered wine glasses and men) than a burning desire to publish the written word.

Reading was much easier and was A Very Good Thing so nobody minded if you spent the whole day curled up in a chair with a book, which I frequently did.

I will now also disappoint you with my choice of reading matter. Enid Blyton was my staple diet, especially the *Mysteries* series and *The Famous Five*. From the one I developed a longing for my own shed in which I could solve crimes and from the other I began to share George's longing to be a boy.

In fact, and I've never told anyone this before but I'm sure it's good for me (see later chapter on Writing as Therapy), I so wanted to emulate George and convince the world of the seriousness of my intent that I fashioned a small penis out of pink plasticine and attempted to attach it to my stomach (I had two sisters and was a bit vague on anatomy).

These days I would be taken for counselling over such gender issues but back then my mother just smiled indulgently and my older sister informed me scornfully that I certainly wouldn't want to be a boy when I grew up (I am still waiting for this happy state of affairs to arrive) because all boys were smelly and vile.

She was quite right in that I've never wished to be male since, except occasionally when wishing to pee outdoors without the entire world seeing my bottom.

The shed never materialised either – ours was full of cobwebs, hairy spiders and rusting tools. I asked my father if he could clear it out to allow me to keep my disguises there together with a tin of biscuits and possibly a dog. He said no.

What he did do was bring home a tape-recorder and suggest that I write an adventure story of my own by dictating it into the microphone and we could worry about typing it up later. This seemed a good plan.

It was to be about a girl called Lucy who was a gypsy and lived in a caravan and met a man with a bullet embedded in his head. But I got as far as describing Lucy sitting on her caravan steps, twiddling with her gold hoop earrings and feeling bored, and got bored myself.

Later, I wrote excruciating teenage poetry about death and suicide and the futility of life and sometimes I wrote a few words that might have made a good first paragraph of something if I'd ever got around to finishing it which I never did.

Later still, after my parents had separated and the whole family were being more than usually bonkers, I wrote a series of short vignettes for my sisters, parodying everyone's worst excesses of dysfunctional behaviour which, gratifyingly, made them laugh, which was a welcome change from all the weeping and wailing that was going on at the time.

But I didn't have the discipline for anything more. I managed to pass a couple of A levels (despite spending most of my sixth form years asleep) and get a place at university to read English. I asked them to hold it open for 12 months (I wasn't an early pioneer of the gap year – I was just bone idle) but by the time I was due to go, I had a flat and a dodgy boyfriend and a job teaching English to bored-looking Germans and that was that.

I spent the next decade or so doing this and a whole heap of other jobs from marketing to promotions to running a couple of small businesses (I did get the two telephones but could never afford the male secretary) and back to teaching again when the last of these entrepreneurial endeavours ground to a halt in the recession. It was hardly what you'd call a career.

I also spent two years copywriting for a tiny advertising agency, creating

5

video-scripts for a company that made wallpaper, writing radio voice-overs for a local taxi company and producing acres of unexciting brochure copy. But I was no nearer coming up with anything that anyone would ever want to publish except for a few newspaper ads for double-glazing.

And then I got married and had a baby (I'll spare you the details of the birth – I'm sure you've already got one of those friends who likes to describe her 18 hours of labour and being stitched from ear to ear) and spent months wandering around in sick-stained tracksuit bottoms and a daze and apart from scrawling "Whose stupid idea was this anyway?" on the wall above my husband's snoring head after my nineteenth night of no sleep, writing was never further from my mind.

Until one day, when my brain cells had all but totally atrophied, Shelagh – she was the aunt who won the Whitbread prize for her children's book (do try and keep up!) – sent me a short story competition entry form she'd picked up in a bookshop.

It was the eponymous Ian St James award, then one of the major writing competitions around, offering the lucky winner publication in an anthology and a substantial cash prize.

Ready by now to think about something other than poo textures, I sat down and wrote my first, whole, short story. It was about a woman who couldn't have any children because she'd had to have a hysterectomy (Sigmund Freud – eat your heart out) and was absolutely diabolical.

It eventually got published in a small press magazine that had about six subscribers and one of them wrote in and said it was the worst thing she'd ever read. I entered it for the Ian St James Awards. It didn't win.

But what it did do was introduce me to the whole new world of the Wannabe Writer. Inside the entry form was an advert for a magazine called *Acclaim* published by one Merric Davidson (very sexy telephone voice – more of him later) and I decided to subscribe.

I found *Acclaim* listed other writing competitions – quite a few of them – and also carried an advert for a new small press magazine called Quality *Women's Fiction* (QWF) which was calling for "stories with strong female characters who approach life with honesty and forthrightness" and claimed to have a "particular penchant for humorous stories". They were running a competition, too. So I entered that as well.

By now I had a repertoire of five stories, written in snatched moments when my small son was asleep – which wasn't often.

I sent all of them to the *Real Writers* Competition – another of the bigger and more respected contests of the time – and one of them, *In Sickness* – a jolly little tale of throwing up on one's wedding night – made some sort of long list. Almost at the same time, I heard it was one of several "runners-up" in the QWF competition.

Carried away by this small smidgeon of success I signed up for regular appraisals from *Real Writers* and Lynne Patrick, who runs the joint, looked at other pieces of work, offered advice and gave me immense encouragement.

One day, after suggesting a few small changes to a story I'd sent her, she casually remarked that it was the sort of thing that the women's magazine, *My Weekly*, published and gave me the name of Liz Smith, the fiction editor, saying that it might be worth popping my story in an envelope and sending it to her. I was surprised and flattered but did not hold my breath.

Three months later, Liz wrote to say she'd loved my story and they'd buy it – a moment of such pure joy and excitement that I knew I had to do it again soon.

Which was a good move, as four years elapsed between getting the letter and the story appearing in the magazine (TIP ONE : always get drunk when you get the acceptance – if you wait till you see something in print, your liver could have given out).

That first sale was in December 1995. In the next three years I wrote many more stories for women's magazines, eventually being published by pretty much all of them. I also wrote stuff not suitable for the magazines for the small press, and had various pieces published in competition anthologies. I went on some writing weekends, began to meet other writers and started to fantasise about writing a novel.

I had a vague idea of what it would be about – a woman and the buy-to-let market (as well as writing, I had bought an old dilapidated house with a builder friend with the idea of converting it into flats and renting it out – a steep learning curve!).

But a whole book still seemed too huge a project to undertake. I would open the "novel" file on my computer, write a paragraph, re-read it, think "that's crap", close the file again and start another short story. A week later, I would open the file once more, add another two paragraphs, conclude that these had made it even worse and close it down.

This went on for about a year until I had five thousand words. They were total drivel and I had no idea where the other 85,000 were going to come from. And that's how it might have stayed had I not opened *The Times* newspaper one morning early in 1998 and read about Wendy Holden.

Wendy was a journalist who'd just got a six-figure deal on her first novel *Simply Divine* (Headline). She'd written a diary piece for *The Times* charting her progress from writing the opening chapters, to landing a top agent, to bashing out the rest of the novel early in the mornings before she went off to work. She relayed the thrill of the auction and the gathering momentum as big publishing houses wooed her with offers attached to bottles of Krug.

Thoroughly over-excited by this and overlooking the fact that Wendy had several things I didn't have, e.g. a great idea, a great marketing hook and great writing ability, I sat down at my computer on a great wave of naïvety, truly believing that if only I could churn out another twenty-seven chapters the same thing would happen to me. Ha, ha, ha.

I wrote like mad, carrying a laptop around with me wherever I went, and finished the first draft of my novel in October 1998. I then spent the whole of 1999 getting it rejected by what felt like every agent in London.

Looking back now, I don't know how I could ever have expected instant success. The fact is that writing is like anything else: music, or painting, dancing or sport – you start off not that good and then you keep practising and you get better.

There are always exceptions and some writers really do hit first-time lucky, but if you look down the best-seller lists you will always find others who really struggled to make it.

Novelist Sophie King (the journalist Jane Bidder) had eleven novels rejected before *The School Run* (Hodder) became a hit. Even the amazing Joanna Trollope was quoted in the *Independent* in 1999 as saying: "It's taken me 20 years to be an overnight success."

And even when you have been published, it's not all a fairy tale. There are days when the muse descends, the words flow and you read them back and take a smug pleasure in your erudite pronouncements and unique brand of wit and feel thoroughly delighted with yourself and think how damn lucky you are to be paid for something that you enjoy so much (if you are being paid, which isn't always a foregone conclusion) and days when frankly you feel it would be easier to pull your own teeth or be put in charge of making John Prescott look sexy.

In short, writing is a funny old business. Nothing else has ever given me such extreme joy or left me in deeper despair but I cannot now imagine doing anything else. How about you?

Becoming a Writer Part Two

Could it be for you?

People become writers for all sorts of reasons. For some, as we've discussed, it has been a burning ambition since infancy. Others fell into it. Jeffrey Archer famously relates that he decided to try to write a book because he'd lost his job and needed to make some money (though it's a mistake to imagine that the one always leads to the other) and struck gold with *Not A Penny More, Not A Penny Less* (Pan).

Novelist Mil Millington was wooed by publishers who loved his website. "Sickening, isn't it?" he says. (Yes, frankly it is!)

Frederick Forsyth says his becoming a novelist was "a fluke". Back from two years in the war in Biafra in December 1969 he too had no money and thought he "might make a few quid with a one-off novel, then go back to journalism". (Obviously Messrs Forsyth and Archer achieved their aims – deservedly so – but if you are only after the money it is probably a safer bet to rob a bank.)

Carole Matthews says she writes because "I'm a complete control freak and love the thought of shaping my own worlds", while Claire Calman, who gets my personal best-title-ever award for her first novel *Love is a Four-Letter Word* (Black Swan) declares in the front of that lovely volume that she decided to write a book when she discovered that it mainly involved drinking coffee and looking out of the window.

Freya North ditched her PhD and sat down to write a book because she couldn't find the sort of book she wanted to read in any of the bookshops.

But most writers would not really be able to pinpoint where the urge came from. "Never for a moment have I wanted to do anything else," says Sarah Harrison. "Writing isn't just how I earn my living, it's what I am, my identity."

Many describe it in terms of a compulsion they have no control over.

If you don't feel like this it may not be too late to take this book back and change it for one on keeping goldfish. Because it's hard enough even when you are driven; it's going to be a non-starter if you'd just as soon paint the spare room.

The good news, however, about being a Writer is it requires no special qualifications and Writers come in all shapes and sizes.

Some appear to be prosperous, respectable, pillars of the community; others look like they live in a cardboard box and are assumed, quite frankly, to be barking.

It would be a generalisation to say that most writers are slightly unhinged, but certainly it is one of those professions where dubious mental health, eccentricity and peculiarities of habit need not be a barrier.

As always, it helps if you are gorgeous, thin, rich and famous but it's not essential. The short, fat and ugly have made it to the top as well.

The only thing you can't do without is a real longing to write and the determination to find the time to keep doing it.

Other things are useful:

- A private income or rich partner (don't think you'll be the next JK Rowling – you won't)
- Children that like to watch videos – on their own – for hours on end
- Hang-over cures
- Tissues
- Chocolate
- A computer with a printer
- Pens and notebooks
- A copy of *The Writer's Handbook* or *Writers' and Artists' Year Book*
- A good imagination
- A ruthless streak
- An ability to spend hours staring into space, muttering to yourself
- A sense of optimism of the bottle-being-half-full variety
- A bottle that is at least half full.

You do not need:

- Any notion of having a "proper job"
- A desire to work regular hours
- A faint heart.

It also helps if you have an idea for a book.

So You Think You've Got a Book in You?

Everyone has a book in them. This is a myth put about by taxi drivers who invariably think their own life story would make the greatest best-seller of them all. It wouldn't. And even if one does have the sort of exciting and chequered past that would make a hair-raising piece of fiction, one is not necessarily equipped with the talent to write it.

It is a strange thing that few people assume, in the absence of any evidence to the contrary, that they can paint pictures worthy of the Royal Academy, sing like Pavarotti or play the guitar like Segovia.

Yet all sorts of otherwise sensible beings imagine that if they only had the time they could knock out 90,000 words that would get snapped up by the publishing world and then fallen upon by a grateful public.

Writing a decent short story is hard enough. Writing a book can be excruciating. There are those who are fond of making comparisons between writing a book and giving birth. The analogy is supposed to centre around the nine months and the pushing and the wonder of creation at the end of it.

For me, it is the fact that you forget the sheer agony and the fact that you longed to castrate your husband with the forceps, and actually start to believe it didn't hurt that much and it would be a jolly idea to do it again.

And when you do, second time around is even worse. It never gets any easier. It is a terrible, all-consuming, neurosis-inducing way to earn a living.

On the other hand it has its advantages. You can turn up to collect your child from school still wearing your pyjamas and slippers and other parents will only whisper "She's a writer, you know," instead of thinking you're being taken care of in the community.

You can ask all sorts of personal questions and friends will be flattered to think you are using them for research instead of getting pissed off at how nosey you are.

And you can stare out of the window for hours on end with a strange expression on your face and a glass in your hand and pretend you're working.

Earning money, after all, isn't everything (if you think any differently, don't try to be a writer). But before you start, are you the right personality-type to attempt to write a book? Try this quiz and see:

Quiz: Have You Got What it Takes to Write it?

1. Overall, how would you describe yourself?

a) You are a healthy outdoorsy type who believes in fresh air, plenty of exercise, eight hours sleep and three square meals a day. (0 points)
b) You love *Eastenders* and The *X-Factor*, animals and small children. You are interested in others and think the secret of a happy life is a matter of give and take. (5 points)
c) You are quite capable of spending sixteen hours slumped in the same position at your desk while chain-smoking. (15 points)

2. On your desk is:

a) A notepad, a pen, a ruler, a bottle of mineral water and a small potted cactus. (0 points)
b) All the above plus some unpaid bills, a pile of letters you really must answer soon and several Post-it notes with telephone numbers on them from people you're going to call back. (5 points)
c) Books, more books, an overflowing ashtray, an empty wine bottle, a packet of nurofen, five highlighter pens, several lists, a telephone directory, last night's pizza crust and an article you cut out of Sunday's paper about venereal disease. Also cat hairs, lipstick, batteries, dictaphone, camera, four notebooks, tippex, condoms and a two foot pile of paper that you haven't got to the bottom of since 1986. (20 points)

3. You are in the High Street when an old lady is knocked over by a bicycle.

Do you:
a) Call 999 from your mobile, cover her with your jacket and begin mouth-to-mouth resuscitation. (0 points)
b) Scream loudly, wave your arms to attract attention and carry out a citizen's arrest on the cyclist until the police arrive. (1 point)
c) Borrow an onlooker's camera-phone to photograph the scene, make a quick diagram of the blood stains on the back of a fag packet and start interviewing the bike rider: this could be very good background info for chapter twenty-seven… (25 points)

4. When you were at school were you:

a) The class bookworm, editor of the school magazine and winner of the English prize three years running? (10 points)
b) Often in trouble for talking in class, caught smoking behind the bike sheds and eventually expelled for having a torrid affair with the French teacher? (15 points)
c) You didn't go to school much. You lived in crushing poverty with ten siblings and only attended lessons every second Thursday when it was your turn to wear the only pair of shoes. (30 points)

5. What is your favourite daydream?

a) You win the lottery, give up work and while away your days sipping champagne on the white sands of the Bahamas. (0 points)
b) You lose three stone, have a face-lift and get swept off your feet by (depending on sexual preference) a gorgeous romantic, muscle-bound hunk or a huge-breasted blonde of twenty-one who wants you to be her sex slave. (5 points)
c) You are sitting on the sofa with Richard & Judy after making your acceptance speech for the Booker prize. (20 points)

6. What is your general philosophy on Diet?

a) Even if it is just you, you eat at set times and cook a proper meal with fresh vegetables. (2 points)
b) You try to eat well but if you're really busy you'll have a quick sandwich at your desk. Cooking is so time-consuming. (10 points)
c) If you realise you've had nothing but chocolate, crisps and cans of cider for more than a week, you take a vitamin pill. (20 points)

7. How much exercise do you take?

a) A healthy body makes for a healthy mind. You go to the gym three times a week, play tennis, jog and wear a pedometer so you can check you've done your 10,000 steps a day. (3 points)
b) You walk the dog most mornings and do a bit of yoga when you remember. (10 points)

c) You are occasionally forced to sprint to the postbox on the corner at five-thirty so you can catch the last post. (You then have a lie-down.) (15 points)

8. How clean is your house?

a) Very clean. All it takes to keep on top of it is a quick run-round with the hoover and a damp duster before work each morning and a proper going-over at the weekends. (0 points)
b) You do the important bits – e.g. kitchens and bathrooms for hygiene reasons – but really can't be worrying about the rest of it until the dust begins to show. Life's short. You'd much rather read a book or write a letter. (5 points)
c) Nobody's died yet. (15 points)

9. You have an important report to write for work that your boss needs a week on Friday. Do you?

a) Sit straight down and do it all. Never put off till tomorrow what you can do today. (0 points)
b) Work an hour on it each day until it's finished. Build in a day for checking it over and making any minor alterations before giving it in. (15 points)
c) Think about it all the time, but leave any actual writing until Thursday at 9pm. Sit up all night to finish it, drinking double espresso and slapping yourself round the face to stay awake. (25 points)

10. What is your partner most likely to shout at you in a row?

a) You never listen! (5 points)
b) You never talk to me! (5 points)
c) We never go anywhere! (5 points)
   Or
d) All of these, plus reminders you that you are selfish, egocentric, bad-tempered, self-obsessed, given to scribbling notes at inopportune moments and making strange muttering noises, that you miss mealtimes, forget appointments, shout at the children when they want to use your computer and you haven't had a proper holiday for ten years. (40 points)

Now add up your score. Add 120 bonus points if you can say yes to any of the statements below:

– I am a famous celebrity.
– I am a famous footballer.
– I am a famous footballer's wife who weighs six stone.
– I have won *Big Brother*.
– I have not won *Big Brother* but I have been on the programme showing my enhanced breasts/sex-change scars/predilection for vibrating toys or displaying some sort of dysfunctional behaviour and then shagging the person who did win it, live on camera.
– I am an MP who's been in prison.

Conclusions

0–30 points – I would never be discouraging enough to say you cannot be a writer because it takes all sorts, but this choice of career may come as a bit of a shock. Have you thought about taking up embroidery, golf or train-spotting?

31–60 points – while you're still displaying worrying signs of normality, there are some flashes of potential here. At least you have a bit of life experience to write about.

61–200 points – you show definite promise and could develop well as a writer given the right circumstances and encouragement.

Over 200 points – you're probably a writer already. If not – get typing now!

Over 300 – you are probably in prison.

Having a Go

How, Why, When?

Still determined to have a go?

Let's start with the basics (those who've already been writing for some time may jump straight on to the chapter on Writer's Bottom – you probably need to). If you've never written before, you need first to decide on your method.

Personally, I have to use a computer. I can only write by typing straight onto the screen. I like to be in my writing room at home, on my main computer – though when deadlines loom I can manage on my laptop pretty much anywhere.

If I try to write in longhand, I get frustrated, start scribbling and usually can't read my handwriting afterwards. This is the main problem with the old chestnut – beloved of all How-to-Write books – of keeping a pen and paper next to your bed to record flashes of inspiration visited upon you in the night.

First you have to wake up sufficiently to make the notes (not easy after a bottle of Beaujolais and a large Scotch), and second, they need to make sense in the morning (ditto).

Other writers differ, of course. The best-selling novelist Jill Mansell writes all her novels in longhand and doesn't even divide them into chapters until the end. She says it saves time as she used to waste a lot of it thinking about how much of a chapter she had left to write and where they would start and finish. Now she writes one great continuous story and chops it all up at the end.

She can't type so someone else does that for her when she's finished. She uses a Harley Davidson fountain pen (and I thought they were motorbikes) and blue ink and writes on the right-hand side of A4 pads, leaving the left-hand side free for corrections.

The novelist and actress Barbara Ewing also likes to write with "a flowing pen" on lined paper. Frederick Forsyth uses an electronic typewriter and Tippex. I couldn't possibly do this as I change my sentences constantly as I go.

If you are rich, you could lie back on a chaise longue sipping champagne and dictate to a secretary. I don't know how anyone could work like this either – I take my hat off to the late Barbara Cartland.

I can manage the bubbly but whenever I try to dictate – even into a dictaphone with some marvellous idea I've had while driving, I falter and stumble, keep going "urm" and "argh" and talk rot. If I have the marvellous idea on the way home from the pub, I can't even understand it.

These days there is voice-recognition software of course, which wouldn't be any good for me – see above – but might be OK for you.

Different writers have different methods of organising work, too. I do divide my novels up into chapters as I go but I keep each novel in one huge Microsoft Word file.

It's easier then to scroll back and forth, use the "find" button to check if you've been repeating yourself or use "find and replace" when you suddenly realise you can't call the dreadful mother-in-law, Kitty, because that's the name of your awful aunt and she'll recognise straightaway where the evil old bag's eccentricities came from. It also means you can keep tabs on your total word-count, which I do obsessively.

Novelist Lynne Barrett-Lee keeps each chapter in a different file; Claire Calman sometimes writes it all in the wrong order and puts it together afterwards – please don't ask me how. All I can tell you is that miraculously, it works.

Bloody Computers

There is no doubt that writing on a computer is quickest and easiest and most suited to endless re-writes but if you're going to use one for your magnum opus then for God's sake BACK YOUR WORK UP.

I can't tell you how many computer crises I've had over the years (vastly diminished since I started going to a proper computer person to solve my problems and buy my software instead of using a crook who built his own dodgy machines and installed the pirated stuff) and how much work I've lost when the power supply has suddenly given out or a virus has started eating my hard drive.

It has never been easier to safeguard your work. Programmes like Microsoft Word have a built-in back-up facility and you can buy all sorts of dinky little memory sticks to copy your novel/article/story on to at the click of a button. You can then carry it around in your pocket or handbag, so should – sadly – your house burn down, or your laptop get stolen, you will still at least have your work-in-progress close to hand.

Jane Bidder (Sophie King) describes herself as "paranoid" about backing up onto floppies. She sends copies of any current manuscript to her children at university for safe-keeping and always sends one to her agent if she goes on holiday, in case something happens to her computer.

As it might well. Which is why having two computers is better than one, and keeping work on a second hard drive, or emailing anything precious to a friend to look after, is always a good idea.

It is one of Sod's many laws that just as the creative juices are really flowing or a deadline is looming, then that is the moment your screen will go blank, the machine will refuse to turn on or, as once happened to me, there will be a nasty burning smell and the motherboard will fizz and die.

Or you will do something stupid to it yourself. Such as:

Spilling Things

It is a scientific fact that the volume of liquid left in a receptacle is not in direct proportion to the amount that will spread all over your desk, soak every bit of paper in a five-metre radius and drip into anything electrical.

What appears as only a quarter of an inch of cold tea while still in the bottom of a cup can totally flood a room.

Try to train yourself out of leaving any sort of cup or glass anywhere near your keyboard especially if it contains red wine. This not only goes absolutely everywhere but your workspace will smell like a brewery for the next three weeks (not good with a hangover).

The worst thing you can do is knock it into your keyboard (I am an old hand at this). If it happens to you, speed is of the essence. Turn the keyboard straight over so that all excess liquid pours out over your lap or carpet, disconnect it, blot with kitchen paper and then use the hair-dryer vigorously backwards and forwards over the keys until it appears totally dry.

It still won't be, so then put the keyboard in the airing cupboard overnight. I have saved a couple of keyboards this way. I have also had to buy several new ones.

Everyone has their story to tell of losing work and deleting the wrong thing. Jane Bidder's anxiety stems from the time when her then three-year old turned the power off, in the days before computers backed up automatically, losing her a chapter and causing her to throw "a toddler tantrum" herself.

The children's writer Chris d'Lacey describes his worst writing moment ever as when five days before the deadline for his book, *Fire Star* (Orchard Books), he overwrote the complete updated manuscript with a much older draft.

For those who are already coming out in a sweat of sympathy I can reassure you that fortunately he had printed it out the night before – the one and only time he'd done so in ten months of writing.

This sort of thing may well happen to you but try not to get suicidal when things go wrong.

I remember the day that I was sitting in my writing room, crying with frustration and despair because my computer wouldn't work and I was so behind with my second novel, which was due to be delivered imminently.

And then the news came on. It was September 11th 2001. It sort of put things in perspective.

A Room of One's Own

Where you do it?

Again, opinions vary. The novelist Sarah Duncan has a perfectly nice study but likes to write in bed. I remember Claire Calman telling me that she couldn't get into her study for all the unfiled paper, so she wrote in the kitchen. Jane Bidder favours her dining room, Jilly Cooper sometimes writes in a gazebo at the bottom of her garden. Freya North takes her laptop to the library. Some writers, famously, go to cafes.

Personally I'm with Virginia Woolf. If you want to write, you really do need a room of your own. I understand this isn't always possible and indeed there was a time when we had just the one work space in our house.

It was a room downstairs we call 'the office'. I was allowed one small end – just enough for my computer and a pile of about six books – while my husband spread himself over the remainder. We had two regular and enduring arguments which we were both quite capable of keeping up for days, the thrust of which was:

1) (mine) How was I expected to write to the sound of him sniffing/shuffling/sighing? and
2) (his) Whose fault it was the room was always untidy?

It wasn't just the need to irrefutably prove my point on both counts that made me move upstairs. It was his announcement that he intended to work from home full-time (it being bad enough having people tramping about the place in the evenings without hearing them droning down the phone for eight hours during the day as well) and the sight of our guest room languishing there large and empty.

What is more important here, I thought, as I heaved out the double bed. Accommodating frilly curtains and matching duvet for a few tedious relatives to sleep under twice a year, or one's own creative space?

Now that I have it, I cannot recommend one's work area too highly. If you have to put your mother-in-law in a home, do it! Kick out the lodger, make the kids share a bed, sell the dining room table or halve the kitchen but get yourselves a room of your own. And if you can, make it a large one.

For then you need to equip it. The following is not of course exhaustive but comprises my own personal checklist of essential items .

I. A fridge. Immediately I had the room, I requested a new fridge for

Christmas, and the family – thinking this heralded my possible return to the kitchen and things housewifely – fell over themselves to buy one. That is, until the dimensions of my dream gift became apparent. My writing room fridge is less than 20 inches tall. It sits discreetly behind a wooden door reminiscent of the best sort of hotel mini bar and contains rations for all eventualities.

Present contents:

- One bottle champagne – just in case
- One bottle of white wine – in case not
- Two cans cider for when wine runs out
- Chocolate milk, chocolate plain (to cater for all moods)
- Upmarket, hand-fried ridiculously expensively-packaged crisps you don't want the rest of the household getting their hands on
- One apple to kid oneself one doesn't eat crisps and chocolate all the time.
- One bottle of mineral water – for flushing out toxins from same.
- Nail varnish – various colours. Because it's true what the beauty pages say: the cold does not stop it going lumpy.

The fridge's purpose is dual.
a) You can impress visiting journalists (come to interview you on your forthcoming best-seller, naturally!) by whipping out a perfectly chilled Macon Blanc Villages from what they thought was the stationery cupboard.
b) It saves forays to the kitchen for sustenance and the risk of being embroiled in some distracting domestic task like having to feed the children.

I also recommend:

- A leather-topped desk in front of wall covered with books on shelves (for being photographed at looking studious)
- A computer on computer desk for writing on
- A sofa for lying back and thinking on (or surreptitiously sleeping hangovers off)

- A stereo system for listening to the radio or playing classical music and pretending you're Inspector Morse
- Oil-burning-aromatic-vaporising thingies for breathing in uplifting and creative aromas (they don't work but it makes the room smell nice)
- Open fireplace for drinking sherry in front of in depths of winter (and screwing up rejection letters and hurling onto flames with hollow laugh during all seasons)
- Perfumed candles, hand-embroidered cushions, fetching ethnic throws and fresh flowers to prove to husband you were artistic, tasteful and capable of keeping a beautiful room all along while he was just an untidy slob
- A kettle and teabags
- A telephone for taking calls from thrilled editors.

Having fitted it out, firmly set the rules.

1) No kids in it at any time – particularly anywhere near the fridge. (Children cannot be trusted not to fiddle with the coloured paperclips or the pile of Post-it pads in this season's six summer shades. They also talk.)
2) Adult visitors by arrangement only and not at all if the door's closed (which probably indicates you're stuffing down contents of fridge or undertaking some quick research into erotica with the nice young man who delivered the envelopes).
3) A clear understanding that you disappear in there as early in the morning as possible and do not emerge until someone else has done the washing-up.

Next, you have to stick to these…

NOW I'VE STARTED...

Discipline and Displacement

When the novelist Carole Matthews started writing she was still working full-time. When she came home in the evenings, after a twelve-hour day, she used to tie her leg to the desk so that she had to sit and write. "Otherwise," she says, "I would wander about and suddenly find my outstanding pile of ironing very attractive."

I love this story and think it goes a long way to explaining why Carole is the enormously successful author of eleven best-selling novels and I'm... not.

As well as talent, which Carole has in spadeloads (this could be another clue) you do need immense dedication and discipline to keep writing when you are busy, exhausted, have children or a job or both, or really any sort of other life at all.

A lot of successful writers got that way by burning the candle at both ends. Wendy Holden still had a full-time job while she was writing her first book, author Sue Welfare wrote for three hours in the middle of each night, the novelist Elizabeth Buchan got up at dawn so she could write a page each morning before seeing to the children and then going off to work.

Kate Long applied for an Arts Council grant to cover childcare fees and put her children in nursery for the summer holidays and wrote her first novel, the wonderfully-titled *The Bad Mother's Handbook* (Picador) in just eight weeks.

If you are still in this first flush of enthusiasm – joyfully bashing out short stories in every spare minute you get and just wishing you had a lot more of them – you may well be unable to imagine any circumstances in which ironing would be preferable. It must be lovely, part-time writers say wistfully to me sometimes, to be able to write all day.

Not necessarily.

For a start there is Parkinson's Law which states that 'work expands to fill the time available for its completion'. You may think that if you didn't have to go to work, you would churn out thousands of words a day, completing a book in a matter of weeks, but it doesn't always work like that.

When I first started writing and had a small baby, the only guaranteed writing-time was a half-day a week while my mother took care of him. The amount of work I used to manage to cram into those few hours was amazing.

Now, when, in theory, I have all day, every day, to write to my heart's content, I can find myself with an overwhelming urge to clear out the airing cupboard or arrange my envelopes into neater piles, and get to Friday wondering how it is that a week's gone by and I've only written 782 words and a shopping list.

If you are now bitterly thinking that the chance to get distracted would be a fine thing and I don't know how lucky I am to have all this time to engage in time-wasting activities and that you would easily write all day if you only had the opportunity and weren't bogged down with the kids, four jobs and a batty mother-in-law who's taken it upon herself to come and live with you and never stops talking, then all I can say is: you'll learn, and try the tips below:

How to Write When There's no Time:

1) **Think about getting up an hour earlier when everyone else is asleep.** When I'm getting to the end of a book (which always takes longer than planned) I sometimes rise at four a.m. to guarantee three hours of non-interruption and have stayed up all night on occasion. I do not, however, recommend you consider any of these options if you have very small children because you must be totally exhausted already. Wendy Holden says, when looking back at her early writing days of doing just that, "compared to having two children under three…. it seems like a holiday now."

2) **Think about going to bed later and write while everyone else is asleep.** N.B. If you like a drink in the evenings you might find you don't understand any of it in the morning but at least your word count will be up.

3) **Be alert for all chances to write.** Get yourself a nice notebook and carry it around with you, jotting down thoughts and snatches of dialogue, sentences that spring to mind or how you are feeling at a

particular time, whenever you get the chance. In the dentist's waiting-room, for example, outside the school gates or when you have to stand around in a queue. Remind yourself that there's nothing like being prevented from writing to make you really productive when you finally get the chance.

4) **Join a local writing group** so someone else is forced to look after the kids and you have a guaranteed evening a week to focus on your desire to write. Meet others who share your difficulties and can give you support.

5) **Pretend** you've joined a writing group and go and write in the pub.

6) **Swap childcare with a friend.** If he or she writes too, so much the better but strike a pact in any case. Have her kids round to play while she does her embroidery or car maintenance, in return for her having yours while you bash out a short story.

7) **Forget** all that talk about the perils of too much TV and embrace the video machine as the greatest of childcare inventions. Tell the children you're all going to watch a favourite film and once they're absorbed, you can scribble things on your lap and make the right noises at the exciting bits.

8) **Write during Sports Days and school plays.** The moment your own offspring leave track or stage, whip out your pen. Put it round the playground that you are a freelance journalist and nobody will think you rude. On the contrary, they will be delighted, assuming you are taking copious notes on the feats of their little darlings.

9) **When your spouse asks what you'd like for your birthday**, request a day to yourself. Earmark a weekend where he or she takes the kids out and leaves you in blissful solitude at your desk. (N.B. This is unlikely to go down well on your wedding anniversary.)

10) **Establish the ground-rule that writing is just as important as Golf or Going Shopping for Shoes**. Drum this into the kids, too. Remember that being bored is character-forming. Let them get a feel for it.

Finally comfort yourself with the thought that if you write ALL the time you won't have anything to write about.

It is part of the process that you need to reflect and recharge, wander and ponder, see people, live life a little – otherwise you'll have nothing to say.

Talking to the postman is a crucial part of a writer's day's work. And all airing cupboards need a tidy sometimes.

What am I Going to Write About?

You may be brimming with ideas but when I started I wasn't. I used to pick up women's magazines and read the stories and think: "Wow, that was a good idea! How did she think of that?"

I would sit on a plane and read a Ken Follett or a Minette Walters or a Barbara Taylor-Bradford (my tastes are nothing if not eclectic) and be bowled over by the intricacies of plot, finding it totally inconceivable that I could ever think up anything like that (on which I was right – I still can't).

I wasted hours of potential short-story writing time smacking my forehead, shrieking "Think! Think!" knowing I had the spare hours, and the inclination (and it might be some time before the two coincided again) but a head quite empty of creative thought.

I would go for long walks and go over and over scenarios, news stories, other people's lives, searching for something plot-shaped I could hang a story on.

Sometimes in desperation I just stole somebody else's plot – justifying this in my head by remembering that there are only supposed to be about fourteen plots in the whole world (I'm not going to list them because I've never found out what they are – I just know one of them is Romeo and Juliet) and was not above posting a story off to *Woman* that was a direct rip-off of one I'd read in *Woman's Realm*.

Then one day when I'd had a few short stories published in the women's magazines and was desperate to write another one but was fresh out of ideas, something happened to change my life.

My son locked me in a cupboard.

We rather grandly call this cupboard "the utility room" as it houses the washing machine. I was bending over, shoving in the socks, as you do, when I heard the door close and the old-fashioned latch-type key turn in the lock. I banged on the door hard and shrieked, "Let me out!"

"Can't," came the reply. It was ten in the morning, and my husband wasn't expected home until six. My mobile phone was high on a shelf precisely so it couldn't be reached by small fingers. My son was two and a half and effectively alone in the house. I pride myself on keeping a cool head in a crisis (a rule I make exception to in the case of large hairy house spiders, or occasionally the tops of tomatoes I mistake for same) so I did not panic.

Remember those Enid Blyton manoeuvres with keys where you jiggle with a piece of wire, slide a sheet of paper under the door and back towards you with the key on it? This does not work in real life.

We eventually effected the Great Escape by me bashing out the bottom of the door and, with my face wedged in the gap, instructing my son to call 999 on the landline until the police turned up and kicked seven shades out of the front door.

Later, one of my friends, to whom the whole thing was unaccountably hilarious, wiped his eyes and guffawed, "I suppose you'll be writing one of your stories about this…"

Actually it hadn't occurred to me but seeing as there was the broken glass to pay for I had a go.

I sat down and faithfully wrote out everything that had happened and sent it off to *Woman's Realm*, now sadly defunct. The fiction editor was a lovely woman called Sally Sheringham with whom I've sadly lost touch – Sally, if you're out there please give me a call – who was incredibly generous with her time and would send handwritten notes explaining exactly what was wrong with a story and why she couldn't buy it.

This one, she said, was "too much of an incident" and "not enough of a story". At first I didn't know what she meant, but I thought about it and once I did, I realised that this was THE most important lesson I have ever learnt about short-story writing.

It sounds simple but it does have to be a STORY. What I had done was simply relate what had happened to me. There was no real conflict – no moment of change.

OK, so I was stuck in a cupboard and I needed to get out and then things changed in that I did, but looking at it afterwards, there was no emotional change, no real story. I sat down and began again. I kept the middle pretty much as it was but I wrote a fictional beginning and end. I was about to start trying to describe it then but, hey – life is short and I've got all the rest of this to write, so I may as well paste it in. It went like this:

"He's going to drop that!"

Liz turned to see the hedgehog cup plummet from the edge of the table. Milk splashed and splattered across the tiles.

"Oh dear," little Jacob said calmly.

David gave an almost inaudible sigh but Liz exploded.

"He's got two parents you know, why didn't you grab it?"

"Because I have to go to work," David snapped back. "And I haven't time to get milk all over me."

"All right," she said tightly, grabbing the kitchen roll and a cloth and smiling at Jacob to reassure him. He grinned back, unconcerned, pushing his toy bus up and down the table with roaring sound effects.

"He's going to knock something else off in a minute," David said irritatingly and she felt like screaming.

"Just go, will you? You'll be late."

David kissed the top of his son's head. "I don't know what time I'll be home. Last meeting's not till five."

When he'd disappeared, she stopped mopping and looked hopelessly round the messy kitchen. Their mornings were often like this now. He always seemed to be criticising her. She tried to understand, knowing he was tired and working harder than ever. Money had been tight since she'd given up work but they'd agreed she should stay at home with Jacob and it wasn't as if she was having a rest all day.

Liz looked ruefully at her small son. He was lovely. Everyone said how bright he was, but he could be such a handful.

"Oh it's terrible twos," more experienced friends told her, laughing. "He'll be off at school before you know it." But sometimes, the days seemed fraught and endless and she longed for the time when she, too, was in a smart suit, briefcase in hand, downing a quick cup of coffee before rushing off to work.

She wiped her hands on her tracksuit bottoms and cleaned up Jacob's hands and mouth.

He put his arms around her and gave her one of his sudden hugs before he raced away.

She smiled. At moments like these she was filled with indescribable love and would have happily had six Jacobs. She sighed. David would be horrified by the thought of any more. He didn't seem to think much of her abilities as a mother. She sometimes wondered if deep down he regretted ever starting a family. Jacob came back into the kitchen proffering the battery from the remote control.

Once she and David had talked all the time. But Jacob had been such a terrible sleeper for so long that they'd spent the first two years in a blur of exhaustion with hardly the energy to open their mouths. Now when they did, they just seemed to end up growling at each other.

Liz picked up the washing basket. At least if David was going to be late home tonight, Jacob would be asleep. She'd cook something nice and they could have a glass of wine and swap news of their days as they'd used to. Then perhaps she could explain how she was feeling – calmly – and find out how he was too.

She went into the glorified cupboard they grandly called the utility room and began to load the machine. Jacob lay on the floor outside, pushing a tractor in noisy circles. She pushed the last small sock into the machine feeling more positive. She clicked it shut and straightened just in time to see the door closing against her.

"Don't, Jacob," she called. As she put out her hand to push it back open she heard the sickeningly sure click of the key being turned in the lock.

"Jacob, please open the door!"

After that I told the story of the key and the phone and the boys in blue turning up pretty much as it happened, just leaving out my foul language and the fact that I'd had to have a large sherry to get over the ordeal and making it a nice cup of tea instead and then back to my imagination for a fictional ending. The sort beloved of magazine fiction editors at the time. It went like this:

Later when Jacob was safely in bed, exhausted, she watched as David poured drinks, dreading his expression when he heard about the splintered door and bill for new glass.

"You all right?" he said, "you look a bit pale." He handed her the glass and she thought how tired he looked. "What sort of a day have you had?"

She began the story, not looking at him, turning the wine glass in her hands watching as the ruby red liquid caught the light. She felt tired and tearful, but she kept her voice as matter-of-fact as she could. When she'd finished, Liz still could not raise her eyes, waiting for the recriminations, longing for him to understand how badly she felt. But there was silence and when she looked up his eyes were full of tears.

"Oh Liz," he said, and she was in his arms.

"The door's broken," she sniffed, "and the glazier cost a fortune."

"I'll fix it," he promised, "and it doesn't matter."

"I know I've been awful," he said later still. "I suppose I've resented having to go off and leave you every day. I love you both so much. I'm so proud, but I suppose I've felt a bit jealous of all your time together here while I'm at work."

Liz looked at him amazed. "We could always swap," she said lightly.

"You'd probably make a better mother than I do."

"You're a wonderful mother," he said, "but maybe we will…" He smiled. A warm, teasing, loving smile she'd forgotten. "…when we have the next one."

You may be feeling nauseous but fiction editors like a bit of reconciliation, even if we all know that in real life he'd moan about the cost of the replacement glass, she'd tell him how petty-minded and selfish he was and they'd both walk round each other with a face on for a week.

I sent the new story to *My Weekly* who promptly bought it. It was published in 1997, illustrated – somewhat inexplicably – with an angelic-looking child holding a basket of fruit.

It was a real watershed moment – the realisation that everything that happened to me – good or bad – was a potential story. And it was particularly satisfying to earn money from something that had gone horribly wrong.

I am not one of life's natural Pollyannas, given more to swearing, stomping about and swigging back large gins in times of crisis than counting my blessings, but it has been a peculiar comfort to think that something worthwhile can be extracted from everything.

I am speaking for me personally, of course – rather than claiming any positive slant on your cat being run over or your granny being washed out to sea – but writers generally in need of inspiration or publicity can do worse than to look to their traumas.

After the cupboard incident it was a kind of game I played with myself. Anything that cost me either financially or in terms of worry or stress, I sat down and wrote about and tried to either earn the money back, or justify it happening by it making me a few quid.

So when I reversed into an empty Ford Fiesta, smashing its headlights and necessitating several long phone-calls with its sexy-voiced owner (I never met him and he probably looked like a gnome but a Scottish accent always does it for me) it rapidly became a tale of intrigue and romance for *Woman's Weekly* which – just about – paid for the damage.

After a rat burrowed its horrible ratty way into our garage and gave me the screaming ab-dabs, the Infestation-Man's fee for a dozen high-tech traps and enough poison to wipe out the population of Milton Keynes was met by a jolly account of a mythical rodent and a birthday surprise. I made a large profit on that one.

Which cannot be said for the story of the woman whose washing machine, dishwasher, toaster and central heating system all packed up in the same week. But you get the idea. Don't cry over spilt milk, as I always say. Write about it!

Especially as you will then be following the age-old advice to "write what you know". I totally believe in this, not only because I don't want to spend weeks mugging up on the daily life of a moth-keeper in the sixteenth century when I can create a modern-day hero with a job I've had myself, but because I consider that if I have done it or felt it, I have a much better chance of making it come alive.

I'm sure we've all had the experience of reading a passage in a novel and being left with the distinct impression that the writer has no first-hand knowledge of what they are describing: watching someone die, say, or seeing a kitten being born.

One book that shall remain nameless charts the various affairs of a married woman with younger men. I happen to know that the author has been happily and faithfully married to the same, older, bloke since she was seventeen. And – to me – it shows!

When the writer really knows what they are talking about, it shows too. Which is why sometimes even the most mundane events can totally grip. I remember being enthralled by a short story which simply described the sensual way a young male assistant packed a woman's shopping. May sound odd if you didn't read it yourself but I could so totally identify with the writer's feelings that it worked on every level for me. I would be stunned if that particular supermarket experience hadn't really happened to the writer concerned.

But nothing happens to me, I hear you wail. So what do you do when you run out of events worthy of recording? Start plundering what happens to others, of course!

I once earned £250 simply by retelling the hysterical account of another mother losing her child in Asda, after hearing it in the playground (she reminded me recently I never did share the fee with her); the exploits of my sister's mog have led to publication in *Your Cat* and what her plumber got up to made more than one magazine story.

In fact I realise now, after years of fancying myself as a creative type, that in fact I have the imagination of a pea. All I have done is write down everything that's ever happened to me, joining dozens of near-suicidal moments into an attempt at romantic comedy or scraping the family barrel of dysfunction and general barminess to bring gravitas to a think-piece.

Use everything, I always urge other writers, if someone has misguidedly booked me to do a workshop and I am called upon to dispense advice. The mad, the bad and the hilarious – shove it all in.

Your subject matter doesn't have to be earth-shattering. The hallmark of all successful writing is the emotional truth it contains – that is why writers like Maeve Binchy and Joanna Trollope are so popular. Both write about fairly ordinary goings-on but in the sort of intimate and insightful way that will strike a chord with every reader.

So look to your own life – really look – and you'll be surprised what you'll find. Then draw on it.

In one's first novel, of course, this is to be thoroughly expected. Everyone knows this is where you make your favourite jokes, air all the issues you rant about when you're three sheets to the wind and take malicious pleasure in providing a very obvious description of your traitorous ex – he with the vinyl fetish and smelly feet.

Certainly in my first book – *Raising the Roof*, in case by some oversight you've never bought it – I let it all hang out. The near-bankruptcy, the duff sex, the time I first discovered I needed a face-lift – they're all in there.

So, indeed, are my experiences of the mentally ill and my capacity to fall dangerously in love with anyone who rescues or protects me. All have served me more than once. I have written short stories, newspaper columns, advice pieces, articles for both broadsheets and tabloids on the same subjects.

For my second novel I drew on the experiences of a friend (that's my story and I'm sticking to it) who began an affair. As she was a good friend, and her husband was a tosser, I agreed to be her cover when she was really more creatively engaged.

She would provide a detailed run-down of the evening we'd allegedly had out together, usually whispered down the phone at some ungodly hour of the morning – *Cocktails in Bar Seven, pasta in Luiginis, we had to wait 45 minutes for a cab, that's why I wasn't home till 1 a.m....* – but I lived in fear of saying the wrong thing to her husband, who definitely had a whiff that something didn't stack up (perhaps the fact that she left to meet an old school-mate dressed like Liz Hurley and came back with her buttons done up the wrong way) and wasn't above interrogating me the moment she left the room.

Word of my nerves-of-steel got around and soon I was doing three of them. Three restaurants or nightclubs to remember – three girly nights out to be word-perfect on next time they met us for dinner with the right bloke in tow. It was stressful but, oh, what a peach.

"I should be running this as a business, " I quipped. Thus my second novel *Perfect Alibis* was born. These days such agencies really exist (and I thought of them first!) but back then it was entirely a work of fiction, featuring an agency giving married women watertight alibis and providing get-outs when things went wrong.

The old man's found pictures of you naked? The agency would not only tell you what to say but ensure you came out smelling of roses while he grovelled apologies for his suspicious nature.

He phones when you're *en flagrante* three hundred miles from where you said you'd be? No problem. I made it all up but for certain individuals it would sure have rung some bells.

Suppose someone had recognised themselves? Funnily enough, they never do. Or they do but they're wrong. When that book came out, the editor of my local newspaper, a good pal, had a marvellous idea for publicity. He made me the front page story: AUTHOR LIFTS THE LID ON THANET'S LOVE CHEATS, implying that respectable, middle-class locals were quaking in their boots in case they appeared in my story, and offering a phone-in number if anyone did spot who the lead characters were.

WH Smith sold out of copies on the first morning and several readers rang in. They all cited philanderers I'd never heard of and for months afterwards people would sidle up to me whispering that they "knew". One glamorous middle-aged woman, known for her charity work, was actually heard boasting that I'd used her in my book. I'd barely met her and still dread to think which individual of few morals she imagined she was!

By the time I got down to writing a third novel, I was the co-owner of a wine bar. I was a sleeping partner (or drinking partner, to be more accurate).

By agreement, my two business partners did the hard graft. Friday night was my only shift behind the bar while the rest of the time I swanned about, drank the profits, and watched and listened.

Again it felt like a gift. Wonderful characters came in and out – who laughed, cried and fell off their bar stools. We saw relationships blossom and fail, feuds simmer, seductions attempted, drinks and secrets spilled.

The central plotline in book three, *One Glass is Never Enough*, is a fictional love story, but for the backdrop – three women running a winebar – I had so much material I barely knew where to start.

In promoting my various novels I have embraced the publicity trail with open arms. I've been screamed at on *Kilroy*, shared my lack of cooking prowess with the nation on *Ready, Steady, Cook* and attempted to have my hair dyed the same colour as my book-jacket on *The Salon*. I mashed potatoes for *Just for Starters*, fell out with the production team on the *Russell Grant Show*, gave hot tips on playing away on *Loose Lips* and managed to smash a large piece of crystal on the set of *The Heaven and Earth Show*.

What does this tell you? That my fourth novel will probably be about Daytime TV.

After that who knows? By the look in the mirror it might be about facelifts and botox but I no longer worry over what I shall write about.

When stuck, I descend into fantasy (why, oh why, don't men like that exist in real life?) but generally, because I spend months faffing about and there have been large gaps between books, by the time, kicking and screaming, I finally have to get down to the next one, something else has happened to inspire me.

Which is why I do not fall gratefully on every offer of a life story to enthuse me. Even though barely a month goes by without someone emailing with the suggestion that I might like to write up their enthralling time in prison/as a Westminster mole/trekking single-handed across the Sahara or – most recently – a detailed breakdown of their ten-year project to turn a dilapidated shed in a remote corner of France into a salt-water spa (gripping stuff – the first three chapter outlines deal entirely with the plumbing).

So if you're really stuck for ideas just get out and talk to other people – the nuttier looking the better. As journalist Richard Morrison from *The Times* said, when I asked him if he'd ever wanted to write a novel: "Real life is so fascinating – why make it up?"

Other Ways to Get Ideas

Kate Walker – the author of 50 Mills and Boon Romances – thinks of a writer as a magpie: "picking up bits of interest that glitter here and there".

Kate is inspired by snatches of conversation she hears on the bus or train, stories in the newspaper, things on TV. Although, interestingly, when she watches Soaps and TV dramas, she doesn't just pinch their ideas, like I might. She asks herself: how would I write it differently? How could I write it so that it ended up in a different place? You could try this, too.

And since there *are* only supposed to be about fourteen plots in the whole world (if you know what they are, do write and tell me) you needn't feel guilty about turning to the classics and using those if you're really stumped.

I think someone's already written a sequel to *Rebecca*, but what would have happened to Jane Eyre if she hadn't eventually got it together with Mr Rochester? Suppose Oliver Twist had never been rescued from Fagin? (You can always update things by having the little blighters pinch mobile phones and rip off credit cards and giving them an ASBO or two.)

Or, turning back to the TV, let us imagine for a moment that Pauline Fowler were not a dreadful, manipulative old dragon (hard to picture I know) and had not met her maker on Christmas Day 2006. What sort of further misery might she have inflicted?

If you don't like *Eastenders* (you strange person) you can do this sort of thing by hanging about in the street. As Lynne Hackles, author of *The Handy Little Book for Writers* (NAWG Publications*)* says in that fine tome: "See the old lady waiting for the bus? What's she been doing for the past eighty years?"

Lynne also recommends keeping an "ideas box" where you keep all the bits of paper on which you've jotted down your various ideas. You could also add interesting cuttings, pictures, or objects. See it as a sort of lucky dip for when you're feeling jaded.

My friend Lesley Gleeson, who's sold more stories to the women's magazines than you could shake a stick at, as well as spending a few years as a literary agent and then a jewellery designer (very nice stuff actually – take a look at **www.coburgcrafts.co.uk**) would use as her starting point six words chosen at random from a book or magazine.

It was all a bit witchy as she had a special pointing pencil and always said that if she couldn't find the pencil, she couldn't choose the words. But it worked. Sometimes she used pictures as well.

Carole Matthews mentions the *Daily Mail* as a good source of inspiration. Freya North rates newspapers too.

"Snippets!" she cries with enthusiasm. "I am obsessed with snippets and have a whole stack of cuttings from newspapers and magazines."

There are worse things to be obsessed with (I once met a bloke who did unbelievably nasty things with raw liver and cling film) – and if cuttings light your creative fire, get snipping.

When I last spoke to Freya, she was writing about a character who sleepwalks because she'd read a piece about a teenager found fast asleep along the arm of a crane.

Short-story writer Penny Alexander talks of ideas springing from "a feeling, a taste, a word , a saying or phrase... but most of all, drawings or photos, especially of the human face."

"If you open yourself to the possibilities," says crime-writer Zoë Sharp "the ideas bombard you from every direction. News items, documentaries, chance overheard remarks in the street, disconnected thoughts. You practically have to beat them off with a stick. The difficulty is filtering out the good ideas from the bad ones..."

I do think she's right. I certainly find the more ideas I get, the more I get. Sounds clumsy but it's true. It is as if you get attuned to the potential of everything around you. Others may not always understand this.

So try and control the gleam in your eye when your best friend comes sobbing to tell you that her husband has absconded with the bloke from the Garden Centre, or his boss was discovered in the Ladies at the office party, adjusting his suspenders.

You can get away with demanding all the details – they'll probably feel better for getting it off their chests. But whipping out your notebook is a definite no-no.

Novelist Judy Astley also gets her ideas from "anywhere and by happy chance". Inspiration for her novels have come variously from: a list of topics to be covered in a course of self-defence classes, a search for an old boyfriend, holidays she's been on, an artist community near her house and a conversation with her sister-in-law.

And once, in the case of *Seven for a Secret* (Black Swan) her book was a "kind of sequel to a movie I once saw". The film in question she says was "fairly naff". It was *Twinkle*, starring Susan George as a young schoolgirl who marries a quite famous older writer. "I saw it again on TV a year before I wrote the book and thought: I wonder what would happen if she sort-of never got round to mentioning the early, dissolved marriage and the man came back into her life again?"

A lot of authors describe that "what if" moment when explaining how ideas come to them, including Frederick Forsyth, who explains: "something starts a germ of an idea; something I heard, saw, read. Then it intrigues, grows and grows... "

Novelist Kate Harrison works in a similar way. "Something in the news might combine with a topic or question that fascinates me and a character or "what if" question will pop into my mind and I run with it..."

Suck it and see, in other words, and if it doesn't work, you can always abandon it. As Kate says cheerfully: "I write a lot of opening paragraphs/chapters before deciding the idea I loved yesterday isn't any good."

But that's OK, too, because by then you'll have had an even better one. And if you haven't, you can always watch *Eastenders*...

Ten top ways to get inspired

1) Consider the words of writer Mil Millington: "I can't think of a single occasion when something external has sparked a novel into existence. I simply stare at the wall and ask myself, 'What interests me?' Now ask yourself the same question: What interests YOU?
2) Start with an emotion – fear/guilt/anger/ecstasy – and imagine what someone might be driven to do in its most extreme state. Then what would happen?
3) Take a picture of a stranger from a magazine or newspaper: give them a name, a job, a family, a secret. Then write about how they must be feeling right now.
4) Read poetry till you find a poem that strikes you in the heart. What is it saying? Now write a story or plan a novel with the same message.
5) Visit your most gossipy friend and ply him/her with wine.
6) Have a few glasses yourself.
7) What are you an expert on? Write about that.
8) What do you wish you knew more about? Research that too.
9) Watch a soap.

10) Stare at the wall. (N.B. This works best if you adopt a peculiar expression and flap your hands mysteriously at the same time so that the family think amazing things are happening inside your head and you must not be disturbed. If you repeat often enough you can probably avoid having to take the children swimming/the rubbish out/any sort of responsibility.)

Genre

Even if your ideas are only half-formed (and many a fine novelist starts a book from that point), the general consensus of opinion is that you do need to be fairly clear on what genre you're writing in.

An agent will want to know so they can tell the publisher they are going to try to flog you to. The publisher will want to know so their sales team can tell the bookseller. Book-sellers want to know because they have to decide whether your book is going to sit on the shelf marked Crime or Romance. So you need to know, too.

If you are already halfway through something that is "a sort of part comedy-thriller, part historical romance with a murder in it," you may think this is a silly system and that you are proud to be gloriously mould-breaking and genre-less. You may also have recently met me at a party. I know I smiled and said: "Gosh that sounds fascinating," but I was privately thinking: "You'll be lucky."

Because silly it may be, but that is how it works. If you can't be categorised, agents and publishers and booksellers are going to scratch their heads and wonder what to do with you.

Before you say it, yes I know, I know, that every now and again a book that defies all pigeonholes is a runaway success. The example that leaps most readily to mind is *The Curious Incident of the Dog in the Night-time* by Mark Haddon (Vintage) – a brilliant book that is very difficult to classify.

And, sometimes, something even more unexpected captures the book-buying public's heart, proving that it's not just novels that can take the world by storm.

Lynne Truss was a lovely writer with a devoted following in *The Times* when she wrote *Eats Shoots and Leaves* but nobody really expected a book on punctuation to hit the big time. The initial print run was just 10,000 copies with the publishers, Profile Books, looking at a niche market only.

To date, that book has sold over three million copies worldwide, its success (totally deservedly – it's terrific!) due largely to word-of-mouth. This, for me, is the stuff the very best daydreams are made of and I suggest that all any of us can do is hang on to the lovely proof that these miracles do sometimes happen.

So it may happen to me, I hear you cry. Yes, you may be lucky and produce another such tome. You also may not. I wouldn't like to put you off if you're sitting on something totally unique and gob-smacking but unless you are entirely sure you are, and don't want to be dismissed as a mad person, my advice, if you're starting out, is to stay on the safe side.

Decide in your own mind whether you are writing a Thriller or a Saga or a Memoir or a Romantic Comedy or whatever and pitch it as that. Sadly we like to put things in boxes and if your idea won't fit any of them, it will put people off.

And for goodness sake pick a genre you WANT to write in. Do not just go for something that is IN at the moment, or is hotly tipped to be The Next Big Thing. I'll tell you why. Firstly, by the time you've spent a year writing it, a year trying to sell it and the publishers spend a year preparing it for publication, the IN will be OUT and everyone will be busily reading something else.

Secondly it's hard enough writing a novel when you're totally passionate about your subject; if you're just trying to follow the crowd you'll have no chance. And thirdly: nobody really knows what the Next Big Thing will be until it is.

As literary agent Simon Trewin says: "It is impossible to predict. I wish I did know – I'd have forty best-selling authors." Publishers, he says, are "bad at setting trends and only know how to follow them."

And even if you knew what the next big thing was going to be, would you necessarily be able to write to it?

If you've taken a vow of celibacy, for example, and are living on a shoestring, you might be short of ideas for a sex-and-shopping bonk-buster, and if you're only eighteen you may struggle with Granny-Lit.

I firmly believe that we have to write what we write – I wouldn't attempt any sort of Living-on-Raw-Cabbage-and-Abstaining-from-Alcohol Lit even if the plot fairy had appeared to me in a dream and told me this was next year's sure-fire winner. And I wouldn't try historical fiction either. Not now, anyway.

Some years ago I heard Carolyn Caughey, an editorial director at Hodder & Stoughton, speak as a member of a panel at a writing conference. Asked what publishers were looking for at the time, she said most of them "would kill their granny for another Georgette Heyer".

I went straight home and phoned my agent, The Fearsome One, to enquire if I wrote anything like the good Georgette, only to hear strange snorting sounds on the other end of the line as she became almost hysterical. "Oh, that really is very funny," she said eventually when she'd stopped cackling. So we'll take that as a no, then.

As Suzanne Baboneau of publishers Simon and Schuster says: "Be aware of what books in your 'area' are working, and why, but don't simply try jumping on a bandwagon – those authors who survive beyond their first or second books do have something unique."

Most publishers would agree that which genre you choose is irrelevant in the first instance. What they are looking for is a damn good story – a page-turning, rollicking good read.

Simon Trewin says the successful books are those that, regardless of genre, will appeal to reading groups. "Aim to write a book you can imagine twelve people sitting around discussing," is Simon's advice. It seems good to me. If there's one thing I've learnt about the whole book-buying business it's that word-of-mouth is everything.

And the best books come from those who really believed in what they were writing for its own sake, not just because something similar was on the best-seller lists.

But if you're not really sure what sort of genre is for you, here is a quick guide:

Popular Genres

- **Romance** – Girl meets Boy, spends 300 pages tied up in events that conspire to stop them shagging each other, get a shag in eventually, live happily ever after.
- **Romantic Comedy** – as above but they fall out of bed while doing it.
- **Science Fiction** – one of them shags an alien.
- **Erotica** – both of them shag anything with a pulse.
- **Thriller** – Boy is part of MI5, Girl turns out to be international diamond

smuggler. Shag each other sporadically while foiling plot to kill the president.

- **Who-dunnit** – Boy is disagreeable old professor who is bumped off in his library with a blunt instrument (possibly a piece of lead piping). Girl is interfering old woman from the same village who knits a lot and tackles the mystery of who did the dirty deed.
- **Crime** – Sexy Police Inspector solves above.
- **Fantasy** – any of the above but set in strange-sounding land, in strange-sounding future with characters whose names nobody can pronounce.
- **Historical Saga** – set in past. See Romance but add in corsets.
- **Contemporary Women's Fiction** – add in diets and soul-searching.
- **Chick Lit** – add in Chardonnay.
- **Lad Lit** – add in football, beer and hilarious masturbation scenes.
- **Mum Lit** – add in screaming brats, scheming nanny and a 4x4.
- **Granny Lit** – add in zimmer frame.
- **Memoir** – add in poverty, child abuse and pretend any of above happened to you.

To Plan or Not to Plan

OK, so you've got your great idea, you know what genre it's in – you're ready for the off. What next? Do you just sit down, start typing, hope for the best, see what happens? Or do you plan everything you're going to write to within an inch of its life? As usual, opinions differ.

Did you ever see that documentary following Minette Walters while she wrote *The Shape of Snakes* (Pan Macmillan)? I got palpitations just watching her as she reached the halfway point in this amazingly complex psychological thriller – which unravels the mystery of who was behind a twenty-year old murder – and still had no idea who had done it herself!

The end result was gripping to the extreme – I was spot-welded to that book when I read it, as I have been to all of hers – but I cannot begin to think how she managed it. Apparently she writes all her books like that.

She says she never knows who the guilty party is when she starts and only starts "whittling down the suspects" when she's halfway through. "It's like flying by wire. You embark with nothing, just a tightrope across a chasm. It's a much more enjoyable way to write because I have to work it out along with the reader. If I don't know who did it until half way, the reader is going to be fairly fazed as well."

I stand in awe.

For Frederick Forsyth, on the other hand, planning is "lengthy and meticulous" and lasts about a year. "Only when I am ready do I sit down. By then the story is finished but simply unwritten. It is in my head, supported by the mountains of research material I have collected."

After that, he writes it in 45 days which he describes as "just a long chore. No creativity – that is what the previous twelve months were all about."

Jill Mansell's novels are born from the setting first, then names for characters, then jobs, then a starting point, then, as she puts it, it's "Ready, Steady, Go!" She does make plans – on several bits of A4 sellotaped together and covered in minute writing.

And it really is tiny. Her normal handwriting is of average, unremarkable size but unless you have 20/20 vision and then some, you're going to have to employ a magnifying glass to read one of her charts. She had a revelation about this while we were talking about it.

"It is exactly how I used to revise when studying for exams," she remembered, "by cramming all the info into as small a space as possible. I hate plotting!"

Bernard Knight, author of the "Crowner John" series of historical mysteries, has tried to avoid it at times but admits that if he tries just to start on page one and hope, then he "fizzles out". Bernard starts with a "flow-diagram of who's dead, whodunit and why" and then builds up names of characters and a general plot synopsis. The plan he says, "usually goes off the rails" halfway through the book but at least gets him that far.

Novelist Isabel Wolff also needs to know where she's going and constructs a detailed synopsis which can take up to five months to complete. "Hatching the evil plot is very difficult," she says, "and I tend to tie myself up in mental knots over it. I usually start with the heroine's job – and then build the storyline from that. Once I know what the heroine does, then I begin to know who her friends are, where she lives, what her tastes are, and what has happened to her in the past to make her the woman she now is."

Novelist Kate Long, an ex-teacher (say no more!) is nothing if not a planner. "Novels start with a time-line which extends down two lengths of A4, onto which I jot the main events of the plot. Then I 'interview' my main characters and generate pages of notes on them. Next I do time-lines of their lives so I have the back-story in place, and I do any research that's needed, for instance what a particular job might entail, or what it's like to live in a certain place. Only when all that's sorted do I start to write, but by that time the ideas are usually clamouring to be set down."

If it were me, I'd be clamouring to lie in a darkened room with a towel over my head – it all sounds too much like hard work.

Caroline Graham, author of the Inspector Barnaby novels that brought *Midsomer Murders* to our TV screens, has a method that sounds easier.

"I start writing," she says, "when characters come along to tell a story." This too, though, can have its drawbacks, as is apparent when Caroline adds cheerfully: "Nobody has turned up for the past two years…"

"Do you plan?" I asked Freya North. "Nope," she said. Her approach is the scientific one of "Start with the first word of the first chapter and haul the whole book out until the final full stop".

Claire Calman also avoids starting with any rigid plot or plan although she does make notes on character, setting and themes. "I've noticed that the greatest leaps forward in my writing are always, without exception, entirely unplanned."

Carole Matthews does plan – producing what she calls a "fairly extensive plot" but says "the book never quite turns out that way".

Dorothy Koomson says simply: "I know where the story starts and where it's going to end and then I work out how to get from one to the other."

This is sort of how I do it too – I think!

For the truth is, that – once again, not unlike having a baby – afterwards I can never quite remember what I did, except that I made a lot of fuss about how much it hurt.

I only know that writing a book always involves lots of Post-it notes, torturous-looking charts and lists of "things to go in," most of which make little sense six months later and are nowhere to be found in the finished chapters. But quite which bits I planned from the beginning and which came to me in a flash of inspiration halfway round Tesco's I am never quite sure.

As I have explained, I wrote my first book on a great wave of optimism. If you had asked me shortly after I sold it, I would have told you that it flowed out of me at a merry rate of a couple of thousand words a day, that I made it up as I went along (basically, as I've told you, just putting in every single thing that had ever happened to me and every joke I'd ever wanted to make) and that I was a dream to live with while doing so.

Turns out this isn't how my nearest and dearest remember it. "You were a nightmare," said one friend with feeling, while the huge piece of white card I had my "Plan" on at the time – an artistic arrangement of frenzied inter-locking circles in black felt-tip, faded Post-its, splashes of red wine, and a corner that looks suspiciously as though I sobbed all over it and then tried to eat it – bears almost no resemblance in plot terms to the finished book.

Still, once the magic sale had come, I thought it would be plain sailing from then on. Sign the contract on the two-book deal, live in state of perfect joy, knock out second book in three months flat … Excuse me while I lie down and have hysterics.

Writing my second novel was the real nightmare. Basically because I had the fantastic idea but no clue whatsoever what to do with it. As time marched on (a year sounds like a terrifically long time to be given to write a book but believe me it can gallop) I planned and I re-planned and I tore the plans up and I burst into tears and spent the day in bed, waiting for the plot fairy to descend.

In the meantime, I wrote anyway, hoping that something would happen and it would start to make sense. It didn't. Even at 60,000 words, I didn't know what I was doing. My writing-room was a sea of plot-plans. Everywhere I looked there were feverish Post-it notes – TAKE DOG OUT! PUT CHARLOTTE BACK IN? MILLIE 37? (NO!! BEEN MARRIED 23 YEARS.) WHAT WITH GEORGE MOTHER DEMENTIA?

Thank God for Sadie Mayne, my very patient editor, who helped me to turn this dog's breakfast into something legible (she'd left Transworld by the time I'd written a third book – I think it was a coincidence).

I swore then that I would never again start writing anything without having a very firm framework in mind. Consequently it took me about three years to produce another novel.

None of which is terribly helpful to you except that it is best to remember that there is no plot fairy. There's just you, plodding away writing the hundreds – that make up the thousands – of words that hit the screen as mostly unintelligible rubbish but which with time and manipulation will eventually become the proverbial silk purse from sow's ear. "It's all in the edit!" a wise friend once said to me, and so it is.

I also want to tell you that it is exceptionally hard work at times and a bit like banging your head against the wall – very nice when it stops – but maybe I am not the rule. Other writers claim to adore the whole process. I particularly loathe the sort that gush about how they forget to eat when they're deeply engaged with their protagonists and are driven to get out of bed at 3 a.m. because they've had such a divine idea for chapter twenty-seven. (I also make small plasticine models of them and keep them in my pin drawer.)

I am not like that. What I most adore is typing "The End" and getting on with all the lovely bits of being an author – like going out and talking about it.

But in the meantime, I muddle through and try hard to be organised. I have approached each book in a different way and in my time have tried a whole host of varying methods of wrestling with what often feels like a huge barrow-load of steaming spaghetti that I must somehow fit into a neat casserole dish.

Things that work for me may not do anything for you. As you will have seen from earlier in this chapter, it is different for everyone and you will have to find your own way of doing things. All I can do is share a few of my own and others' tried and tested methods:

The Post-it and Card Approach

This is how I dealt with my first novel and I can recommend it. Mostly because it keeps everything contained – a concept I am thinking particularly fondly of right now, since my writing room looks remarkably like that flat in the advertisement for Yellow Pages, where the girl upstairs thinks the nice young man has been burgled and they've trashed the place, but in fact he always lives like that (until of course, he lets his fingers do the walking and hires a cleaner to tidy up after him).

Anyway, it wouldn't work with this book I'm writing now because I have about five hundred pieces of paper from a host of authors who've generously shared their know-how with me, lying all over the floor, but this is how you can do it normally.

Get a really big piece of card (you can buy it in sheets at stationers or craft shops or those small and helpful printers that do leaflets and business cards and photocopying and the like) and lots of Post-it notes (if you are particularly anal you could get them in different colours and do a spot of colour-coding according to who the major character in each chapter is or which plot strand you're concentrating on).

Then the idea is that you write notes on what will be in various chapters or scenes and stick them on the card – the beauty being that you can move them about into a different order every time you realise things need a bit of re-working.

Post-its, of course, come in all shapes and sizes these days, so if you're feeling particularly witty or ironic you could use lip-shaped ones for the love scenes, speech-bubbles for the chapters heavy on dialogue, arrows for major plot developments etc., but let's not get too carried away.

The main thing is to have a visual aid in front of you that gives an overview of all the major goings-on in your novel. You can add new ideas, screw up old ones and rearrange the order of events to your endless content.

On the card itself you can scrawl general notes as they occur to you – about people's habits, appearances, the name of their cat etc. The card can be pinned to a wall or left on the floor, rolled up and shoved out of sight if nosy relatives come to stay and you're forced to let them sleep in your study. (N.B. This is not to be recommended if you can help it.)

The Index Card Method

This is a variation on the above but designed to help you think up a plot in the first place. It sounds quite a good idea and I've heard various authors mention it over the years.

As far as I can gather it goes like this:

You take a packet of index cards and first you write down the names of all your main characters – one on each card. Next you work out whose view point you're going to be working from. Let's say you're going to alternate between your hero, your heroine, the shady serial killer intent on bumping the heroine off and the alcoholic ex-cop who will eventually eschew the bottle and save the day.

You do a bit of basic maths – calculators permitted – and you work out that a novel of 90,000 words may contain approx 30 chapters of 3000 words each, or you can work in scenes instead – you may have two or three scenes to a chapter – and say that if the average scene is 1500 words you're looking at 60 of them.

Then you say, OK, so I've got four viewpoints going on. I want the hero and heroine to take up the bulk of the action as they grapple with the strange phone calls and sense of being followed etc., with Shady just appearing from time to time to chill us with his twisted thought processes, and the odd rambling from Drunk Cop to keep us up to date with his battle of the booze.

Let us say 20 scenes from the hero's perspective, 20 scenes from the heroine's and then ten each for Cop and Killer. Now what you do is write each character's name a few more times on a few more cards until you have the right number for each of them.

Then you brainstorm – writing down any ideas for scenes or chapters that hit you – not worrying at this stage whether they hang together or indeed, make any sense. You can write some extra ones on blank cards too, if you have the brilliant idea – eg. Shady is finally trapped in a telephone box by the crazed dog that belonged to his seventh victim, set on him by our now-sober policeman – but are not yet sure whose viewpoint it is going to be from. You keep writing – everything and anything that occurs to you as a possible runner – and then you give the cards a good shuffle and spread them all out on the floor or table and see what you've got.

Hopefully one of those scenes will strike you as perfect for a strong and gripping start and something else will look like a natural conclusion to things. Then you start playing about with what you've got left – putting them into some semblance of order.

Discard any scenes that on second inspection look too dull for words, or anything that just doesn't fit with the rest (where the heroine gets abducted by aliens perhaps) and keep moving the others about and see what you get. You may need to write out some new cards to link other scenes together but hopefully you will end up with a basic plan you can follow – or at least will be sufficiently inspired to write out a different one.

I haven't tried it but have been assured it works. In fact I might just give it a go for my next novel, as, once again, I have the beginning and the end but the middle is a bit hazy. Any sort of exercise where you stop worrying about the end product and just bash down thoughts has got to be a good thing. If it just brings one single marvellous idea you can pounce on – and it probably will – then it's always worthwhile.

Some novelists use a similar method to keep track of the plot once the work is actually in progress. Lynne Barrett-Lee doesn't use index cards as such but says, "I certainly jot down a list of key scenes at some point – on the computer – then print them out, cut the page into strips and play around with them till the order seems correct. Once I have that, I re-sort them on screen and start adding any linking scenes I need, in much the same fashion."

Sarah Duncan says she does it after she has completed the whole of the first draft – she writes a summary of all her scenes on cards and lays them out in front of her so she can get an overview of the structure of the novel and see if it can be improved. This sounds like an excellent idea to me.

She says: "It's much easier to see the novel overall, and if there are any holes. I think it's a help psychologically, too. My novels are over 100,000 words long and all that paper can be daunting, but a little pack of index cards somehow makes it manageable."

Magazine writer Penny Alexander uses cards to help her keep track of her serials. When I spoke to her she was mid-way through one for *The People's Friend*. "I've put descriptions of characters on cards so they're easily accessed, and their eyes, hair or teeth don't turn a different colour part-way through," she explains. She starts her planning with a "flow diagram" to see connections and what-ifs, but later uses a card system. "It is all about getting the threads back into some kind of logical order."

Thread Charts

I first came across one of these in a workshop run by novelist Jean Chapman (thanks Jean!) but lots of different writers use thread charts or a variation on them. These too can be very useful as a visual overview of what's going on and I find them helpful in making sure I'm keeping all the different strands going and haven't started a minor sub-plot in chapter three and then forgotten to mention it again for the next sixteen chapters. They work a bit like this:

Let us imagine we are writing a novel about a girl called Lucy who has just got a new job in an old people's home – it is probably called something like *Sunshine Towers* – and who battles away dealing with wee and the odour of cabbage by day while, in the tradition of many a fine contemporary tale, drinks too much Pinot Grigio and searches for a better boyfriend by night.

In between times, she worries about her mother, who has begun acting strangely, sees her best friend Tina, and frets over how she can go about reducing the size of her bum (better not become a writer, for a start).

At work, Matron – a peculiar woman with a dodgy past – makes life difficult, but Lucy strikes up a friendship with inmate Aged Arthur who is away with the fairies most of the time but enjoys occasional moments of clarity (usually when Lucy has sneaked him in a rum and coke) in which he is able to offer some thought-provoking pearls of wisdom on love and life (think discerning readership/book clubs/*Richard & Judy* etc).

Lucy gets him a three-legged Pekinese from the local Animal Rescue Centre (think Nation of Dog Lovers) which Ned, the kitchen-hand and chief cabbage-chopper, takes for walks in a wheelbarrow.

As Lucy gets through more blokes than Arthur has hot dinners (Matron is siphoning off the catering budget), her mum disappears and her friend Tina gets increasingly pregnant while refusing to admit who the father is.

Driven to despair and exhaustion by this convoluted and mostly pointless plot, Lucy trips over a stray commode and breaks her ankle. Rescued in her moment of agony by a knight in an apron, she realises she has been in love with Ned all along.

Just as it strikes them that they will never be able to afford to ride off into the sunset, Lucy's mum reappears to reveal that Aged Arthur is really Lucy's granddad and not ga-ga at all but assuming a false identify to test Lucy to see if she is morally fit to inherit the secret family millions he has wrestled back from Matron's porn empire.

The shock sends Tina into labour and who will be the father? Has Aged Arthur got more lead in his pencil than even Matron suspected? Was it Tom, Dick or Harry or – Quelle Horreur – will Ned the chopper be forced to abandon Lucy and face up to his duty? Only a DNA test live on *Trisha* will tell if Lucy's dreams can finally come true…

Our thread chart might look something like this:

Thread Chart for:
The Lacklustre Life of Luckless Lucy by A. Wannabe

Chapter No	Lucy at work	Aged Arthur	Lucy's Mum	Lucy's Love Life	Matron	Pregnant Tina
1 Mid Jan	First day at work	Introduce Arthur			Enter Matron	
2			Home – mum being being peculiar	Out evening meets Tom		First mention Tina
3	Bed pan incident with Mabel	Arthur loses his pyjamas			Trouble with Matron	
4	Lucy helps in the kitchen – meets Ned	Arthur has his bunion looked at. Discussion about dogs	Mum still being peculiar	Chatted up by Dick		Arrange see Tina
5	Wakes up with Dick. Late for work	Loses teeth! Ned has idea about rescue dog			Matron gives first verbal warning	
6 Two weeks later	Morning off to pick up Pekinese	Arthur gets dog	Finds strange receipts in washing basket	Light flirtation with guy from animal rescue	Mysterious goings-on in storeroom again	Tina reveals she is up the duff
7 Three months have passsed. It is Easter Monday	Bad hangover Calls in sick		Heart to heart with mum–reveal truth about bingo nights	Spots Harry across crowded room		Tina still throwing up – NB pregnancy will be showing

N.B. It can be useful to note the date as well as the chapter number as if, say, you want Tina to give birth in the final chapter, you need to check the rest of the action takes nine months too. Don't forget Christmas, birthdays etc. If action takes place over several years, they need a mention sometime!

Spider Charts

The lovely Katie Fforde told me about these. She heard about them from her publicist at Random House, Charlotte Bush, whom she describes as "the most efficient person on the planet".

Spider Charts are good in the very early stages of planning when you are really just brain-storming ideas with yourself. The following example is the sort of spider chart Katie used when she was thinking about her novel *Practically Perfect* (Century).

This is the tale of Anna, a newly-qualified interior designer, who buys a cottage to renovate and sell on. All sorts of things go wrong but she is fortified by her neighbour, Chloe, who as well as the wine and sympathy presents Anna with a rescue greyhound. The book, described by *The Independent* as a "witty and generous romance" also, naturally, features a good-looking bloke on the horizon. So Katie's initial spider chart looked a bit like this:

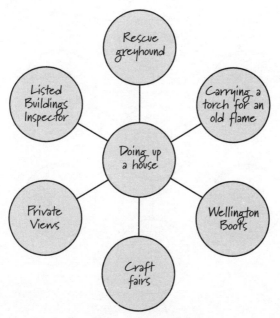

She knew she wanted to write about house renovation – she had just had her own house fairly extensively re-worked and says: "I never waste anything that happens in my own life" so that was the main blob in the middle, then – as she had all the associated ideas – she added further blobs. Sometimes two blobs might have a definite connection – e.g. the Listed buildings inspector and the greyhound – so these are joined by an arrow. If you want to know where Wellington boots come into it, you'll have to buy the book!

Obviously there is no end to how many blobs you can have so, let us just imagine for a moment that she had decided that the greyhound would need an operation and have to spend two days at the vet's and in the waiting room our heroine would meet just the right carpenter to make up her kitchen cupboards and, through him, she'd find out about a dog show, which would later be the scene of a fine dramatic climax. Meanwhile, at one of the craft fairs, the heroine's interest in 18th century chamber pots is reawakened... Then it might end up looking like this:

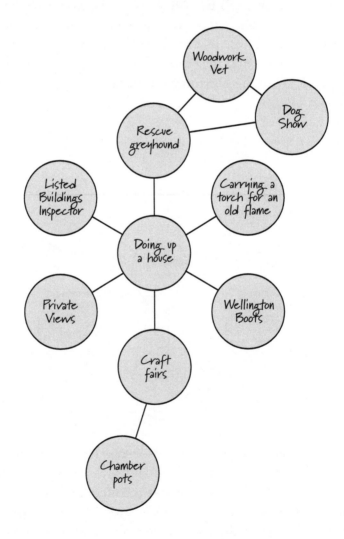

Katie says she starts with one of these, "follows her nose" for a bit and then writes a synopsis proper as she goes along. She also recommends a "backwards synopsis" as a useful tool – particularly if you get to a sticky patch. For example, she says, imagine that you know how your novel is going to end: the couple in a clinch on a beach in the Bahamas (mmm, yes please!). But, unfortunately, you are stuck somewhere long before that. Start working backwards from that final scene, is Katie's advice. Ask yourself how they are going to get there? Fly, presumably. How do they get to the airport? Why did they choose the Bahamas? What had happened just before that? And so on.

Thanks Katie! This is something I shall try too.

The Wallpaper Roll

This is another tip from Lynne Hackles – she uses a roll of wallpaper to make a wall chart similar to a thread chart (she would!).

She uses the back of a long piece ruled into columns – which she keeps tacked up somewhere prominent. She lists her characters across the top, with the chapter headings or numbers down the side.

Then in each square she makes brief notes about what each character might get up to in that particular chapter. The beauty of this, I imagine, is that because you can keep on rolling it out – it could hang all the way down the length of the wall – you can have an overview of the whole book in front of you without having to mess around with sellotape.

Or it might just be her being bonkers again.

Black and White Boards

Barbara Erskine, the sweet old-fashioned thing, plans out her novels on a blackboard with chalk.

Which reminds me that one of the most useful things I have ever bought for my office is a mini white-board and dry-wipe pen which stands next to my computer and on which I can jot down deadline dates, sudden thoughts and things I mustn't forget and then have the satisfaction of erasing them with a small cloth once they're done (it's the little pleasures…).

If you have the wall space, a big white board could serve as a useful place to plan out a novel – again very easy to alter, as new ideas come along or the order of events change. Can also be handy to cover up damp patches.

Grow a Novel in a Folder

I don't know who first thought of this and I've never tried this either, but it sounds excellent in theory.

You take an A4 ring-binder, lots of paper and a hole punch. Let's say you've thought of what your first chapter would be – let's suppose it's Samantha's and Robert's wedding day and everyone is expectantly assembled in the church.

But at the bit where the vicar says: Do you take this woman? Robert shakes his head and strides out of the church, leaving Samantha in floods and her father mightily pissed off that he's just wasted ten grand on a marquee and a lot of poached salmon.

You know the second chapter is going to be ten years later where we discover what Samantha and Robert have been doing since. The ending you have in mind is them getting married again, older, wiser and in the registry office (her old man isn't going to be caught like that again) where maybe they will prepare to live happily ever after or – if you're one to harbour grudges – Samantha will do exactly the same to him.

Anyway, what you do is write some brief notes on those three chapters, and put them in the folder in chronological order. (If you can get hold of some numbered file dividers, so much the better.)

If you're a writer who likes to work with pictures you could stick a photograph of a bride that looks like Samantha might in with the first chapter, and if you've got a useful cutting from the newspaper in which a jilted bride describes how the experience scarred her forever, pop that in too.

Ditto the feature in which a psychologist explains why some men are terrified of commitment.

When you have the brilliant idea of Robert having a terrible car crash and Samantha who – guess what – is now a physiotherapist (someone's got to do it) being the one to get him back on his feet (cue hilarious scene where she kicks his crutches away from him and stamps on his bad leg) – jot it down and add this in. Yes, together with the research into what sort of things a physiotherapist actually does when not exacting sweet revenge.

Gradually your file fills up and your novel grows. If you decide the car accident would serve the plot better if it happened in chapter three instead of thirteen, you can simply unclip the pages and move them forward.

Again, it keeps all the info in one place – which helps one feel more in control of what can feel like a very unwieldy project – and saves research notes getting lost or forgotten (I frequently come across cuttings I had intended to consult two books ago and never did).

And if you're getting stuck or bored on chapter two – there'll be notes in there to start you off on a later chapter instead.

Mind the Gap

And talking of getting stuck ….

This is my own favourite novel-writing method, which I employed when writing my third book – *One Glass is Never Enough* (put it on your shopping list now).

Playwright Angela Lanyon so named it, after listening to my explanation of how it works in my workshop at Writers' Holiday (more of that later) entitled *Novel Writing – Where do I Start?* (a bloody good question if ever there was one). It is perfect for those who frequently grind to a halt out of frustration, boredom or just that oh-god-where-do-I-go-now? feeling.

Though I would say at this point that if it's the second one, ask yourself why you are bored. Because if you are finding the endless description of exactly what your hero had for dinner before he spent a scintillating evening discussing accountancy with his mother, a bit of a yawn, then the chances are your readers will too. If the narrative is getting tedious, even to yourself, ask yourself how necessary it actually is.

Remember there's nothing wrong with writing: "Samantha was starving, having spent her entire lunch-hour queuing in the post-office waiting to get the parcel weighed."

There's no rule that says you have to describe everyone waiting in the line and the fact that the bloke in front of her was clogging up the system by filling in the form for a tax disc for his car, instead of getting it online like anyone with a life, and the exact degree of unhelpfulness displayed by the old dragon behind the counter.

Nor – tempting as it is – do you have to go off into a diatribe on why pensioners who've got all day, every bloody day, to go to the bank or post-office have to descend en masse on a Friday at one o'clock.

But I digress. Mind the Gap works like this:

You merrily write away and when you get stuck or fed up or aren't sure where to go next you write in some capitals like this:

AND THEN SOMETHING ELSE WILL HAPPEN – I'M NOT SURE WHAT – PROBABLY THEY HAVE ANOTHER ROW AND HE'LL CRASH THE CAR. (NB DON'T FORGET TO CATCH UP ON SUB-PLOT WITH STAN.) Then you cut to the really heart-wrenching bit in Intensive Care.

With this method you can write according to mood too. Leave yourself notes on what needs to be inserted later – NEED A COUPLE MORE SCENES OF HER WORKING IN SHOP AND FRIENDSHIP WITH BERT DEVELOPING – and then leap forward to the bits you've been looking forward to – the big love scene or the violent car-chase.

When I got to the end of my last novel it was only 56,000 words long. It grew to its full 90,000 when I went back and filled in all the bits in capitals – which was enjoyable as I could relax then, knowing I had got the story down. It was "safe", as it were, and in front of me, however imperfect, to work on.

Another advantage of working this way is that you never have any excuse to stop because you're on a tricky bit. Your novel continues to grow even when you're feeling bogged down with it.

Because keeping going is the only way. Lynne Barrett-Lee puts a row of qqqqqqq whenever she doesn't know what to say next. I use xxxxx if my dialogue is drying up. It really doesn't matter – the important thing is to carry on slogging and you'll get there.

Eventually.

Suck it and See

And finally – if none of the above appeal to you?

Just start writing and see what happens – you might be pleasantly surprised. Or you might not.

Do remember though that at this stage it is supposed to look like rubbish. So don't let that put you off. Write, write, write. You can sort it out later.

Voice

But *how* do you write it?

A writer's voice is their most important asset. As successful novelist Lisa Jewell says: "A fresh, compelling voice can carry an average story much further than an unoriginal voice can carry a great story."

She is absolutely right, but what is voice, and how can you make sure you've got a good one?

Your voice is your own individual style and sound. The writer's fingerprint, if you like. It is what would make you recognise a book by your favourite author even if the cover were blank.

For in the same way as we all have a unique way of speaking, so we have of writing. It is our own special use of vocabulary, rhythm, sentence length and structure. I don't believe it can be taught – it is something that develops naturally with practice.

The more you write, and the more you RELAX while writing, the more it will become apparent. And you'll know when it has.

In the meantime, I can only advise: Don't try to imitate another writer; don't strain to use long words or try too hard to be "literary" or highbrow. Just keep writing, the way that comes naturally to YOU and your own distinctive voice will emerge.

I think I probably have two "voices" – one for when I am being "light" and another slightly different one for when I am being more serious and "literary" (it doesn't happen often).

I can look back at early pieces of writing and see how self-conscious some of them were, how formal or wordy; how I seemed to be trying a little too hard. As I read on, I see how gradually I found a style I was comfortable with and how both voices came about.

I remember distinctly the first time my "humorous" voice really established itself. I was writing a story I called *Carla's Gift*.

It has since been published in the charity anthology *Sexy Shorts for Christmas* (Accent Press) but at the time, I wrote it to send to editor Jo Good. It is the tale of a woman learning to have her first orgasm (and is quite chaste really, if you are already having the vapours). "Is QWF ready for this?" I asked, in my covering letter. "I don't know about QWF," Jo replied, "but I certainly am!"

What struck me about the experience of writing it was the way it just flowed out – I wrote it straight off, in little longer than the time it took me to type it. It felt simply as if I were talking to the page. It felt "right".

I knew then that, try as I might to be a literary genius, my natural "voice" was rather more lowbrow.

To prove my point the story began like this:

> What do you say to a woman who has just had her first orgasm on the top of the multi-storey in a Ford Fiesta?
>
> *Congratulations* was the word that sprang to mind but the others were strangely silent.
>
> 'Good for you,' I muttered to a cold shower of black looks.
>
> I have always liked Carla. I liked her when she was married to Stuart and so I like her still. Round here, however, things are not so simple. I had witnessed a definite ripple of unease running around the circle of women I call my friends ever since Stuart walked out of 25 Arnold Drive and Carla – dry–eyed – walked out into the world and started to enjoy herself.
>
> It was as if they feared that having gasped her way to ecstasy with her garage mechanic today, the next logical step would be tempting away their husbands. Frankly she was welcome to mine. If she could stir Norman into producing the merest erect nipple, I'd cheerfully buy her gins all night. And quite honestly, by the look of the other lot's assorted and spreading spouses I thought they should be jolly grateful for any spark of enthusiasm injected into their drooping genitals too.

I wrote that back in 1996 and my voice has of course developed again since. I think I am less wordy now, and write even more simply but I can see in the rhythm and the phraseology the seeds of the way I write today.

Keep writing – anything, everything, entering competitions, experimenting with different subjects and moods – and keep reading, and your style will emerge too.

And when it has, you're halfway there. For it may be difficult to come up with a totally unique plot – we'll go there in a minute – but your voice is your very own.

Losing the Plot

Whether you plan it exhaustively, or pray it will come to you once you begin, there is one thing you must have if you are going to attempt a work of fiction and that is: A Plot.

"Books without plots are like bodies without skeletons," says Katie Fforde. "Very unstable."

But what is the secret of a good one? "Sex," says Wendy Holden succinctly.

"Power," cries June Tate.

"It must appeal to oneself," declares Barbara Erskine.

"It should be fast-moving, with constant peaks and troughs throughout," offers Bernardine Kennedy, while Claire Calman speaks of the importance of the "tension between anticipation, delivery and surprise".

"I think of writing novels as being largely a matter of 'problem solving,'" says Isabel Wolff. "How do your characters interconnect in a way that doesn't depend on coincidence – i.e. bumping into each other in the supermarket the whole time? What – or who – connects them? How are they going to change during the course of the book? How do you move your characters around the story – or even just into another room – in a way that is believable? These are the problems that writers have to solve all the time – and it can really do your head in."

What all these authors are listing, of course, are the ingredients that contribute to what every single great book has in common – its page-turning quality. The thing that makes it "unputdownable" as reviewers are fond of saying these days. Whatever it is that makes us have to read on, that keeps us glued to the print while the dinner burns.

The hallmark of a brilliant book is that it keeps its readers agog to know what happens, to care deeply for the characters, to suspend their disbelief so that they forget it is just a story and are totally transported into that other world.

Easier said than done? Of course. Which is why out of the hundreds of thousands manuscripts produced each year, only a few make it. But why shouldn't one of them be yours, if you too have that gift?

And either you do or you don't. No point trying to be a second Jilly Cooper or John Grisham – aim to be the first one of you!

So stick to your own voice, as Lisa Jewell advises. "Trying to emulate another writer's style is a sure route to writing a rubbish book," she says candidly.

She is right but ultimately you need both – a fresh voice AND a great story or as Sarah Harrison, prolific novelist and author of *How to Write a*

Blockbuster puts it (the capitals are hers!) "STORY FIRST – STORY FIRST – STORY FIRST – STORY FIRST. Oh and did I mention? STORY FIRST." She explains: "It's so much easier to say something if you have something to say."

And do make sure that story is believable; you want nothing to bring your reader up short. To make him or her stop and think: THAT'S not very likely. It's the sort of thing that always disappoints me in a book, however well-written.

And if, worse, I come across a real inaccuracy – a plot twist that couldn't possibly have happened for example – it can put me off completely.

Which brings us neatly on to:

Research – Do You or Don't You?

Frederick Forsyth carries out what he calls "relentless research", spending an entire year at it. Minette Walters is also extremely thorough and painstaking – consulting forensic scientists and attending post-mortems as well as the usual background reading.

While I'm writing this, Jilly Cooper is working on a new racing book. "I have about a hundred books to read," she told me. "Biographies of jockeys and autobiographies of trainers and biographies of horses…"

I, on the other hand, err on the idle side when it comes to research and tend to proceed on a need-to-know basis rather than mugging up for months in advance.

Lynne Barrett-Lee works in similar way. "It's all too easy to spend precious writing time jotting down facts, facts, facts, and to put off the hard bit," she says. Research for her "happens organically as a by-product of writing, definitely not the other way around". She says: "I don't allow myself to sweat the small stuff until I reach a point where I need to. As long as I've established there's a patient soul or two who'll fill me in on any detail I need, I simply call them, as and when, while I'm writing."

All of which shows that there is no right or wrong answer to how much research you should do as long as, whether it takes six months holed up in the British Library or six minutes on the phone to a friend, you do enough.

Even if you are writing "what you know" you're still bound to have to check something, and check it you must, for as we've said already, your novel will only work if it rings true and you won't achieve that if your facts are wonky.

It is also worth remembering that what we know can only ever be just that – what WE know. By talking to others we can gain different insights or whole new angles on what we thought was familiar territory. Hilary Lloyd, the author of *A Necessary Killing* (UKA Press), is an ex-farmer who drew on her own experiences of living through the foot and mouth crisis for her novel.

Despite her first-hand knowledge, there were still things she needed to investigate. She says: "My experience of the epidemic was traumatic but a novel demands much more than reminiscences and feelings. I needed facts, and details of procedures employed by government and other official departments. I also needed to confirm that my own trauma wasn't unique so I read through dozens of bewildered, distraught or angry messages on internet forums used by rural people at the time, and downloaded enough articles and comment from newspapers to wallpaper the whole of the house. The reading and absorbing of this material gave me a much wider view and helped flesh the bones of my plot."

I did a similar thing when I was writing my second novel, *Perfect Alibis*, by talking to lots of different women who'd had affairs – or as many I could find who would admit to it!

Interestingly, for the same book I asked several friends who'd had appendicitis what it felt like, and was surprised by just how different their accounts were, and how entirely varied their symptoms.

It was a lesson on the importance of getting more than one version of anything one's not been through oneself. Make sure you've got the majority experience down rather than a one-off.

For if you are asking a reader to suspend their disbelief and get totally absorbed in the world you've created, then you owe it to them to make sure that world is as authentic as possible.

I usually do this in one of two simple ways – go on Google or ask someone who might know.

Google is a wonderful tool. There isn't much you can't find out on the internet these days, though a word of warning: do always check more than one source.

I have just spent a sobering half hour trying to find out how many grams of carbohydrate are in a large glass of wine (hoping to shed ten pounds on a crash Atkins-type diet while still getting pissed every night). The answers have been variously 3g, 1.8g, 5g and almost 7g (with the only consensus being the dispiriting news that to lose weight you have to give up the booze).

Asking an expert on the given subject is usually a safe bet – although again, two are better than one. During the writing of my last book, I checked facts with a GP, a gynecologist, a dog-owner, two wine-writers (who contradicted each other), an ex-policeman, a nurse and a solicitor.

I also pored over the *London A–Z*, studied different models of answer-machine and, since the novel is entitled *One Glass Is Never Enough* – suffered several near-terminal hangovers.

And I still missed something. I never want my husband to read anything until after it's published but this time I wished he had. He instantly spotted an irregularity that I had totally overlooked (a bottle of champagne to the first reader to write and tell me what it is. Clue: it will help to be a gardener) and which I've been kicking myself for ever since.

I always think that if you have a scene that is heavily dependent on some specialist knowledge – let's say a scene in the operating theatre in a hospital – then it is a good idea to let someone with first-hand experience – say a surgeon or a nurse – to have a quick read through and check for any suspect bits.

Even if you have that sort of experience yourself, make sure your knowledge is up-to-date. Police procedures, for example, have changed a lot over the years, as have the job-descriptions of teachers. Find someone who is doing the job right now rather than speaking to the old duffer next door who retired in 1976.

If you are lucky enough to get a publishing deal, the copy editor will pick up things that need checking too, but be professional and make sure everything in your manuscript is as accurate as you can make it before you submit it. There's an old adage about keeping going through a first draft, that says: "Don't get it right, get it written." It's excellent advice. As long as once you have got it written, you make sure you've also got it right.

Character, Dialogue, and Things to Forget

If you ask Freya North what the secret of a good plot is, she will say simply:

Good Characters. "The most intricate plot will fall flat if the characters are dull and two-dimensional," she very rightly declares.

We do have to believe in the people we read about , we do need to be able to visualise them. We do have to *care*. And getting those characters to come to life in this way can be hard for the beginner writer. (If you are not a beginner and have written seventeen novels, three screen plays and a four-part guide to Spoon Collecting in the 18th Century, please feel free to skip on once more).

This is a letter sent to my *Writing Magazine* column by a chap called William Harrison – it is a query I have received more than once.

I have joined a writing group and now receive regular feedback on my short stories and the early chapters of the novel I'm attempting. I find this very useful but the same criticisms come up again and again. Everyone says that my descriptions of places are beautiful, my prose almost poetic, but I don't seem to be able to write people. They describe my characters as wooden or one-dimensional. My problem is that I don't really understand what they mean or – more importantly – what I can do to put this right.

As I said to Mr Harrison in my reply, it's frustrating to be told something is wrong with no real guidance on how it can be improved. I can remember getting a critique back, years ago, which said that my story seemed "to strain a little". At the time, I had absolutely no idea what this meant (I have now – it was frightful) so it wasn't much help.

But from the critiquer's point of view, there are some things that are very hard to put your finger on – you just know they're not right. In this case, I imagine what the writing group were really saying to William was: your characters are not convincing.

Poor characterisation happens when characters are not multi-faceted enough, tend to be all 'good' or entirely 'bad' (instead of an imperfect mixture of both, like most of us). Maybe they speak in a stilted or unlikely way, come across as stereotypes rather than individuals, or are simply very hard to imagine.

In other words, they are characters that just don't come alive for their reader. As a writer, the first way to avoid this is to make sure that they come alive for YOU. For if you don't intimately understand the people you are writing about, what hope has anyone else got?

Some creative writing tutors recommend making index cards for each character and noting down everything about them from their hair colour to where they went to school to whether they prefer tea or coffee.

Personally I find the thought of this too tedious for words but the principle behind it is a good one.

You need to really know who you are writing about. The characters in my novels exist like real people in my head. I see them quite clearly as I write about them and can hear their voices (though one has to be careful about saying this too loudly – since non-writers may imagine one has one's own social worker).

And when I read a good novel by someone else their characters exist for me, too. In fact I sometimes find myself thinking about the protagonists from books I read years ago – the hallmark of a successful tale if ever there was one. I can still remember all sorts of things about Tiffany Trott – Isabel Wolff's first heroine – and boy, was I rooting for her all the way.

Isabel describes novel-writing as an "exercise in amateur psychology" and emphasises the importance of building up a psychological profile of your main characters that is absolutely believable – and also consistent. "You can't have your readers sitting there thinking, 'but she wouldn't *do* that'. Your heroine can of course act 'out of character', but you have to provide a cast iron reason for why she would do so – i.e. she's drunk, ill, heartbroken, recently bereaved."

Carole Mathews works for two weeks on her characters, giving them whole background stories which, she says, she then never uses. If you can't face going to these lengths – I'm not sure I could – do hold on to the basic concept of what she's doing, all the same.

Ask yourself about your own creations – do you know not just what they look like and how they sound, but is it also very clear to you how they would react in any given situation? Can you visualise their mannerisms? Are you familiar with their emotional foibles and personality quirks? Do you understand what's behind their positive and negative traits?

Make lists or cards if it helps (just because I do the minimum, doesn't mean you have to) but as Lynne Hackles, author (in case you've forgotten) of *The Handy Little Book for Writers* (NAWG Publications) says sternly: "Your characters should be real to you, like your relatives, and you don't forget about them, do you?" Unfortunately not, I think, is the answer there.

I prefer to compare writing a novel with being in love. In that happy state, the object of your affections hovers at the edges of your consciousness whatever you are doing, and this is what you need to aim for with the characters of your novel. If you can just think about them for a few minutes fairly frequently, you will be surprised how much they will grow in your subconscious and nag away at the corners of your mind and the more they do, the more you will realise about them.

But if you are having real difficulty imagining all this, then the best piece of advice I can give you is: turn to real people. Think of friends, family or work colleagues – can you take inspiration from them? Can the harassed father in your novel fiddle with paperclips the way your boss used to, while talking too loudly on his mobile like the friend you play golf with?

N.B. It's best to fudge things a bit so even if your ghastly sister-in-law suspects you were thinking of her as the blueprint for the carping wife, she'll never be sure. Change her hair-colour, accent and how many children she's got but if you hold a picture of her in your mind as you write you'll do it all the better.

I am often inspired by real people but these days I make a point of altering them. If the interfering mother-in-law in your book bears an uncanny resemblance to your husband's dear mama, then give her a make-over. The original got grey hair? Make this one snow-white. If she's got a sister, give her two brothers. If she's a dog-lover, make her mad about cats. And so on.

In my experience, people seldom recognise their own negative qualities (and that's the only thing you need fret about. Anything positive and they'll be overjoyed to think they appear). So as long as you change the physical details, your boss will never realise the crashing bore in chapter seven is him.

And if ever asked outright, the best approach is to lie. State unequivocally that your fictional characters are just that – made-up – and that if you *have* ever drawn on real people you've combined the traits of several and rolled them into one. Everyone will automatically assume the unflattering bits were someone else.

It can also help to dedicate the book to the person most likely to be offended (my first novel was for my mother!). But I have trained myself to genuinely combine characters now. In *One Glass is Never Enough*, the heroine's best friend, Lizzie, is made up of three of mine. She looks like one, has the personality of another and the lifestyle of a third. And I bet none of them recognise themselves.

As well as keeping an eye on those you know well, watch and listen wherever you go as strangers in pubs, shops or on the bus can be wonderful starting points. I have long wanted to explore the woman who bellowed across our local Tesco, for the combined enjoyment of everyone in the queue, "Tell me the truth now, Mother! Is it his bowels?"

And I have used – quite blatantly – a very drunk man who once came into the bar I used to own. He was so inebriated he'll never remember.

On the other hand, if I am teaching you to suck eggs here and your characters are already like crystal to you but somehow they are still not working for anyone else, then you need to look at how you are putting them across.

Have you described what they look like, demonstrated their strengths or weaknesses, given an indication of their outlook on life? It is possible to be so clear in your own mind about why a character has just stormed out of her best friend's wedding that you quite forget to explain it to the reader. I do that sometimes, too.

When I sent my agent – The Fearsome One – the first three chapters of *One Glass Is Never Enough,* she was not impressed. "Apart from Chloe," she complained, (Chloe is a fairly minor character in the whole scheme of things), "I don't know what anyone looks like! This Danny," she said crossly, "what's his hair like? What colour's this designer shirt of his? Victor? Can't visualise him at all. It's not enough just to say he's tall. And as for Claire…"

It went on like this for several minutes. When she drew breath I got a word in. "What did you think of chapters two and three?" I ventured hopefully.

"HURRRUMPH" came the reply. "I didn't bother with THEM! Go and read some Jilly Cooper!"

I wouldn't like you to run away with the idea that my agent is anything but totally loveable – I adore her – but she is not for the faint-hearted.

You could however do worse than to follow her advice. Jilly Cooper is an excellent example of an author who creates vivid pictures of her characters instantly and is a good point of reference for all of us. Consider for example how she describes Perdita in the opening chapter of *Polo* (Bantam Press), reprinted by kind permission of The Random House Group Ltd:

She was a big girl for fourteen, tall and broad in the shoulder, with pale, luminous skin and a full, sulky mouth. A long Greek nose and large, very wide-apart eyes, as dark as elderberries, gave her the look of a creature of fable, a unicorn that might vanish at any moment.

So visual!

And later – I love this –

a small, fat, bald man with the tiny mean eyes and wide jaw of a bilious hippo…

Can't you just picture him?

I went back and reworked my first chapters and The Fearsome One was absolutely right – I had seen my characters very clearly in my own mind but had done little to convey that vision to my readers.

The same applies to your characters' motivation, personal history and general philosophy on life.

You may feel you could go on *Mastermind* with it but that's not much use if anyone picking up your book is totally bewildered by Fred's determination to ruin his brother's life because you've forgotten to actually put into words the fact that the sibling in question ran off with the love of Fred's life/nicked all the wealth/ate the family guinea pig twenty years earlier.

Above all feel for your characters – love 'em, hate 'em, be furious with them but do feel something. Because your novel will only work if you induce real emotion in us the readers – if you make us care so much for the people you've created (or pinched from the real world) that we simply have to turn the page.

Dialogue

The thing about writing good dialogue, I find, is that generally either writers have a natural flair for it or – unfortunately – they don't.

In the latter case, this is a shame. Not only because their attempts at short-story or novel-writing will be excruciating but because while it is clear that sparkling dialogue is the spice and backbone of a good novel, it is very difficult to explain to anyone else what makes it sparkle.

I have had letters about this at *Writing Magazine* and have only really been able to point out that common mistakes are either to write totally unrealistic, wooden exchanges or to make them so realistic they're unreadable.

On the one hand, it is good advice to urge writers to listen endlessly to how "real people" speak. On the other, one needs to point out that to then write that down verbatim is a recipe for disaster.

As Catherine Merriman, novelist and creative writing tutor at the University of Glamorgan puts it: "Dialogue should not try to reproduce the ramble and repetition and profanity of real speech – pare everything back so it merely gives the *illusion* of real speech."

In other words, the art of writing good dialogue lies in capturing the essence of what people say in real situations without necessarily including all the detail. If you listen to any conversation for more than a few minutes it is not hard to see why.

I was horrified when I first heard myself on radio to find not only that I sounded like Pollyanna on speed but that I preceded the answer to every question by saying "umm" and then "urgh". (If the Director General of the BBC is reading this, I would like to point out that I have improved massively since and should still be considered for my own Breakfast Show.)

I still have a tendency to say everything twice when I'm particularly animated – not the stuff a gripping read is made of – and the husband of a friend is incapable of more than two sentences without adding: "yer know what I mean?" to the end of them (why she doesn't take a blunt instrument to him, I shall never know).

So unless you want to bore your reader rigid you need to filter out such "realities" and instead concentrate on what he or she needs to know, and most importantly, what will move the plot along.

Make sure your characters are not just droning on about what they had for breakfast, to fill in a bit of time before the next piece of action, but are actually telling us something we didn't previously know. Although for heaven's sake employ a light touch and avoid what Catherine refers to as "bad soap territory."

There's nothing worse than a conversation that goes like this:

"Your brother Brian's here," announced Sally. "And I'm getting fed up with him. He probably wants to talk to you about his divorce again. He's been so miserable since his wife, Fenella, upped and left him, hasn't he?"

"Yes, he has," agreed Robin. Mind you, you can hardly blame him – it's not very nice when your wife leaves you for the window-cleaner..."

Slightly more subtle would be:

Sally came back into the kitchen. "Your miserable git of a brother's here again."

Robin sighed. "Give him a break – he's had a tough time." But his heart sank too. Another evening of listening to Brian banging on about how miserable his life was without Fenella...

Dialogue, says award-winning saga-writer Margaret Kaine, is "the best way I know of showing character." To create dialogue that is convincing, she says you must be "completely inside your character's head and heart. And as no two people talk or sound exactly the same, each character should have – even if only in a subtle way – a distinctive voice."

I would just say here, however – be wary of how distinctive. Unless you are Robert Burns, I would not attempt several pages of regional dialect unless it were absolutely essential, as reading it can be exhausting. Sufficient to slide in somewhere, I think, the fact that whoever is speaking had a strong accent. Or as Mil Millington eloquently puts it:

"If all your middle-class characters' dialogue is written perfectly normally – as though they have no accent whatsoever – but you feel the need to have any working-class or regional characters' words written phonetically ("It's yer 'eater, missus – yer gonna need a new un.") then, instead of doing that, you might want to consider picking up your keyboard and rhythmically smashing yourself in the face with it."

Having said that, do try to think of how people actually speak – remember that spoken English is quite different from its written form – we use contractions, leave sentences unfinished and do not always use very precise grammar or formal terminology. Well, not usually.

I once judged a short-story competition for a writing group and was then asked to go along to one of their meetings and give verbal feedback to the entrants.

I highlighted a piece of dialogue in what was supposedly a modern-day story by one of the non-winners. It went something like this:

"But hear what I have to say," cried Cuthbert. "For I can tell you that Henry is touched by tragedy. Daily he laments the loss of his dear-departed forbear..."

"The thing is," I explained kindly, "real people don't talk like that."

"I do," came the earnest reply. There were nods of agreement around the room. "I'm afraid he does," mused one of the others.

Hmm. He might do but most people don't. They certainly don't talk like that in most offices, the average supermarket or, come to that, on Radio Two.

If you spend time listening to how people interact you will find that everyday conversation is often a whole series of half-thoughts and non-sequiturs.

"Dialogue is not a game of ping pong," says Catherine Merriman firmly. "All main characters have their own moods and agendas and don't necessarily answer directly questions posed by others. Obliqueness and implicitness makes for interesting dialogue."

People also talk over each other and interrupt and there's nothing wrong with that as long as it doesn't become too confusing. An argument, for example, might quite logically go like this:

> "I didn't think..."
> "No, you never do. Look what happened when Cathy–"
> "For god's sake. That was an accident. And you were the one who–"
> "Don't you dare blame me!"

Be careful, however, about going on for so long in this vein that the reader gets confused as to who is saying what. It always infuriates me if I'm engrossed in a book only to find myself having to stop and trace a conversation back two pages because I've got no idea which character has just said: "I was the one who killed him."

Make sure you break up long screeds of dialogue with some pointers. For example:

> "I hate you!" Cathy shook her fist.
> "Please don't be like this." Jim tried to put his arm around her.

Also try to avoid very long chunks of speech by the same person without some respite. If they really must go on at length – they are explaining exactly how they came to be standing over the inert figure of the vicar, God help him – then do break it up by the speaker lighting a fag, mopping his brow or beginning to pace the floor. Or have his listener do it.

For this reason, I find it very helpful to not only hear my imaginary characters in my head when I'm writing dialogue, but to actually visualise them and see what they are doing. This also helps to prevent one from stating the obvious. For example, let us imagine we have a situation where two people are stuck in a lift. One is late for a meeting, the other is frightened. How might the conversation go?

John looked around him. "Oh damn! The lift has stopped."

"Oh no, I'm claustrophobic," said Mary.

John walked over to the panel of switches by the door. "Hang on – I'll press the emergency button…"

I hope you are by now being sick in a bucket because this little scenario is about as likely as me winning the Booker Prize. It will be completely evident to both parties that the lift has ground to a halt so there is no need for John to point it out. He'd probably just let out an expletive and look at his watch.

If Mary has a problem being confined in small spaces, she'll feel immediately uneasy. But she's more likely to display this by breathing deeply, clutching her throat or looking around her in panic rather than by calmly announcing the medical name for her reaction.

And hopefully, unless John is completely dense and useless, he will already be pushing the red button rather than talking about it.

Remember also that you can convey an awful lot with gestures as well as words.

"I don't think you are telling me the truth," she said angrily…

could sound stilted, whereas

"Come off it!" She banged her coffee cup down on the table.

might be a little more natural.

Having said that, different characters will express themselves in different ways and dialogue is one of the main ways in which you will reveal what your protagonists are all about.

Some people do become very icy and formal when angered, others splutter incoherently. The person who says in a tight voice: "I don't think so," is not the same as she who cries: "You've got to be joking!" and different again from the bloke who sneers "Are you having a f**king laugh?"

"Keep it short and snappy whatever the mood," says gritty-novelist Bernardine Kennedy, whose books are all dialogue-led. "Nobody, except maybe a politician who doesn't want to be interrupted, speaks in long drawn-out sentences that go on and on like orations."

Bernardine's advice is to read part of the dialogue out loud, preferably taping it so you can play it back to see how realistic it sounds.

Margaret Kaine recommends reading aloud too. "And not just quietly to yourself, but as though you were reading it to a group of people. There's no better way of revealing flaws."

If you have friends with time on their hands you could read it with one of them, both of you taking different parts and see how that feels.

In the meantime, keep listening to others talking, at work, at home, on the bus, in the street. Listen to radio plays, take in a some decent films or even watch *Eastenders*. Though the latter comes with a warning: if suddenly all your characters are saying: "Wot's going on?" you'll know you've overdone it.

Oh, and for God's sake, lay it out and punctuate it properly. It looks terrible if you don't.

Remember that

1) Commas and full stops go inside the speech marks and if the speaker hasn't finished his sentence then you only use a comma – not a full stop – after you've shown who he is. (Catherine Merriman has taught me during the writing of this book the correct term for this is "attribution". She means "he said", "she asked" etc. You live and learn in this game.)

Compare and contrast:
"It's nearly time," said Gregory, "to open the port."
"It's 8pm!" announced Gregory. "Time to open the port."

2) Question Marks go inside the speech marks when they are part of the quotation and outside when they are not. So it is:
Gregory was becoming agitated. "Have you got the stilton?"
But
What would he do, I wondered, when Amanda declared: "I've eaten it."?

Catherine Merriman has also drawn my attention to the importance of a new indented paragraph when speakers change and the need to join narrative action to speech if they belong to the same person.

Because I am now thoroughly bored with Gregory and his port – he'll have gout the way he's going – I shall use Catherine's examples below:

> 'What did you say your name was?' Kate asked the question offhandedly, as if she didn't care.
> 'I didn't.' Roy threw the ball in the air and waited.
> 'Oh.'
> Roy smiled.

Catherine Merriman who, remember, is a creative writing tutor at the University of Glamorgan, so she knows what she's talking about, also reminds us:

1) Don't use semicolons, colons or brackets (parentheses) in dialogue. For gaps use ellipsis…or dashes – . For speech cut-offs or brackets use dashes.

2) Beware over-use of the exclamation mark. Don't use to indicate humour. Use for loudness: 'Come here!' he bellowed. Or genuine exclamations. 'Oh drat!'

For my own erudite pronouncements on such things please read on.

The Tedious Bits – Stuff You Must Remember

Grammar and Punctuation

Yes, they do matter. Nobody is going to take you seriously if you think potatoes has an apostrophe or you witter on about having "less" apples* instead of "fewer" (my pet hate – I've even heard the BBC get it wrong).

*Footnote: Use "less" only when the noun is uncountable e.g. one speaks about having less time/space/money. "Fewer" is for countable nouns e.g. apples, children, five pound notes. If you can't work out whether a noun is countable or uncountable (even after this excellent explanation) ask yourself if you could have three of them.

If English is your first language and you're even half-educated, you should use good grammar instinctively. And there has been absolutely no excuse for poor punctuation since Christmas 2004 when everyone in the land was given a copy of *Eats, Shoots and Leaves*.

About Layout

Which yes, I know, you've heard a hundred times before but just you volunteer to judge a short story competition and you will be amazed at how many writers still haven't grasped these basic requirements. So, just in case:

Even if you do the first draft longhand, the final manuscript must be typed or word-processed, double-spaced on one side of the (white) A4 paper only. Green ink or pink perfumed notelets will say: Mad Person.

Put your name and the title of the book as a footer on each page and make sure you NUMBER them. Literary agent Simon Trewin cites unnumbered pages as one of his pet hates. "What are we supposed to do if the manuscript falls on the floor?" he enquires. "I haven't got time to do a literary jigsaw!"

Use a decent-sized font. 12 as a minimum. Some of these commissioning editors might be gorgeous young thirty-somethings but a lot of agents are of an age to need reading glasses. If it's in tiny print they're going to be fed-up before they start.

Use wide margins.

Use Spell-check.

Double-check spell-check yourself. It will pick up spelling mistakes but not usage errors. E.g. It will think "The dog gnawed at it's bone" or "Look over their – the children are with there parents" is quite acceptable. (N.B. if you do too, I suggest you give up now and go back to your stick-insects.) You can of course, switch on Grammar-check as well but it will drive you insane, and quite frankly you're going to be doo-lally enough by the end of this already.

Things You Can Forget

I think it was Somerset Maughan who said there are three rules for writing a novel but nobody knows what they are. For the moment, if you're just starting out, forget any notion of "the right way" and just get it down on paper in the best way to suit you because **the most important thing of all is:**

YOU'VE GOT TO FINISH IT.

Hundreds of thousands of people start a book. Some of them may be totally fantastically, ground-breakingly, earth-shatteringly, toe-curlingly good writers or brilliant story-tellers. But we will never know because round about chapter seven (or two) they gave up.

If you want to be a writer – a real one – you have to keep going. As Lisa Jewell says: "Don't expect it to be easy. Don't expect it to be fun. Do expect it to be a complete nightmare."

But keep going and get to the end and – there you will have it – a first draft that you can begin weaving your magic on.

Just try your best to:

Keep the plot going forward
Keep us wanting to turn the page
But above all –

...I'LL FINISH

Keeping Going –

Discipline and Displacement Part Two

Jeffrey Archer describes himself as "a very disciplined writer".

His routine is to write in two-hour slots, from 6–8 a.m., 10 a.m. – 12 p.m., 2–4 p.m. and 6–8 p.m. "In between, I go for a walk, eat or watch a film."

I find this wholly admirable and almost impossible to imagine. I wish fervently that I was like that but sadly the best laid plans...

A few months ago when I realised that it was a year since my last novel was published and I hadn't got nearly far enough with this book, I stopped and attempted an in-depth analysis of where my time disappeared to.

I was writing one weekly column, two monthly columns and the occasional article for the national papers. Let's say eight days work a month. So how come I was so behind? I looked hard at my life. Even leaving aside the occasional urge to clear out a cupboard and the odd long lunch, there should still have been more time than there was.

In theory I was writing from nine-ish in the morning – once I had dropped my son at the bus-stop, emptied the dishwasher, kicked any crumbs out of sight under the kitchen table and done the *Times Two* Crossword (important for limbering up brain and staving off Alzheimer's).

Once upstairs in my writing room I pretty much stayed there all day – with maybe a quick expedition to the kitchen for sustenance around lunchtime – until the son came home again and fell in a starved heap at my feet. You would think therefore that I would be churning out many thousands of words. It seemed not.

Sometimes, it's true, I made phone calls to my publisher and at other times The Fearsome One called me (I have learnt not to call her unless I have something Very Important to say. Otherwise I get short shrift and told to Get On With It).

Occasionally I gave a talk to 12 people who looked as if they wished they'd stayed home to watch the shopping channel and I do have a mild addiction to sudoku.

I also have fingers in a couple of non-writing pies which can be time consuming but mostly I thought, I was sitting in my writing room, apparently writing. So why was I producing so little? In desperation, I called in a Life Coach called Angela Brier-Stephenson (**www.anotherjourneybegins.com**) and she revealed all.

Emails: the Hidden Time-eaters

Questioning me on my morning routine, Angela discovered that once I am in my room I make a cup of tea (green with lemon – very good for you – full of antioxidants) turn on the radio, switch on the computer, open Outlook Express and – now I learn – that's where it all goes wrong.

I send emails. I've always begun this way. It's a chance to catch up with the gossip, share a bit of angst, describe my hang-over… It's a warm-up before the real writing starts. Even if it now transpires that the warm-up becomes a full-blown work-out and suddenly it's lunchtime and I've sent seventeen, received nine and haven't even opened the file marked "Finish Urgently". And when I do start writing? I'm still checking them.

When I was a smoker, I'd light a fag if I didn't know what to do next; now I hit the "Send & Receive" button. Stuck on how my heroine's going to be back in the bathroom by the time her double-crossing lover shins up the drainpipe? Look for emails! Realise chapter three's a dog's breakfast? Send a couple of replies.

I wouldn't dream of replying to a hand-written letter mid work-day, but a quick click to switch programmes and I find myself exchanging news with a long-lost cousin from the dubious branch of the family or swapping dirty jokes with a dodgy journalist I once met at a party.

At the height of my email addiction (I am thinking of forming Emailer Anon for other sufferers) I once sent 486 in one month. Even if they were only 100 words each – and a lot of them were an awful lot longer than that – that's half a novel!

And because I was typing – I thought it was work. It's got to stop, said

Angela. So I had to go cold turkey. No emails till lunchtime, then hands off again till five. (I've only caved in four times since writing this page.)

Other writers have a similar problem with the dreaded net. "Wireless broadband is the biggest killer," says Kate Harrison. "I usually begin by having to research some vital fact and an hour later I'm still reading people's blogs or sending gossipy emails."

Freya North, who used to hail the library as the perfect place to write precisely because she couldn't use her mobile phone or check her mail, was emailing me in October to say "horror of horrors they now have wireless connection and I am helpless not to check my emails every 30 secs. Consequently, my new novel still has 50,000 words to go with a Christmas deadline... "

Which I found very comforting.

I expect she got it finished because sheer panic is a great incentive. It's when a deadline looms that I get up at 4 a.m, or don't go to bed till then. When the anticipation and excitement kicks in because the end is in sight, the adrenaline flows and I am a thing possessed.

But at the beginning of a book when the computer screen is horribly empty and there is that proverbial mountain to climb? I'd rather feed the goldfish, put the socks in pairs, refold towels, or colour-code my magazines. Many writers, at that point, feel daunted.

Judy Astley is the author of fourteen successful novels. She says: "I get Writers' Block every day and am permanently sure I'll never write another good sentence."

But as she says: "The secret is to start typing even if it's complete rubbish... Nothing gets written unless you're actually sitting on that chair."

So sit on it, is the obvious answer.

But when it isn't going well and you write a bit, read it back, realise it is bilge and, anyway, you have no idea what to write next because you're fed up with your heroine's whining already and you're beginning to realise the brilliant idea you had in the night for what to do with the hero once he's lost both legs in a car crash and his wife's left him, now seems far-fetched even to you, it is all too easy to wander off and put the kettle on, make a phone call or check for emails. All I can say is: Don't!

Routine

Some writers have a rigid routine, others say they have no routine at all, but you will find what all successful writers share is some sort of regular output – however they achieve this.

Prolific novelist Fiona Walker, who writes a big fat book a year, describes herself as "hopelessly undisciplined".

"I am often at my desk first thing in the morning with ambitious intentions to write several thousand words by teatime. There then follows a long bout of displacement activity. Almost inevitably, I don't really get going until late afternoon and then I can find myself writing through the evening and at times, right through the night."

This is the crucial point – she gets there in the end. When I first met Fiona, she had just done a sixteen hour writing stint!

Katie Fforde starts work at 6 a.m. and keeps going until she's completed a thousand words, "hopefully before 9 a.m. when the phone starts ringing."

Jane Bidder "steels herself" not to answer the phone and expects to produce about 2000 words between 9 and 11 a.m.

Chris d'Lacy sets himself the goal of 500 words a day.

It really doesn't matters what sort of routine or target you have, as long as you have one. And do make it achievable – better to promise yourself you will write 250 words a day and reach that goal than set yourself the impossible task of writing five thousand and feeling a failure.

Don't expect it to flow all time. On a good day, your fingers may fly over the keys, barely keeping up with your imagination – on another you may have to drag it out of yourself, one sentence at a time.

"Writing is cold-blooded hard labour," says Bernard Knight. "Like digging holes in the road."

And the only way to get those done, is to keep shovelling.

What to do about Writers' Block

I'm not entirely sure what true Writers' Block is – but I certainly recognise what horror writer Cari Crook describes as "Writers' Can't Be Arsed" – when it just all seems too much like hard work – and what I would call "Writers' Crisis of Confidence" when I'm trying to make excuses for myself.

This is not so much the stereotypical picture of the anguished author staring at a blank page, pen poised, only to find no words will come, but that what does come isn't what you'd hoped for and the disappointment and frustration makes you think you might as well give up for now and go and have a long lunch instead.

Sometimes this can be the best possible solution and you'll be amazed at how many fresh ideas you have after a nice bottle of Macon and a couple of hours listening to your best friend's marriage crises or a spot of eavesdropping into those of the next table.

But obviously you can't do this everyday – it's too expensive and you'll end up like an elephant. Also you won't get anything published or earn any money.

"My bank manager doesn't allow me to have Writers' Block," says Carole Matthews briskly, while June Tate, author of ten sagas, agrees:

"I can't afford it. I have a contract so writing is my business."

June does acknowledge that sometimes things "go slowly" and she finds that "retail therapy" never fails to get her going again. Presumably as she then has to keep writing to pay for it!

Other authors have their own ruses to keep it at bay.

"Cry but carry on," advises the writer and actress Helen Lederer, while Bernardine Kennedy types "a line of very rude words" across the page and then she too, moves on to a new bit.

"When I am stuck," offers Caroline Graham, "I beat my head slowly but firmly against the wall…"

"Don't beat yourself up," says Freya North. "Give yourself half an hour to have a Curlywurly, buy some tat on Ebay, read a tabloid newspaper and then get back to your work."

"I rewrite my last page," says Jill Mansell, "tricking my brain into thinking I'm on a roll."

"Don't stare at a blank page or screen," advises Bernard Knight. "Get something down. You can always erase or edit it the next day."

"Nurse's block? Lorry driver's block?" asks novelist and creative writing tutor Alice Jolly. "I've no patience with the idea that you have to wait for inspiration to strike. What you have to do is turn up at the page every day."

Romantic novelist Kate Walker, who has written no less than fifty novels for Mills and Boon and who is contracted to produce three a year (!), takes a similarly no-nonsense approach: "Writing is the science of BICHOK – bum in chair, hands on keyboard – and staying there." But if she feels really blocked – "when I feel the story has just died and there's nowhere I can go with it" – she goes for a walk or does "some job I hate like ironing" and lets her mind daydream. "I've been through the 'this book sucks' stage so often that I know, even when I am despairing, it will probably come right in the end."

I think that's a very important thing to hold on to. It can also be useful to go back a few pages, or chapters and re-read what you wrote the day before or even a month ago – you might feel so thoroughly impressed with yourself you'll start again with renewed vigour and even if it only makes you want to immediately start editing it, this will kick-start the creative process again.

And if none of the above work then just grit your teeth and do it anyway.

"Certainly not!" said Frederick Forsyth, when I enquired if he got Writer's Block. "More wimpery!"

The esteemed author, who has written fourteen more books since his famous bestseller *The Day of the Jackal* was published back in 1971, writes ten pages a day. "It's a job, that's all," he declares. "Get on with it."

Top Tips for getting it written

1) **Always Write First**. If you say you'll "just" clear up the kitchen, make your phone calls or put the washing on before you start, the whole morning will disappear.
2) **Set yourself targets** – I will not move from this chair until 11 a.m./I have written 500 words/got to the end of this chapter. Then stick to them.
3) **Leave the answer machine on.** Especially if you have a mother. Or are one.
4) **Do not check for emails.**
   Emails are the very worst form of displacement activity there is. With broadband it's all too easy to stay online, to keep your emailer open and have the 'you've-got-mail' beeper chirruping away. If you want to get anything done at all, keep your email programme firmly closed until you're ready to stop writing for the day.
6) **Tie your leg to the desk.**

Keeping it Going

Even if you are strict with yourself, follow all the above rules, stay seated and keep those fingers moving, some of us are better at keeping concentration than others.

I remember chairing a panel at the Guildford Book Festival with the amazing Penny Vincenzi (who has sold no less than a staggering four million copies of her books) and lovely Fiona Walker who also sells in shedloads. Fiona was talking about writing all night long, Penny spoke about how she gets "a sort of post-natal depression" whenever she finishes a book. I began to think I was not a natural.

Both spoke of characters filling their heads, of being totally consumed with their plots and living, breathing, sleeping, whatever novel they happen to be currently immersed in. This was a worry.

My head tends to be filled with phone calls I must make, emails I've not answered and what cunning ruse I might use to blag my way on to *Richard & Judy*.

When I wake at four a.m. it is not to fret over what happens in chapter twenty-seven but with a sudden idea for a stunning non-fiction book I'll never write, a thought for my newspaper column and the revelation that I could always rewrite the piece *The Guardian* didn't want and very probably pitch it to the *Daily Express*. I remember several bookstore managers I haven't schmoozed with lately, the ideas I had a week ago for an article for *My Goldfish*, and the perfect answer to the current problem that's been sent in for my monthly advice slot in *Writing Magazine*.

These moments of enlightenment are generally interlaced with thoughts of bills unpaid, deadlines looming and the realisation that I've still not renewed my subscription to the Society of Authors.

This, my friend Lynne Hackles (see later chapter on Friends Called Lynne) said reassuringly, is because I am a "butterfly writer." People like us (she says she is one, too) always have too many things on the go because, apparently, we have an enquiring mind, many different creative talents and a need for the constant stimulus and endorsement of the frequent sale. This makes me feel better even if deep down I know it is a polite way of saying I lack focus and direction.

It does help if you can eat, breathe and sleep your novel – if it is all-consuming. In fact it helps with anything you write. But once again life can get in the way and sometimes it is very difficult to clear your head and get to grips with what to write next and this is the time, I think, to go for a walk or a drink and stop stressing about it.

I am incapable of sitting doing the same thing for longer than an hour or two anyway. I have to get up and walk around and do something else. Sometimes I get heartily sick of whatever I am writing – particularly if it is a long thing like a novel – and I need to stop and write a newspaper article, one of my columns or even a long angsty email to one of my writing friends moaning about how I need a change.

This is how I am and I have tried to stop fretting about it. On the one hand it means I have only written three novels in the time some of my friends have produced six, on the other hand, I've also written for most of the women's magazines, several national newspapers, have three regular columns and a pretty portfolio of cuttings I can peer at when I start to wonder what I do all day (email mostly – as we've discovered).

The important thing if you want to be a writer is to write. And to find a way to do it that fits in with your life. Marina Oliver, the author of over fifty books including *The Beginner's Guide to Writing Novels* (How To Books) was recently writing two books at once. But others have written to me at *Writing Magazine* to ask how the hell they can keep the impetus going when they have a full-time job, unsupportive spouses, dozens of demanding kids and no peace and quiet? With difficulty, is the short answer, but there are things to be done if you want it enough.

If you haven't got the time or inclination to do long stints at the computer actually writing, the important thing is to keep whatever you want to write, when you do have time, in your mind.

Sarah Duncan has a busy and varied life, teaching Creative Writing and juggling family as well as writing. She advises: "Write something every day, even if only for 10 minutes, to keep the story fresh in your mind. EVERYBODY can find 10 minutes – lock yourself in the loo if you have to."

I would also say: keep a notebook with you at all times and scribble down any ideas that come to you. Never imagine you'll remember them without doing this – you won't, especially if you're busy. Keep re-reading those notes, in the odd times you do have free, and try to add something every time – even if it's just a sentence.

Make a pact with yourself that you will always think about your novel when doing a certain task – e.g cleaning your teeth or tackling the ironing (if you bother with the latter, which I don't if I can help it). It may not be easy in the beginning but what I can tell you is that the more you do this, and the longer your work-in-progress gets, the easier it will become, until you can think of little else.

There comes a point where you cannot help but be consumed. Then you will spend endless hours staring into space, ignoring everyone and before you know it, you'll have got a divorce, had the kids adopted, been sacked from work and be welded to the computer after all.

Even then, don't be hard on yourself if progress is slow. The reality is that writing a book is hard. For a start, there's the sheer number of words and the vast amount of information and ideas you need to keep in your head.

Remember this is a first draft. A hole-ridden, glitch-filled, jumble that can all be sorted out at the end.

I sometimes look back at early drafts of my novels and they read like the ramblings of a madwoman (some might say they still do) but it reminds me that everything can be cured in the edit.

If you're stuck on this particular bit of the story, then leap forward and write a bit you are sure about. Even if you don't yet know how the two will link up, don't worry, it will come to you later.

Add something every day – even if it is only a sentence or two. Open the file on your computer or re-read your longhand whenever you can, to keep in touch with your characters. Think about them constantly. If you keep feeding the conscious mind, you will be amazed what the subconscious comes up with.

Gradually a hundred words will become a thousand and that will become five thousand. Then ten thousand will become twenty and that will become thirty. Which is – I will warn you now – a particularly grim point as you seem to have been writing for ever and are only a third of the way through.

But you still keep going and then you're suddenly at 50,000, over half way, and before you know it you've written three quarters of your book and the light's started shining at the end of the tunnel. Then the hard work begins! But don't get bogged down with that just now. Just keep writing. Even when it's not going well.

Ironically, I am having problems with writing this bit. I have so much to say I don't know what order to say it in. I keep cutting and pasting and it's starting to confuse even me. What chance will you have? In the last hour I have checked for emails, phoned a friend and gone downstairs for some houmous and crispbread. This is not the way to deal with it.

Expect your writing to look confusing at first. It may be disjointed and have gaps in it. You will repeat yourself, use clichés and produce whole paragraphs that will make you cringe when you read them back later. This is how it is. The trick is to keep going anyway. For every exquisitely-written, beautifully-polished, cunningly-plotted novel you've ever read there was once an author looking at an early draft with something close to despair.

It is the nature of the beast.

But you can't put anything right that isn't there in the first place. You have to write it in the first place no matter bad it is. No excuses. No short cuts. No fretting over the end product. Just get something – anything – down. Bash, bash, bash. Sort it out later.

Or simply remember the wise words of Katherine Mansfield:

Better to write twaddle, anything, than nothing at all.

Waste Not, Want Not

Eventually, however, you will have to sort the twaddle from the wheat, as it were, and get down to editing it all. No need to worry too much at this point – just get to the end of this first draft. But there is something worth bearing in mind as you go.

I have no idea who first said: "Murder Your Darlings" (the internet variously attributes this to Ezra Pound, F Scott Fitzgerald and Sir Arthur Quiller-Couch – if you wanted proof of what I was saying earlier about websites contradicting each other, there you have it) but it is a good piece of advice to pass on to you here, even if I am extraordinarily bad at following it myself.

It means that if you have fallen in love with a particular piece of your writing, beware. Or as the American writer Elmore Leonard once (allegedly – if I spend any more time on Google I shall never get this book finished) said: "If I come across anything in my work that smacks of 'good writing,' I immediately strike it out."

This may strike you as rather an odd approach but the theory is that if we, the writers, are particularly proud of something then it is probably self-indulgent or superfluous and will serve no good purpose in moving the plot along.

Instead it will stand out like a sore thumb and break what has been described as the "fictive dream" – in other words it will jolt the reader out of their reverie and they will no longer be so absorbed in the story, and will suddenly realise that the bath is overflowing and the kids haven't been fed for two days.

I know where proponents of this theory are coming from – I look back at some of my early work that I thought was the dog's bollocks at the time and see it in all its self-conscious, pretentious glory – but as a general rule I think it is largely tosh.

Sometimes we are proud of a piece of writing because it is bloody good. Because just for once, everything has flowed out exactly as it should and it all works. Now I've got a bit of experience, I wouldn't want anything to be published that I wasn't proud of, so if I followed old Elmore's advice (if it was him) then that would be 100 short stories, three novels and about 750 articles that would never have seen the light of day (is that a wistful look I see in your eye?).

What I would say, however, is that however fond you are of a particular sentence, paragraph, scene or chapter, if it doesn't really fit with what else you've been writing, then It Has To Go.

Let us suppose you are writing a murder mystery set in the village of Little Twerpshaw. You might have decided that your hero, George, works for the butcher. Early on in your novel you have a hilarious scene where Mrs Scroggins (your first victim) comes in for her lamb chops and your hero gets mixed up and sells her pig's trotters instead.

You are immensely pleased with this bit – it makes you laugh out loud even though you wrote it yourself, and you feel it beautifully illustrates the juxtaposition between the sexually-repressed and pseudo-genteel existence of our hero among the potted palms at home with his Aunt Agatha, and the raw reality of the blood-streaked chopping block at work. Or something.

However, round about chapter seven you realise that George is going to have to be a postman instead.

How else can he contrive to be wandering up the garden path of the vicarage at 6 a.m.? (Even the good reverend's wife would not want her mutton mince delivered that early). It strikes you that if George is a Postie, he will also have ample opportunity to note the way Mrs Scroggin's curtains are usually open by 6.43 a.m. and be the first to raise the alarm when they are still closed at 10.30 a.m. (her not popping in for her Friday kidneys would not have the same impact) and will be expertly placed to have the inside knowledge required to tell us that Mrs S. received a mysterious pink envelope on Valentine's Day and from the look on her face, it wasn't from Mr Scroggins, either.

This sorted, all that's needed is a quick re-write and the provision of a bicycle and a sturdy pair of boots and Georgie Boy's transformation is complete.

The trouble starts, I can tell you from experience, when – loath to waste your fine scene in *Scragend and Son Master Butchers* – you start trying to work this in somewhere else.

Always a mistake. This is the time to take a deep breath and your best deleting finger and get rid of the offending section. It doesn't have to be forever – you can cut and paste it instead, saving it in a file called "Scene in Butchers" and stored away in a folder called "Bits To Use Sometime" somewhere in a drawer or far-flung corner of your hard-drive – but remove it for now, you must.

Otherwise you will spend precious hours trying to create another character to be the butcher – one capable of making the same jokes as George did, without sounding like another George; will be forced to send Mrs Scroggins off meat-buying when she should be signing for a parcel at home; and will therefore realise that now you need to rearrange the whole order of events so this little encounter has some semblance of significance until finally, you end up bringing only to that original scene the indefinable "so what?" factor.

In a very early draft of the opening of *Perfect Alibis* I wrote a scene where my heroine, Stephanie, was flat on her back with her feet in stirrups undergoing a smear test. It was supposed to introduce us to the fact that she'd rather gone off having sex with her husband.

I am particularly neurotic about these little procedures and have been known, after a major bout of hysteria during which my gynaecologist considered early retirement, to have my own tests done under general anaesthetic.

You could say, therefore, that the inclusion of this scenario said more about me than my heroine. Which is probably why, after much working and reworking, I realised it didn't really work at all, took it back out of the book and stored it away for future reference.

I should just have forgotten it.

Instead I followed my terrible compulsion to use "one I made earlier" – a fixation I blame on too much *Blue Peter* in my infancy – and a couple of years later dragged this out of cold storage to try to use it in my third novel.

I was able to justify it. My heroine was having trouble conceiving – where better to introduce this than from the gynae couch with a consultant thoroughly looking into things? (Or up them, to be precise.)

It is never a good idea to force old writing into new. It takes twice as long – by the time you have edited and adapted – as if you had just started afresh and often doesn't ever sit comfortably in its second home.

Even if you wrote it relatively recently, when you try to put old writing in a new context there will be imperceptible changes in style or voice.

But I persisted and shoe-horned it into *One Glass is Never Enough* (Chapter Four, page 36, if you're interested. First line: "Ouch!").

It took quite a while to change the names and move it from first person to third and back again, and alter all the details to fit the new storyline – this time the heroine isn't getting *enough* sex with her old man – and erase all the irrelevant bits and make the dialogue reflect the thought processes of my new heroine, Gaynor, who is a very different kettle of fish from my previous one, Stephanie, but I got there in the end.

It probably took three times as long as if I had abandoned the whole idea and written a new chapter where Gaynor is at the dentist instead or just sitting at home painting her toenails but – phew – nothing wasted.

And do you know something?

Nobody has ever come up to me and said: "My God – that smear test scene – I am SO glad you wrote that."

One of my friends looked at me oddly and said wasn't it a lot of fuss over a mere internal examination? (When she had one of her three fifteen-pound babies, her consultant told her she had a pelvis the size of a bucket so she probably doesn't even notice when she has one.) The Fearsome One said it made her squeamish and my gynaecologist hasn't spoken to me since.

So don't follow my example. A much better plan is to keep everything by all means, but only ever recycle an old piece of writing if IT really fits the plot, not because you've spent three weeks squashing the plot into a shape that will accommodate IT.

And by 'recycle' I mean read it, absorb the content, let it kick-start you but WRITE IT AFRESH. Because we change and develop all the time and however great it seemed when you wrote it the first time, you can probably do a hell of a lot better now.

Basic ideas, however, are another matter.

Every idea you've ever had can be used somehow, somewhere, some day – if you wait long enough. And a lot more quickly if you learn a few tricks of the trade.

If you are writing short stories, say, and sending them off to magazines and competitions you may get a fairly high rejection rate at first. This may be because your ideas are good but your writing needs a polish or – your writing is perfectly accomplished and competent but your ideas are naff.

Let us imagine it is early days in your writing career and it is the former. It may that you can rehash those early rejected ideas and produce new stories later from the same premise.

When I first started writing short stories, there were a few that totally flopped in competitions and I put them to one side. Much later, when I began to gain some knowledge and experience, I saw that the ideas were often perfectly good – it was just that my style was all wrong.

Often it fell between two stools – not being accessible enough for the women's mag market nor literary enough to score very highly in a competition. Once I got to grips with that, I sold or placed pretty much everything I wrote. And sometimes more than once!

This is why I was well-equipped to answer one Denise Collingwood who wrote to me at *Writing Magazine* on this whole subject of recycling:

I have been writing for a couple of years and have got quite a collection of short stories. Some of them have won minor prizes, others have been submitted to Women's Magazines and have been turned down. But what I find frustrating is that there's nothing to do with them next. A lot of competitions will not allow you to enter a story if it has previously won a prize and once a story has been rejected by a magazine, that presumably is that. I hear there's no market for a book of short story collections unless you're already a famous novelist but it's pity to have all this work, and all those plots I struggled to come up with, sitting on my computer and going to waste. Have you got any ideas for stories that are "dead"?

As soon as I read her letter, one name sprang to mind.

Sally Zigmond is the veritable Queen of the Short Story and has won every competition known to woman. She doesn't enter so many these days as she's working on a novel (hurrah – I can't wait!) but when I was first entering competitions myself, her name popped up on every results list, for every competition, everywhere.

Naturally I hated her – especially when my own entries flopped back onto the mat in their dispiriting SAEs or were never heard of again. But then we met and I discovered that not only was she one of the loveliest people I'd ever met but she was full of hot tips.

I had long wondered at the way she managed to churn out the sheer volume of stories needed for all those competitions and she generously revealed how.

Sally's trick is use the same theme and plot several times. She doesn't have a file for each story on her computer, she has an entire folder, holding all the different versions of what is essentially the same tale. "If the first time it was set in Cornwall," she says cheerfully, "I change it to Scotland. If there was a cat in it, I make it a dog. I alter the beginning, rewrite the end and give all the characters different names…"

And why not! Following Sally's method, you could take some of your favourite stories, give them a face-lift, and – submit them again.

"I bet some editors often don't read more than the first paragraph anyway," says Sally. (If they're in green ink, they might not even get that far!). "So if you change that…"

She does, however have a word of warning. "You've still got to do the work," she says. "If you're going to make changes you must be extra careful with the editing – to make sure that the story still flows and there are no anomalies."

I soon tried it myself, for I too hate to think of work I've slaved over not earning its living. Even now, if I'm suddenly asked for a short story in a hurry, I often look back for an old one I feel particularly fond of and take the essence of it – the theme and basic plot – and then rewrite it in what is, hopefully, a fresh new way, updating as I go.

The toddler might become a stroppy teenager for example, and that thirty-year old who thought she was getting ancient (pause for hollow laugh and rueful inspection of one's wrinkles) is transported a decade to when her life has truly begun.

When I was writing regularly for the women's magazines, I must have produced at least twenty magazine stories around the same basic premise. Namely marital conflict, for some reason (he's working too hard, she's working too hard, they're both exhausted because the baby never stops crying, she thinks he fancies her sister) followed by a trauma (he nearly misses important party, kid gets lost, sister is run over) resulting in the sudden realisation they do love each other after all, a sloppy reconciliation and the promise of a whole new beginning (which, as I've already explained, editors seem to love. Not for the coffee-break read should he sulk for three days, while she threatens to divorce him).

All the stories were quite different, but they sprang from the same idea. Instead of counting the stories on your computer, count how many different ideas and plots you've got – and how many things you could do with them.

Could the tale of the mother who is feeling lost now her child has just started school translate to when her youngest leaves for university? If you've previously written about family tensions over Christmas could this become a wedding? (always ripe for an argument or two).

Perhaps the Easter Egg Hunt can turn into a winter treasure trail, the sun and beach holiday a glorious skiing trip? This way you can use your work again, with a clear conscience about breaking rules, and without risk of irritating editors by sending the same thing twice.

With the added benefit that when you become a famous novelist you'll have even more short stories to choose from for your first collection! In short, don't ever see stories or articles as "dead" but just waiting for reincarnation. With you as the one to give them the kiss of life.

Foibles and Superstitions

Having now thoroughly digressed, we must get back to Keeping Going and Getting It Finished. Which as we have said ad infinitum, are all-important and anything that helps you do that is a good thing, however bizarre. Writers, as I warned you at the beginning, are an odd lot and many have good luck charms or little rituals they adhere to (mine often involve alcohol and don't always work).

You may have no truck with such stuff or you may wish to feel like a proper writer by developing a few peculiarities of your own.

Erica James, the award-winning romantic novelist, transfixed the audience at the Guildford Book Festival with hers when I interviewed her on stage in 2006.

"As far as I'm concerned my writing rituals seem perfectly normal to me," she says. "It's only when I describe them aloud to anyone that they take on a faint air of madness."

When Erica wrote her first book, she had a special pencil to make notes in the margin of her manuscripts. By her second book, she'd acquired a set of red files, a pencil sharpener, an eraser, and a fountain pen which her sons gave her for Mother's Day.

"All these things became vitally important to the production of a new book. Without them, I was sunk. No other pen would do. No other file could possibly be used to keep the pages of my manuscript safe. Why, you ask? Well, for the simple reason, that it was all a matter of luck getting my very first novel published and the only way to keep the luck going was to surround myself with 'lucky' things."

From then on, she says, "things subtly escalated as new ways to keep the luck rolling in presented themselves." These days her top foible is the purchase of a new bone china mug at the start of a new book.

"I drink gallons of tea while I'm writing and unless the mug 'feels right' the words won't flow as they should. It goes without saying that these mugs are sacred; no one else is allowed to drink from them. If that was to happen, the luck would drain clean out of them. Madness? It works for me!"

It certainly does. Erica is the author of eleven best-selling novels and counting.

Crime writer Lesley Horton has two rune pendants. One is the Rune of Odin which is said to bring the wearer inspiration and deeper perceptions in their creative writing. The other is the Rune of Magick which allows: "those wonderful coincidences to occur, enabling success in things which seem impossible to achieve."

"I don't wear them all the time," says Lesley. "But I can always reach for them when I feel the need."

Claire Calman tries to actively avoid getting too attached to things to help her along, although she admits she likes a particular pen. "I sometimes deliberately start using another so I don't start thinking what I do is dependent on the pen."

I wouldn't want to rely too heavily on anything either – frankly I'm neurotic enough – but I must say I like to have fresh flowers in the room and they do have to be in the glass vase that came with the roses my aunt, Shelagh, sent me when my first book was published.

In the winter I like a fire burning or candles flickering. Unless there's a blizzard outside, I need a window open. And I must have the radio on, although not loudly enough for me to be able to actually hear it much.

Jill Mansell has the TV on when she's writing, but says radio or music would be distracting (!) and Lynne Hackles keeps a china ornament of a Lazy Cow on her desk to remind her not to be one.

The actress Helen Lederer also likes to light a candle when she writes. Then, she says it's a case of a "a cafetiere of strong continental coffee and pray".

Kate Long requires a session on Ebay before she opens Word each morning, while writer and journalist Karen Howeld has to do her "wombles". This is five minutes of stream-of-consiousness writing that she carries out to the ticking of a plastic lemon kitchen timer before she starts her real work.

Jan Henley says a glass of wine usually helps the flow though I wouldn't recommend this much before breakfast and Margaret Kaine says she writes best when she's got make-up on.

If push comes to shove, I can write in most circumstances and am more likely to be superstitious about the finished product.

When I was trying to place my first novel, I sometimes used to kiss it first and I always felt it was imperative that it was posted from my favourite local post-office – I'd get all twitchy if I'd forgotten Thursday was early-closing and I had to go elsewhere – so I totally empathise with writer Sue Houghton who will only use green paperclips when sending off a manuscript.

I still, if I send a manuscript anywhere by Special Delivery, keep the ticket propped up on my desk until the said work had got the thumbs up (ripping it to pieces and then stamping on it if it hasn't).

I also find it very difficult to work on anything new while I'm waiting for the verdict on the last bit. Unlike Kate Walker who wants to feel that she always has a book in progress (on a contract to write three a year, she probably needs to have!).

"When I finish a book, I always open a new file labelled 'New Book'," she says. "I set up a page and write 'Chapter One' at the top of it – then a few words even if it's only a hero's name or a line of dialogue from the heroine, then I've always started the next book and I'm never not writing anything."

For some writers it's what they wear – Fiona Walker has a "shapeless grey fleece sweater" that she "more or less lives in" when she's finishing a book.

And for some it's what they don't: freelance journalist and non-fiction author Emily Dubberley swears that her hourly word-count rises if she writes barefoot.

But my favourite tale of all is of a writer, Drew Jagger, who always scours the charity shops when he is at the beginning of a novel to find a hat that his main character would wear and then wears it himself throughout the entire writing of the novel. Marvellous!

But if this all sounds too wacky for you, worry not. When Frederick Forsyth was a boy he saw someone brandishing a lucky rabbit's foot. "It didn't do the rabbit much good and he had four of them," he observes. "I've never believed in charms or talismans since."

And I think we are safe in saying – he's done all right!

NOVELS ARE NOT THE ONLY FRUIT

Just because you like writing or want to be a writer, it does not mean you have to write a novel.

In fact if you can find some other sort of writing to do which gives you pleasure and/or earns you money then I would grab the opportunity with both hands.

Spending months on end trying to churn out 80,000 words that mean something and sweating over the intricacies of plot is not for everyone and I have every respect for the writer who would rather write the mottos inside Christmas crackers or the definitive guide to the history of the teapot.

I also have every respect for the writer who wants to write for his or her own pleasure and who has no interest in getting published at all. (You are probably much more balanced and sane than the rest of us.)

Writing as Therapy

Vanessa Gebbie, a writer and specialised creative writing tutor, is a firm believer in the therapeutic qualities of writing.

Vanessa works with the residents of a drug rehabilitation centre, as well as with the homeless, asylum-seekers and refugees.

"I think it is a great way for people to spill out fears, worries, guilt...anything," she says. "The very action of getting it out and on to paper is almost a metaphor in itself. Sometimes people have said to me "I really didn't know I was hurting about that...""

I have, in a small way, had that experience myself.

Over the years, there have been times when I have been profoundly affected by those around me suffering mental health problems. As I wrote in a newspaper article on the subject: other families had holidays in Spain – we had nervous breakdowns.

In my first novel, *Raising the Roof* , which is essentially a chick-lit-type romantic comedy, I chose to give one of my characters a severe psychotic episode and have her admitted to a mental health unit. I knew I needed to write about it – both because there is still a stigma attached to mental illness (if your sister has cancer, you tell all your friends and get hugs and support; if your brother is psychotic and has just been sectioned under the Mental Health Act, you tend to keep quiet) which I wanted to address, and also on a very personal level I needed to somehow exorcise the very real fear and distress I'd felt when this happened in my own family, by using it in my writing.

I did it for me, but was touched and honoured when a tutor doing some training with nurses working with patients with mental health problems, wrote to tell me he had recommended my novel as useful reading for his students.

When I was writing my third novel, *One Glass Is Never Enough*, I returned to the subject. For in the intervening years I had found that as I began to tell others, tentatively at first, what had happened in my family, so they told me. It seemed everyone had a mother, brother, cousin or aunt who'd had a breakdown, been under a psychiatrist or was still on medication.

A girl I'd known for years suddenly told me harrowing tales from her formative years with her manic-depressive mother, and another friend admitted for the first time that her brother was schizophrenic.

Most said how exceptionally tough they found it – long-term – to cope. How intolerant they found themselves at times – and how guilty that made them feel. It makes me feel guilty too. And frustrated.

It's not that I am not sympathetic or even that I don't understand – I do my own weeping and wailing and I too can wake at four a.m. gripped with a sickening anxiety over nothing very much. But I'm essentially an optimist who can pour a stiff drink, pick herself up and get going again. I do under-stand that others can't but that doesn't stop me getting uptight about it.

For it is immensely hard when someone you love is lost to you. And however much I've read on the subject – if there were a GCSE in Serotonin levels and neurotransmitters I'd pass it tomorrow – and however completely I grasp that it's not the patient's fault, there is still a part of me that can be suddenly filled with resentment.

So I wrote about this – about the role of the carer, this time, rather than the patient. I had Gaynor, the main character, say: "if one in four suffers from depression then three-quarters of the population have a hell of a lot to put up with."

I had intended that to be the end of the speech but before I knew it I'd filled three pages. My fingers bashed away at the keyboard not able to keep up with the stream of emotion coming out of me, as I ranted about how everyone feels sorry for the depressive but no-one gives a thought for those around him or her whose lives are so fundamentally changed, too. I'd known I was angry but not how angry.

I edited back the offending passage but I did write a couple of newspaper articles on the subject and got a very wide response. One wife of a man who had been clinically depressed for twenty years wrote: "We all think those things, but you have dared to say them."

The fact that I am able to is probably what keeps me – just about – sane.

I realise now that my early humorous writings about my family were my way of dealing with them. That I use humour to help me cope with the things that have hurt me most.

Over the years I have written many short stories that were sparked off by something that had upset, disturbed or confused me and more recently I have turned to journalism to offload the same.

It has been especially gratifying to have a local newspaper column for the last few years – one of my problems is that I have an ego the size of Milton Keynes and I DO want everything published – as it is the perfect place to spill out my angst and it has made me feel much better to be able to rant about things that anger me (John Prescott's housing policy, white-van drivers, telephone banking) or describe my sadness when friends have died or one of our cats has been run over.

If you haven't got this sort of public outlet you could start a web-blog (a new one pops up every three seconds, I believe) or keep a diary and who knows what might become of it later?

Several novels have been born as a result of bloggers being talent-spotted by agents or publishers and memoirs have also been big in recent years.

The "unsent letter" has been a favoured therapists' tool for many years and a collection of your own un-posted grief, rage or vitriol may serve as a useful basis for something one day (even if it's only so that you can get pissed one night and decide to post them after all and watch all hell break loose).

Vanessa says of her work with addicts:

I have found that the writing of letters is an extraordinarily powerful therapeutic tool. My clients often write letters, maybe to parents, kids, people they've hurt, stolen from or injured. The letters don't get sent. But the action of writing exorcises a ghost that haunts them, it seems.

She highlights the case of a 40-year-old man who had left school with no qualifications and had not written a word since 'filling out a form for the Social.'

He said, in his first session with me: 'I can't write. They told me at school my writing was awful. I can't spell, I don't know grammar, I'm thick.'

By the end of that session, he had written two letters. One to his dead father and one to the son he'd not seen for three years. AND he had played a game and laughed for the first time since moving in.

Vanessa also emphasises how anything can be a jump-start to the creative process.

I never, ever plan our sessions. I pick up on a mood or a look and take that as a cue. Or I'll jump on a phrase someone says. And give them the credit for setting the writing going, always. Anything is a cue, for me... it's just the way my mind works. A bus will go by the window and we will write about 'journeys I wish I had made/hadn't made'... and the stuff that comes out is like diamonds.

If you are a lover of freeing creative exercises (I am not) Vanessa also recommends trying Flash Fiction. The clue is in the name – it is done in a flash. Sometimes it involves writing within a certain word count (say 500 or 1000 words) or sometimes to a time limit. Therefore the pieces are short. But the important thing is that it is unthinking and unplanned.

The idea is that you simply look at a prompt and write – something, anything – and see what comes out. Devotees of the exercise say it is extremely liberating. Because I am generally lagging behind on various pieces of writing that have been planned for weeks, and whose deadlines are looming in an alarming manner, I admit I have never tried it. But I can see how the writing might be fresh, exciting and unexpected.

Presumably – says she who likes to see everything end up in print – you can worry about what to do with it later.

And even if you do nothing with it at all, it will probably make you feel good. I sometimes wonder why I procrastinate so much and delay the moment when I commit myself to the keyboard for the day because one thing I do know is that writing – particularly if it is going well – makes me happy.

And the good thing about being a writer is that if everything around you is crap and even writing about it won't make you feel better at least you can sit down and make up an alternative.

"I've certainly used writing as therapy," says Sarah Harrison. "After all, one of the pleasures of fiction is that it imposes a kind of order on the messy randomness of life."

Writing as Revenge

This can be therapeutic too and great fun. 'Don't get mad – get your pen out', is a fine maxim for a writer to uphold especially if, like me, you are a bad-tempered old harridan who gets shocking PMT and would quite often like to stab someone.

So far, nobody has ever died in one of my novels but I can quite see how it must be very satisfying to kill off your most hateful relative in fiction to make up for the fact that you are stuck with them in real life.

"I have lost count of how many times I've murdered my mother-in-law," confirms Lynne Hackles, with feeling.

Crime-writer Zoë Sharp takes a more altruistic approach. "I see myself as a kind of literary contract killer. I ask friends, family and acquaintances for a name of someone they'd really like to see dead or guilty and use that…"

Novelist Sue Moorcroft, too, has a simple solution for those deserving retribution – "I give them BO and dandruff"– while Freya North warns: "Anyone who double-crosses me will find themselves in one of my books. I'll make a very basic anagram of their name and write them in as an utterly odious character…"

I don't always bother with the anagram. I first embraced writing-as-anger-management some years ago, when, after a particularly galling domestic, I described in a newspaper column how my husband responded to most crises by turning purple and jumping on the spot.

I referred to his abiding belief that minor accidents were only such when they happened to him. If they happened to me, they became wilful acts of malicious negligence. Whatever went wrong in our house, I wrote, was bound to be My Fault.

The very act of bashing out five hundred words on his exact shade of puce, calling on my readers to join with me in condemning conjugal injustice and enquiring if anyone else was married to such an icon of unreason (the paper immediately had several fervent emails from women wishing to form a support group) was soothing but I didn't realize the full mightiness of pen over sword potential until later.

First my sister phoned up guffawing and asking for "Purple Tim". Then the bloke at the garage said: "you'd better watch that missus of yours, mate" and one of our neighbours, encountered in the post office, shared a similar anecdote about her own cantankerous husband with the rest of the queue, while pointing triumphantly at mine. Great stuff.

But doing it deliberately is one thing – I have also had my revenge on over-zealous traffic wardens, rude shop-keepers and local councillors with a tenuous relationship with the truth – but you have to watch what goes on in your subconscious, too.

Obviously, giving the vilest female character the same name as the witch your husband left you for, or calling the bloke with halitosis and erectile dysfunction after your arrogant boss (and even better, making sure he also drives the same car and has the same disgusting habit of picking his ears) is one of the perks of being an author. But beware of doing it subliminally and upsetting your nearest or dearest.

Got a friend called Lynda married to a tosser called Robin, who's got a dreadful child called Jacob? Check carefully, when gaily writing about boring husbands and spineless mothers who let their horrible brats run amok, that you haven't called them Robert, Lydia and Jack.

I can tell you that it doesn't go down well. Quite unconsciously I have done this myself, in one of my novels, not only very nearly replicating several names but giving the offending character a very similar job and address to A Certain Person in real life. I can't give you any more details because we're only just back on speaking terms.

You might think this is a good way to get your own back. But changing one letter of her name and then gleefully describing the more sordid secrets of the woman who used to be your best friend till she ran off with your plumber, may not be so clever.

If she later dumps him for a lawyer and you can't actually prove what she used to get up to with a monkey wrench, you could be in trouble.

This is probably a good moment to talk about the laws of libel.

A Word of Warning

The laws of libel state that a case can be brought if something you have published exposes another to ridicule or contempt, if it causes the person to be shunned or avoided, or to be damaged professionally.

The acid test is whether it would damage that person's reputation in the eyes of "reasonable" people.

If what you have written about someone happens to be entirely true – your neighbour really does take crack-cocaine and eat small children – then you're OK (as long as you can prove it).

But if, as so often in novel-writing, it is a blur of fact, fiction, speculation and flights of fancy, you could possibly be on dodgy ground, even if in practice it is unlikely that many would have the money or energy to drag you through court.

I must admit I'd never given any of this a thought until I was showing the page proofs of my last novel – set in my home town and very obviously inspired by my time owning a bar there – to an old editor friend.

"Should you be saying that?" he enquired of my reference to the philandering Irishman, whose wife used to knock seven bells out of him every Friday night when she'd been on the cherry brandy.

"Why not?" I chortled. "Even if they do recognise themselves – if the cap fits, wear it!"

"NO!" he said, sternly. "If the cap fits, you can be sued for libel...."

Really? This was a bit of a shock. I had – as I've told you already – been taking from real life for a long time. And nobody had ever recognised themselves (or not correctly anyway) so it had never occurred to me to worry.

With my friendly editor's lurid tales of fortunes lost, books pulped and beautiful friendships ruined for ever ringing in my ears, we looked at the manuscript. I had, as I pointed out, at least changed some details...

"In fact his wife used to beat him up when she'd had seven ciders," I explained. "And really it was a pornography habit, not a real girlfriend, and I've changed their names..."

"Not enough," said the wise one, whose previous long and distinguished career had been working on the tabloids. "Better to make him Scottish, her Portuguese, alter their ages by twenty years and give them a disabled mother living in…"

Better still, he pointed out, to make them a same-sex couple or brother and sister. That way nobody could ever reasonably argue a case for it being the true-life O'Flanagans (not their real name, of course) I was thinking of when regaling my readers with their marital strife.

So it went on. Me highlighting the dubious paragraphs – those where local people would probably guess who had been my source of inspiration – and Ed giving me his advice. The blonde with the six lovers? Make her a celibate brunette. The alcoholic Welshman with the arm missing? Make him Scottish with one leg.

The nasty piece of work who used to make such abusive phone-calls in the middle of the night we had to get the police involved? Surprisingly, I could leave him in. He had no good name to protect.

The bloke so drunk he couldn't stand? He won't remember. The sad old guy who got run over? You cannot libel the dead.

The local councillor with his hand in the till? For God's sake, delete him altogether.

By the time I'd finished changing hair shades, jobs and numbers of limbs still in action, I was thoroughly paranoid. These minor walk-on parts were one thing, but I couldn't do much about the main protagonists, short of writing a whole new book.

"The character that is sort of like you," I ventured to Jacqui, one of my ex-business partners, "I've made her quite bad-tempered in the kitchen."

"That's OK, I was," she said cheerily.

"Your look-alike comes across as a bit bossy," I mentioned to Wendy, the other one.

"I am," she agreed readily, adding that her husband was hoping he was in it and our temporary chef had already ordered ten copies to send to his relatives abroad (whoops – forgot about him!).

"The thing is," said Jacqui, "those that know us will know what is and isn't true, and those that don't – who cares?" Jacqui is a dear friend and a wonderful woman (who hadn't read the book when she said that) but others, remember, may not be so accommodating.

The fact is that I live in a small town and – because of owning the wine bar and because I write for the local press – Jacqui and I are both reasonably well-known.

I called the Jacqui character "Sarah" in the book but there were enough recognisable details in the story for anyone who ever drank in our bar to reasonably assume I was writing about Jacqui even though I had changed her name.

So, although what Sarah gets up to in the book – apart from stomping around the kitchen swearing a lot – is entirely a work of fiction, if I had made Sarah a violent drunk or a secret arms-dealer and local people had then shunned her because of what they supposed were her displays of bad behaviour or illegal practices, she could possibly have sued me for libel by claiming I had ruined her reputation.

In fact I thought about suing myself. For having been reassured by Jacqui and Wendy that I wasn't going to see them in court and breathed a sigh of relief, it was only much later that it occurred to me to consider the third partner in my story. The heroine, Gaynor, is a gorgeous if seemingly-ditzy blonde, with a great body and men falling at her feet.

With toe-curling horror, I realised that half my hometown would now think this was how I saw myself!

I spent the next six months explaining to anyone who would listen that while she might share a few of my emotional foibles, the rest of Gaynor – including the size eight jeans obviously! – was pure fantasy. (I also went on a crash diet and had my highlights done.)

This didn't stop a bloke at my launch party looking me up and down with evident disappointment and saying: "You're supposed to be the sexy one, are you?"

Naturally I made an instant note of his ill-fitting trousers and spreading girth. (His name was Kevin – watch out for him in novel number four.)

For I shall probably continue to give disagreeable old relatives a sex change and friends' nasty brats a different set of disgusting manners. Groping Grahams will still become Gary. Ex-lovers' horrible habits shall remain even if their jobs, clothes and penchant for eating strange animal parts are well-disguised. For me that's half the fun – I know who I'm talking about and hopefully, in the case of the last, somewhere deep inside them, they will too!

But I will not lead YOU astray. You don't want anything to ruin the joy of getting published, so if the possibility of being sued is going to worry you then remember it is better to be safe than sorry.

As my wise old newspaper editor summed up:
If in doubt, leave it out.

Another Word of Warning

There is another good reason not to sail too close to real-life scenarios and that was very ably illustrated by Brenda Whitmarsh who wrote to me at *Writing Magazine* to complain that whenever she drew on "true experiences" she was told her plots were unbelievable or contrived.

> I recently wrote a short story about two people who met by chance after sixty years. It was rejected as 'too unlikely' but this really happened to a friend of mine and I only wrote what she told me. I thought everybody knew truth was stranger than fiction!

Which, as I said to her in my reply, is entirely the point!

Truth may be stranger than fiction but it is also a very different thing.

We know that coincidences do happen in real life but if you are not careful they can look pretty contrived in a novel.

We've all heard of someone who went halfway across the world only to bump into the woman from three doors up, but if you used that as a plot device, editors would be more likely to roll their eyes heavenwards than offer you a publishing contract.

Or, as agent Jonathan Lloyd put it, when I asked him how he would respond to someone sending him a manuscript described as based on a true story, "It is not so much the true but the story I am looking for."

And that story has to convince. The reason we hear about odd holiday experiences, or read in the papers about childhood sweethearts brought back together after decades, is because these events may be fact but they're also very, very unusual. And as writers of fiction we need to be describing things others can relate to.

Short-story writer Sue Houghton told me of a story she wrote that was based almost entirely on a real event. It was the tale of a family friend in his seventies who calmly climbed out onto a window ledge when his house caught fire and called the emergency services on his mobile. Later some smoke-damaged clothes got mixed up with somebody else's at the dry-cleaners, creating more amusement and drama.

The story was rejected five times as unbelievable. Sue, being an old-hand at magazine fiction, accepted this verdict and changed some pertinent details, making the man a woman (for some reason women are considered more prone to clambering about in their nighties and twice as likely to have a phone close at hand) and creating some romantic content.

It was then published in *Woman*.

And therein lies the trick. We must learn to edit our "truth". For example, one could take the basic emotions, feelings and reactions of the couple who met after sixty years but instead of them happening to turn up in the same bar of the same hotel on the same day (a chance in millions) one of them might have been searching for the other on Friends Reunited, or they could have answered an appeal from 'Where are you now?' on Radio Two, or met at a mutual friend's funeral – all far more believable.

And remember that just because something is true it does not necessarily make it gripping. Once, when judging a short story competition, I came across an entry that began: *This is a true account of trying to find somewhere to park in Coventry...*

Whether he (I cannot believe a woman wrote it – this was one who wore a cap behind the wheel) ever did find the elusive space I do not know, for I lost the will to live around the bottom of page three when he was still queuing outside the second multi-storey.

But even if your real-life events are momentous and life-changing, it is very easy to fall into the trap of including too much detail or too much authentic dialogue, all of which may have taken place but do nothing for fostering page-turning quality.

In my second novel, *Perfect Alibis*, I modelled the heroine's disagreeable mother-in-law, Agatha, on a real-life ancient aunt (now deceased).

My editor said she couldn't believe the woman would say such things and when I thought about it, I knew what she meant (after all, I used to listen drop-jawed to the things the good auntie came out with too).

So I had to tone Agatha down a bit in order to make her more realistic even though my original depiction of her was "true".

Publisher Alan Samson explains this by describing a good novel as being "a feat of re-creative imagination" and says "I think texture is important, the feeling of truth, but not literal truth. Not in fiction anyway."

He is totally right, but as long as you bear the above in mind, and are prepared to edit ruthlessly, I still say (as I do ad nauseam) that nothing beats writing from your own experience.

Yes, you can research how it feels to be the mother of a heroin addict, watching him destroy himself before your eyes and you may be able to write a convincing novel on the subject, but I will never believe it won't have that extra edge of resonance if you've been there yourself.

Which brings us neatly on to:

Memoirs and Life Stories

Lots of people imagine that their own lives would make fascinating epics and it is certainly true that memoirs have become very popular. You may be encouraged by the fact that some of these have been written by quite "ordinary" people but I think we have to be realistic when considering writing one of our own.

Basically, unless we are very famous or have done something truly extraordinary, the chances are that the most fascinated parties will be ourselves.

If you've had a torrid affair with the Prime Minister or have DNA evidence that you are the true father of George Clooney (or *are* George Clooney) then you are probably in with a good chance (and you won't even have to worry about whether you can write – a ghost-writer will be supplied pronto).

But if the only reason you think you're interesting is because your mates down the pub said so – as in *"you're a 'kin laugh you are – you ought to write a book, that's what you ought to do"* – then I shouldn't hold out ever such high hopes of hitting the best-seller lists.

But please don't let me put you off entirely.

The success of books such as *Angela's Ashes* (Flamingo) have shown that we do have an appetite for the details of other people's lives. Since Frank McCourt wrote his award-winning memoir of his poverty-stricken childhood in Ireland there have been a huge raft of books on childhood experiences – many of them totally harrowing.

I am thinking of books like *A Child Called It* by David Pelzer (Orion); *Ugly* by Constance Briscoe (Hodder) or *Remembering Judith* by Ruth Joseph (Accent Press) and I think the market for them is probably unlimited if they are good enough.

And there's the rub.

Unfortunately it takes more than simply having a grim tale to tell. Tragically, thousands – millions, indeed – have their are stories of being beaten or humiliated. Many have suffered from eating disorders, overcome alcoholism or been sucked into drug addiction.

Others have been through incredible, life-threatening ordeals or overcome adversity in some unique way. And there are those who really have had a life so full of hilarious incident that it would make a great source of entertainment. We all – in our own way – have our stories to tell.

What makes some of them stand out is, as comedian Frank Carson would have said, the way you tell 'em.

It's not enough to simply relay an interesting life experience. You have to find your own unique voice, have to grip your reader and absorb them into your world – writing about feelings that they can relate to. You have to, in other words, hold them.

I would say it is probably even more difficult to keep the page-turning quality high with a personal memoir precisely because the contents may be distressing and because of the enormous difficulties of writing about oneself.

When it is *your* story it is hard to be objective about what is truly pertinent to pass on to the reader and what you want to write for *you*. It is difficult, when so close to the truth, to be discerning about which parts of that truth are worth sharing.

All of this is easier if you are talking on a subject that many of your readers will have experienced themselves.

Having read Lindsay Nicholson's beautifully-written *Living on the Seabed* (Vermilion), her immensely moving account of losing both her husband and daughter within a short space of time, I sent a copy to my friend, the one-time editor of QWF I've mentioned earlier, Jo Good.

Jo too lost her husband at a young age – Phill was just 34 when he died of a brain abscess – and I knew she would identify greatly with all Lindsay had written about grief.

She emailed me a few days later to say how much it had meant to her.

Once I started to read it I couldn't stop. It's a wonderful book – so well written.

It really spoke to me. I wish I'd had this book a few months after Phill died.

Jo, whose mother had recently died also, went on to describe *Living on the Seabed* as a book to "treasure and re-read". She said how important its "positive and upbeat ending" was to her and thanked me for "a very special present".

This illustrates perfectly how a good memoir is not just an account of what happened to the writer but must strike chords with others, must contain some emotional truth that they recognise.

I have no doubt that it must have been cathartic for Lindsay to have written her book, although she has said how "scary" it was to put her "innermost thoughts out there for the world to see". But it has also done a huge amount for her readers. That too brings its responsibilities and can have its downside. She explains:

> Of course, you are afraid that people are going to criticise you but actually what I found was that they want to share their own experiences which are very moving. As you can imagine, many of the letters I received were heart-breaking. I replied to all of them but found it incredibly upsetting. In the end I had to bundle the letters up and respond to them all in one go because to open the post every morning and be confronted with terrible tragedy was just too much.

Living on the Seabed has gone into a second, updated edition and continues to sell well.

Other Non-Fiction

A quick look at my current copy of *The Writer's Handbook* reveals that there are 82 pages worth of magazines listed, covering every subject from antiques to jazz to swimming to railways.

All these magazines need a constant supply of articles and features and many of the editors will be only to happy to hear from freelancers.

If you have an area of expertise you feel you could write about, see if there is a magazine to match it (I bet there is) but don't necessarily stop there.

With sufficient research a competent writer should be able to come up with a piece on pretty much anything. There are some obvious exceptions – I would not recommend you attempt to submit anything to the British

Medical Journal unless you have some suitable qualification – but if you keep away from the finer technical details of, say, cycling, then why not? You might not be able to talk with authority on gear-changes in professional racing but you could write a piece on the importance of teaching children road safety and hand signals the moment they've stopped wobbling.

Or maybe you haven't got the first clue about golf. But if your spouse spends every spare moment on the course with his/her cronies, you could probably write an amusing piece on being a Golf Widow/Widower.

Think beyond the obvious and you will be surprised how many subjects you could find an angle on.

As far as a full-length work goes, this is my first non-fiction book so only you can judge if I know anything about how to write one.

Maria McCarthy, however, the author of *The Girls' Guide to Losing your L-Plates* (Pocket Books) (if you get a copy, you can see how I failed to lose mine on page 115) is full of hot tips.

> One: Don't get so involved in research that you put off the actual writing and end up in a mad sleep-deprived rush to meet your deadline.

(Ah – now she tells me)

> Two: Getting the right experts makes a huge difference – lots of people know their subject but find it difficult to communicate in lay language. Hunting around on the internet or going through relevant trade journals is a great way of tracking down accessible experts – or visit **www.expertsources.com**.

> Three: When it comes to getting a book deal, going into detail about the potential readership for your book (e.g no of people in the country who have asthma, restore classic cars, go sky-diving or whatever) can be really helpful. Outline what other books are available in this field and why yours is so much better!

It is worth pointing out here that the beauty of a non-fiction book is you don't have to write the entire thing first before you try to sell it. Unlike a novel, when you should. Yes, I know that you've heard of people who sold their first novel on the strength of three paragraphs, but believe me, you won't. If you've never been published before it really is best to write the whole thing. This is:

a) to show you have the stamina
b) so an agent or publisher can see you know the whole story
c) so they can also see that it doesn't sag in the middle or tail off lamely at the end
d) because if you've never done it before, you won't know you can, until you do.

But non-fiction is different. You can put together a proposal with a couple of sample chapters and, hopefully, get the deal on the strength of that.

These are the instructions The Fearsome One sent me when I first mentioned writing a non-fiction book.

WRITE: a separate paragraph on each of the following:

1. Focus – what
2. Purpose – why
3. Approach – how
4. Readership
5. Competition – compare with other books on same subject.

GIVE: Marketing ideas

PROVIDE: A table of contents
Introduction
List of illustrations (if applicable)
Brief biographical information focusing on the author's
professional background and his or her suitability to write this book
(NB this should be written in the third person).
A list of previous publications
At least one sample chapter.

So I wouldn't dare do anything else but some publishers have their own guidelines for submissions. Jill Hassall is the author of *The Greatest Wedding Tips in the World* (Public Eye Publications March 2008).

Jill read an article about the publishers and their various "tips" books (one of them is the *The Greatest Sex Tips in the World!*) in *Writers' News* and sent off a brief submission. In return she received their guidelines.

"I followed the guidelines very closely, sending off exactly the number of tips they had requested, and sticking to their word count. Lo and behold – I got the offer of a contract."

Jill went for wedding tips as she'd run a wedding car business for 9 years (obviously Write What You Know really comes into its own in non-fiction – little point in writing *The World's Greatest Tips on Slug-Keeping* if you know bugger-all about it) and had picked up all sorts of useful info along the way. "It's amazing what you hear when you're driving a couple to the reception!" she says.

Jill makes the very sensible point that if you have a particular area of expertise and come across a publisher looking for authors for this sort of series, then "get in quickly".

"I'm sure I wasn't the only one to think of weddings," she says. "In the past, I've wasted time 'thinking' but I did this almost immediately I saw the article."

Good for her but remember that in the same way that it is hard to come up with a totally unique plot in fiction, so are you unlikely to be wanting to write a book on a subject that hasn't already been covered somewhere, sometime. (Search the word "Diet" on Amazon – when I last did it, I got 20,449 results). The trick, as always, is to find a different slant, a different voice, some whole new tricks to teach jaded old dogs who've read it all before.

Jill writes fiction too – she's written short stories for the women's magazine market and has had a couple of children's books published. The main difference, she says, is that in non-fiction you are dealing with facts and can't "wander off". (Whoops – something else I should have found out first.) "In a fiction piece," Jill explains, "you can actually go in a different direction to the one you intended at the beginning as your characters develop. With a non-fiction book, you have to stick to your plan."

Sue Moorcroft, who as well as being a novelist and short-story writer, writes occasional articles, too, agrees. "My big problem is not being able to 'bring on a man with a gun' if I feel the piece is lagging! Fiction is so flexible in comparison."

Penny Alexander, on the other hand, thinks there are more similarities than one might suppose. Penny writes articles as well as short fiction and says: "It's as essential to include emotion in non-fiction as it is in any romantic fiction. Look for an emotional hook along with your facts."

In other words, we are back to finding something others can relate to.

One of my early forays into journalism was a personal, confessional-type piece for *The Guardian's Weekend* magazine about developing teenage-type crushes as an adult. (They called it *I love to love* – you can find it online at Guardian Unlimited **www.guardian.co.uk** if you're interested.)

On accepting it, the editor said she was doing so because "it rang a lot of bells with me – this means it will with readers too." And sure enough, I had a lovely, touching letter from a grandmother in her sixties who said she still got crushes too and that my article had been very reassuring.

If you, too, like the idea of writing for the newspapers, read on.

Wannabe a Journalist?

"I had fallen into a trade where the only necessary qualification, it seemed, was the ability to write plausible drivel while under the influence of alcohol."

So wrote the excellent Richard Morrison in his column in *The Times* in 2006 when reflecting on his entry into journalism thirty-odd years previously. The tradition of lunchtime drinking, he admits, has "withered tragically" since the 1970s but he still considers journalism to be "one of the last great skives of modern life".

I don't know what it's like to do it full time, but I consider journalism to be just about the nicest, most stress-free way to earn money from writing with the added benefit of having the ego boost of seeing your name in print in a matter of days instead of a couple of years down the line, if you're lucky.

I should say at once though that what I mean by journalism is the sort of freelance work I do – writing a weekly column for the local rag, some regular pieces for magazines and the odd piece for the nationals when I hit lucky with the right idea at the right time.

I know nothing about the hard slog of joining a local paper at sixteen and covering village fêtes and weddings and whoever got knocked over in the High Street again, gradually working your way up the reporting ladder until you're covering wars in the Middle East or have become Kate Adie. If this is even how one still does it.

Most of the full-time journalists I know got their jobs by various other routes. Melanie Whitehouse from the *Daily Express* got where she is today by getting on the wrong bus. Stuck with a much longer journey than she should have had, she bought, for the first time ever, a copy of the *Evening News* and spotted a situation vacant: that of a secretary for a national newspaper. She ended up, aged 19, leaving her job in a solicitor's office and going to work for four feature writers on the *Daily Mail* that she describes as "the legendary Lynda Lee-Potter and hugely talented and very naughty theatre critic Jack Tinker, Peter Lewis, the literary editor, a dreadful but totally endearing old rogue; and sweet, kind Margaret Hinxman who was the film critic."

Unlike the "pompous" solicitors, her new bosses made her very welcome. "They took me to restaurants and premieres and introduced me to what was then a necessity for any would-be journalist – the art of drinking and holding your drink…"

It left Melanie knowing she "had to be a journalist" and there followed a series of jobs with regional papers both here and in Australia before she joined the *Daily Express*.

Richard Morrison had a music degree rather than any formal journalistic training. He started out by writing for various music magazines before landing a job as music critic on *The Times*. Gradually this led to "more general stuff" .

"Never say no to any assignment," he counsels. "Don't be too precious to try any area – it might be another string to your bow."

His colleague on *The Times*, Mick Hume, didn't come up by a conventional route either.

In what he now describes as his "revolutionary twenties", Mick and "some comrades" set up a magazine called *Living Marxism*, relaunched in the 1990s as *LM Magazine*, specialising in "edgy current affairs and cultural criticism".

After being sued for libel and closed down in 2000, Mick was head-hunted (ah, the stuff dreams are made on!) to write comment pieces for *The Times*, where he became a columnist.

Award-winning journalist Robert Crampton got into student journalism at university when he realised writing was the only thing he "was any good at" and then got a bursary to become a trainee on *The New Statesman*.

Sara Lawrence, too, went to university and then landed herself some work experience on the *times 2* features section of *The Times* where she went all-out to make herself indispensable. "I smiled at everyone until my cheeks hurt, and I fetched more coffees than I can ever remember."

After a couple of weeks, she noticed a bulging grey post sack in the corner was growing bigger by the day and that the feature writers she was sitting with kept throwing nervous glances at it. Discovering that it was filled with limericks written by readers' kids on the subject of the latest

Harry Potter book, Sara offered to read through them all and make a shortlist.

It took her a week but thoroughly endeared her to Sandra Parsons, the editor, leading to Sara writing the piece on the winners. " Three weeks in the office and I had my first double page spread complete with huge byline."

In her fourth week, she discovered that one of the three junior researchers was leaving. She went back to see Sandra. " I told her I was desperate to be a journalist and could she possibly consider me for the position. She said yes, and that was it."

Sara spent two years at *The Times*, progressing to writing and commissioning others. I had my first thrilling moment of seeing my own copy there when I contributed three sentences on why I like Sudoku.

You may not be in a position to go hunting down a full-time job on a national paper and even if you are, it is desperately competitive. But there is a whole freelance world out there too.

"Journalism is very open," says Robert Crampton. "There are no barriers. If you can find a good story, write it and sell it you can call yourself a journalist. It's not like being a doctor or a lawyer. A lot is done by networking – jobs don't get advertised – it's word of mouth and who knows who."

The late, great John Diamond, Robert's predecessor in the Saturday *Times Magazine* slot would have agreed.

John was immensely kind and encouraging to me when I was trying to get my first novel published. I wrote to him one day, to comment on one of his columns and we ended up exchanging many emails before he died. Once when I congratulated him on a fantastic review of *A Lump In My Throat*, the play Victoria Coren wrote based on his book and experiences, he pointed out that between them he and Victoria had worked for every paper in Fleet street bar the *Sun* and the *Star* and often played poker with the arts editors, while the main editors were all good enough friends to turn up to his parties.

"What are they going to say about me or her other than that we're truly marvellous people?" he enquired. "Everything that wannabe hacks say about it not being what you know but who you know, is spot on."

That may be true – I have seen it myself – but he was also being very modest. He added at the time: "my only defence is that I started off as a school teacher knowing nobody", and that of course is how he'd have stayed if he hadn't been a brilliant writer.

Instead he went on to write for most of the national papers and numerous magazines, as well as writing travel features and radio scripts. He is best known for his *Times* column and his inspirational and humbling book *C – Because Cowards Get Cancer Too* (Vermilion). If you've never read it – do.

Let us remember that whoever you know, you're not going to get very far if you don't have the talent and a fairly unusual one at that. We might all sit at our breakfast tables thinking "I could write that," but actually we probably couldn't.

"Don't confuse journalism with writing," says Melanie Whitehouse. "Being good at one, doesn't necessarily mean you'll be good at the other."

So what does make a good journalist?

"Cynicism, a thick skin, low cunning, perseverance, and unshakeable belief that you are always right," says my old mate Mike Pearce, the now-retired editor of the local newspaper I write for myself.

"A boring willingness to work the hours," says Mick Hume. "And the nerve to write what you believe to be true, regardless of whom it might offend."

"Curiosity about people," says Richard Morrison. "Plus stamina and the determination to tell good stories as accurately as you can."

"But don't tell me you 'like' people," grumbles Mike Pearce. "If so, go off and be a social worker instead. Liking people is not an asset when your day job is asking people how they feel when they've just lost their nearest and dearest, confronting those who want to smack you on the nose, or catching influential people off-guard."

But "empathy" is vital, counters Melanie. "People think you have to be hard to be a successful journalist, but I believe that while a tough exterior helps, a soft inside is a must. How else can you relate to the woman who is telling you how her daughter was murdered, or that her husband beat her up? You need to develop the ability to win someone's trust in minutes, and then not abuse that trust."

Most freelancers – and there are many of them chasing every feature – are either ex-full-timers who've had kids and need to work from home, or general jobbing writers who do all sorts. Or they're little-known novelists who got a taste for it, like I did, when they discovered it's a very handy way both to make a few bob and get your books mentioned.

Everything is faster and more immediate in the world of newspapers and

I like the adrenalin rush this gives me. Though the first time was a bit of a learning curve.

I wrote a piece for *The Sun* when *Perfect Alibis* came out – contributing a few words of wisdom on the thorny question of why married women have affairs.

I had discussed the possibility of doing this with a press agency who told me that someone from *The Sun* would be in touch. I was driving into Canterbury (about twenty miles from my home) to meet someone for lunch when the call came in from Sinead Desmond, from the women's pages. It was about 12.30pm by the time she'd run through what she needed and promised to email me a more detailed brief to write to.

"When do you need it by?" I asked cheerily.

"3 p.m.," came the reply.

Needless to say, I cancelled lunch, turned the car round and went straight back home to switch on the computer. It was very tight – I emailed it off at 14.58 p.m. – but it gave me a huge buzz.

That was unusual, though. Mainly when I write for a national, it is because I have thought up a possible idea and pitched it to someone and they – if I'm lucky – have gone for it. Usually I then have a few days rather than hours, to get the copy in.

I don't know if there is a correct way to do these pitches to newspapers and magazines – I can only tell you how I do it.

And that's like this:

1) First I target my newspaper or magazine, generally by having spotted a similar sort of piece in there by someone else. For example, reading the *Guardian's Weekend* magazine showed me that they liked first-person confessional/true experience type pieces, so I approached them for my piece on infatuations.

2) Next I find out the RIGHT PERSON to contact. This is terribly important. It is absolutely no good just sending off an email to someone you've seen in *The Writer's Handbook* listed as features editor. He or she may be the person you need, but equally they may not. Editors get shifted around, magazines get revamped, jobs change. If you don't know anyone else to ask (once you make one contact you'll have someone to whom you can politely enquire of others) then do phone up and ask very specifically who edits the parenting or travel pages. And what their email address is. Although these days you can usually work that one out for yourself if

you've ever dealt with the publication before – most will follow a format. E.g. Firstname.secondname@thenewspaper.co.uk

3) Then I email them. I keep it short, light and friendly. Tell them who I am, what I have done ("I am a novelist and freelance journalist" will suffice – no need to list every last thing you've had published and the details of your cycling proficiency test) and briefly outline the article I have in mind. For example, this is what I said in my email to Hannah Pool who commissioned my "crush" piece:

> Would you be interested in a piece on Crushes? I am thinking of an "I still get them" piece – the teenage-type obsession/fantasies about people in "authority" (they are not usually sexual and not necessarily just men!). I am talking Bank Managers/policemen/the kid's history teacher/anyone who has helped or "rescued" me in some way. This would be tied up with my theory that the stronger, more independent and emancipated a woman is, the more there is a secret desire to be dominated/nurtured/rescued. It is all about fantasy. I would point out that one usually comes out of the crush very rapidly after a reality-dose. E.g seeing your gynaecologist walking round Sainsbury's in old tracksuit bottoms with breakfast on his jumper and two whining kids at his heels.

She emailed back fairly rapidly and bought it.

N.B. make sure you include clear contact details – especially a mobile phone number. If an editor gets no reply from the landline because you're pushing a trolley round Sainsbury's yourself, they may be too busy/not bother to phone back and buy someone else's article instead.

Have something ready to show them. When I started out, I was often asked to send cuttings of previously published pieces. These days, most commissioning editors have a quick look at my website (which, although I say it myself, is jolly good) or assume that because I have written three novels, I can string a sentence together. Although Melanie Whitehouse tells me the one does not always follow the other when it comes to writing features.

It is Melanie's job to commission them from people like me – that's how I met her – and she has kindly offered tips of her own on both pitching for features and then writing them.

- Know your market. Don't, like so many PRs, pitch inappropriately. It is irritating, time-wasting and loses you credibility.

- Be persistent but patient – many features editors are so understaffed and under pressure that they can't reply to all their emails. Having said that, they will usually home in on good ideas and get back to you, so if your ideas don't hit the spot and they don't respond, don't pester. Take it elsewhere.

- Make sure you get a precise brief and know exactly what is expected, when the deadline is and what you will be paid and when. There's nothing more annoying for a writer than to accept a sloppy brief from a lazy commissioning editor, spend days trying to make it work and then to get the article returned because it isn't what was wanted. 'I'll know what I want when I get it,' was what one features editor used to say to writers. Unfortunately, she lasted longer than she should have.

- Stick to the brief you've negotiated, including format and word count. There's nothing more annoying for a commissioning editor than to get copy that doesn't fulfil his or her requirements. If things don't work out as planned, inform your editor and discuss how best to proceed.

- When writing your feature, never leave an unanswered question in the reader's mind. When you refer to something, make sure it is qualified the first time, not halfway down the article.

- However daft the queries on your copy, try to keep your temper. It can be hard but it will stand you in good stead in the future and you won't get a reputation as being 'a bit difficult to work with'.

- Cultivate a friendship with commissioning editors, and suggest you meet up with those you like occasionally. Don't waste their time with long, chatty phone calls – the curse of the freelance may be loneliness but you don't want to alienate those who employ you.

Thank you Melanie! It is worth inwardly digesting these nuggets of advice and maybe even writing them on the wall above your bed because the one thing you can be sure of, whichever editor you approach, he or she will be inundated with other hopefuls.

Miles Kington, the humorous writer, broadcaster and *The Independent* columnist, once worked for *Punch*. He recalls:

Readers would send us hundreds of pieces each week, thinking they could write as well as us. Maybe they could. But how could we use their stuff?

THEN WE WOULD BE ADMITTING THAT THEY COULD WRITE AS WELL AS US. We used to divide the pieces up and share them out, and if any showed promise we would circulate them round the staff. They usually fell at the following hurdles.

1. Not funny.
2. Might have been funny at the time, but not when written down.
3. The writer thought that a funny story or funny incident was funny in itself, but it is the way it is written that makes the difference.
4. They could also be dismissed as "The day the washing machine broke down" or "This is a comic incident which happened to me in the war and all my friends have persuaded me to send it to Punch". Oh, false friends.
5. Too much like Alan Coren or P G Wodehouse or someone.
6. Not enough like Alan Coren or P G Wodehouse or someone.The only pieces we accepted were quirky ones which we couldn't categorise.

Sometimes we would get a really nice piece which didn't fit in with Punch. An analysis of supermarket trolley behaviour perhaps. In fact, we did get that once. I wrote back and suggested that the writer should send it to a grocery magazine, which probably needed humour much more than Punch did. He wrote back later and said he had done so, and it had been accepted, and he had been paid much more than Punch could offer.

Miles also offers his four golden rules of writing. (Mr Kington is much better-known and far more experienced in the ways of journalism than I am – so I am repeating them even though they may seem barely relevant and I had to delete number four as I didn't know what he was talking about).

1. Don't send articles to Punch, which no longer exists.
2. Get a good agent, or, if you can't get a good agent, take a good agent hostage and force him/her to represent you at gunpoint, which might also make a good plot for a novel.
3. If all else fails, write a cookery book.

The prolific columnist, writer and broadcaster Rosie Millard has words of advice too:

I would say probably the most important thing about being a journalist is to read the paper you want to write for. Every day. If you want to be a columnist, read the columns. If you want to be a feature writer, ditto. Work out what makes a good story. Then set about finding ones of your own. Remember every story needs a top line. Can you explain the story in 10 seconds or less, or one sentence? If so, it's probably going to work. It also must be original but not necessarily terrifyingly so. i.e 'Don't buy a dog for Christmas' has been done to death, but 'Don't buy a parakeet for Christmas' probably hasn't. Oh, yes, and NEVER invent your quotes…

Rosie is an excellent example of a writer who turns her hand to all sorts of subjects and apparently never lets anything that happens to her go to waste. Quite apart from her regular spot – *Tales of a Landlady* in *The Sunday Times* – she frequently pops up on other pages; one minute it's the difficulty of holding on to your nanny, next it's travelling with children on trains, or how broke she is (everything is relative) and the joy of making homemade chutney for cut-price Christmas presents (give me a break!).

Sometimes she phones me up for quotes for her Buy-to-Let columns and I still like her, despite her making me sound like Ann Widdecombe's rather more right-wing grandmother every time.

And talking of columns, it's a funny thing that every novelist I know seems to dream of having a column in a national newspaper (well, I do anyway – editors please note!) while most journalists will mention a long-term ambition to write a book.

Sara Lawrence has already realised hers. Leaving *The Times* for work on the *Daily Mail*, as "lots of the people I most admired used to cite it as the greatest journalistic training they'd had" she quickly became disillusioned with the very different set-up. The paper commissioned far more pieces than they could ever use and it took Sara a month to see anything of hers in print. "I became more and more demoralised as piece after piece was binned," she says. "Writing for the spike becomes incredibly tedious." (You see – it isn't all glamour and expense accounts – you heard it here first.)

She began writing a book at the suggestion of her friend Julie Burchill, finishing it when she was made redundant from the *Mail* some months later.

The result was *High Jinx* a "21st century take on Enid Blyton's *Malory Towers*, complete with sex, drugs and rock and roll".

Her agent, Robert Caskie, sold it for fat sums both here (Faber & Faber) and in the USA and also negotiated the TV rights. So you see – it can happen!

When we were last in touch, Sara was sipping champagne cocktails on

Bondi Beach in Sydney, while writing the sequel. It was January here and cold, grey and raining. I was totally thrilled for her and not at all jealous.

But to get back to columns, everyone wants to write one and only a special few will get the plum job of doing so. Once again "it's not enough just to write well," says Mike Pearce who has hired a fair few columnists in his time. "Have you anything new to say?" he enquires, "and a convincing argument as to why anyone is going to be interested in hearing *you* say it?"

He is summing up exactly what makes a columnist successful – his or her ability to either surprise us with something we've never thought of or to cover well-worn subjects in an original way. This may be in terms of the language one uses (Mike once told me that he gave me my column on the strength of a joke I made in my begging email) or the unusual insights one shows.

Yet again you are looking for that recognition from your reader: the YEEESSS factor.

Or, as Robert Crampton puts it, far more eloquently: the best sort of column "articulates something that has not yet solidified in other people's minds".

I admire Robert's columns hugely. He is an excellent writer with a very clever turn of phrase and a good line in being hilarious about dead hamsters as well as more common preoccupations such as eating too much or being a funny shape – his accounts of eating 72 assorted canapés (it may have been more) and going to be fitted for a handmade shirt are genius. But the best example of this was a piece he wrote in Beta Male, his *Times* column in May 2004 in which he listed all the things he didn't like.

I have no idea if he did this because absolutely nothing else had happened to him that week and he was desperate for subject matter – and he can't remember either – but it worked a treat. A bit of it went like this:

> I dislike most things about most hotels. Blond wood, kettles with absurdly short flexes, weird light switch configurations, shower controls you need a degree in hydro-engineering to fathom, fire doors, soap in little packets, milk in little cartons, butter in little sachets (in fact any form of portion control), banqueting suites, a stingy supply of teabags and being called Sir.

I had never thought about it before but yes – the flexes on hotel kettles ARE ridiculously short. Unless you unplug them from the wall you can barely upend the bloody kettles to get the water in your cup. And no – there are never enough teabags. And it wasn't just me. Robert was inundated with emails from other readers who had the same grievances. They all identified exactly with what he was saying but had never thought to say it themselves. So the column did just what it should have done.

In simple terms, we are talking that 'YEESSSS' quality that has you nodding away and jabbing the paper with a gnarled forefinger, shouting "Quite Right Too!"

India Knight quite often has this effect on me – though I don't always remember to read her now the powers that be have moved her to another section of *The Sunday Times* (why do they *do* that?) and Shane Watson certainly did when she wrote a hysterical and painfully accurate account of the typical female day for the ST's *Style* Magazine – explaining what makes us all so grumpy (we hate our clothes, have bad hair and are fat). I felt a particular empathy for her "waking thoughts": "Why, *why* the third bottle? Did I finish off the pizza at 2 a.m.?"

Others are simply very amusing (Jeremy Clarkson: I couldn't exactly empathise the week of his self-administered rectal examination but I still laughed like a drain), compulsively irritating (Michael Winner) or just totally wickedly hilarious – what a sad day it was for us all when Michael Bywater upped and left *The Independent*.

I loved him best when he was ranting and being unrepentantly abusive – very un-pc but what a way with words. I particularly recall him describing certain women as "burping pallidly out of their chain-store slag-wrappings" (the dreadful man) and was highly amused by his column in *The Independent* in January 2004 where he mused on those ads that were headed "Why not be a Writer?"

Anyone can be a writer. Why not? Your life is your own. You'd have no pension, your old age would be one of destitution, you'd have to fight to get paid peanuts, you'd be behind with the tax (and don't even mention the VAT), you'd be unmortgageable, unmarriageable, intolerable; you'd have piles, emphysema and cirrhosis; each day would begin in panic as you realised you were behind schedule, bereft of ideas, played out, washed up, knackered and skint; the only people who would speak to you are editors nagging, duns dunning, and other writers ringing up who put the phone down when you say "Hello" because they were only calling to see if you were dead so that they could move in on your patch.

I posed the same question to him when I was foraging for insights for this book and he sent a page of replies. I'm not sure all of them are printable but they are very funny so I'll share some of them with you later on.

All of these great writers may make it look easy but that is their talent. Robert Crampton takes up to two days to write each column "even if it reads as it if is just dashed off!".

The main trick, as Robert says, is the deceptively-simple-sounding "keep your readers in mind".

"It's no good just writing for your mates," he points out. "No good just writing about life in the particular chunk of North London where all the other journalists live."

Although that particular area has stood Richard Morrison in good stead. One day after changing his barber he got to wondering why all the barbers in North London are Cypriots. "I got a lot of response to writing about that," he says. "It's the little things that strike a chord!"

Or the big things indeed. Both Isabel Wolff and Helen Fielding got such a huge response to their columns on the life of the single thirty-something that these were turned into best-selling novels.

But sometimes you have to say what everyone is NOT thinking as well. Melanie Whitehouse rates the ability to go against the grain. "A great columnist will stick their neck out," she says. "He or she will have the guts to say what they really think and feel even though they know they might get a flood of hate mail. It can be horribly personal at times."

I know this myself from my own small column in the *Isle of Thanet Gazette* (part of the Mirror Group). I receive regular missives from a nameless correspondent – known affectionately in the *Gazette* offices as 'Anon' who berates me for talking about myself (she has clearly not grasped the point of a personal column) being dull and uninteresting and talking rubbish. Why don't you give up? she wants to know on a monthly basis. I realise that it would leave a hole in her life if I did so, I keep going.

Readers also write in to tell me I drink too much and to suggest remedies for my liver. One week I mentioned this and my most favourite missive ever came in response. "In my opinion," an elderly gentleman wrote, "Jane Wenham-Jones does not drink enough. If she did, she might find something sensible to say…"

Short Stories

Writing short stories is a great training ground for writing something longer one day and is also very pleasurable and satisfying in itself. I know several successful short-story writers who just stick to that and have no particular desire to write a novel (and why should they!) but it is also true that several great novelists started out this way and then moved on.

Minette Walters leaps immediately to mind, as does Kate Atkinson. Both wrote for the women's magazine market in their early days. Having to write to a word count is a good discipline and encourages you to make your prose sharp. And writing for huge-circulation magazines is also living proof, if you decide to go the novel route later and are trying to woo agents or publishers into taking a look, that that you can string a sentence together and understand what makes writing commercial.

It is quite competitive – magazines like *Woman's Weekly* get 1000 submissions a month. But they have the weekly magazine and a bi-monthly Fiction Special to fill and fiction editor Gaynor Davies says she is always open to new writers. The guidelines state: "We welcome stories on a wide range of themes and moods, for instance, warm stories about children, teenagers and family problems of various kinds; love stories, funny stories and even stories with a crime or thriller element, so long as they are not violent, threatening or too incredible. In other words, fiction that grips the readers rather than sending them to sleep!"

Both Gaynor Davies and her Assistant Fiction Editor, Clare Cooper, are immensely encouraging to new writers. Everything is read, even if at times it takes a while – the WW guidelines ask you to allow up to 16 weeks for a reply – and they will often take the trouble to explain why a story hasn't quite made it.

They are looking for up-to-date characters in modern situations and I know from my own experience – I have written for them many times – that humour always goes down well, too. Gaynor sums up: "The ideal *Woman's Weekly* story is imaginative yet convincing enough for the reader to believe in it completely."

At *My Weekly*, Fiction Editor Liz Smith also welcomes submissions.

"I'm always short of good, contemporary light-hearted themes, off-beat romances and stories about children." She's particularly interested in those children being girls for, as she explains: "For some strange reason little boy stories are more prevalent and illustrations of these are not so widely available."

Both magazines will send you guidelines if you write to them, enclosing an SAE. *My Weekly* also offers them by email – send to **myweekly@dcthomson.co.uk**

The queen of magazine fiction, Teresa Ashby, has sold over 1500 short stories and ten serials to women's magazines. You must, she says, "know your readers inside out." Teresa reads all the magazines she writes for, "from cover to cover" every week. And even after all those sales, she works as hard on each story as she always did.

"Write it. Read it. Rewrite it. Read it. Rewrite it. Read it," she advises. "Keep doing this until you can read it from beginning to end and not want to change a single word. And when you think it's perfect, put it aside and later read it again and see what needs changing. Write with your heart and read with your head."

She is totally right and I would add – as a quick list of must-dos:

STUDY the magazine you want to write for – a *Fiction Feast* story will be a different kettle of fish from one published in *The People's Friend*. Read several copies – not just one.
SEND for guidelines if the magazine has them.
STICK rigidly to the recommended word count – if there are no guidelines available, count the number of words in previously published stories.
SUBMIT one story at a time, enclosing an SAE and a short covering letter. Do not send the same story to half a dozen magazines at once – you might think two editors wanting your work is a good problem to have, but you will probably just annoy and alienate both of them.
SHRUG – when you get a rejection and send it out again. There are all sorts of reasons why a story might get turned down and there is no reason why the next editor – if you adapt it to suit their magazine – won't buy it instead. Tenacity is the name of the game. (My record for a magazine story was eleven outings – and about eight re-writes – before I finally got that cheque.)

If the magazine market is not for you, either for reasons of preference (some writers are incredibly sniffy about it – more fool them) or ability (it takes a certain skill that not all writers have – even those who are wildly successful in other fields), and prefer your short fiction to have a more literary bent –

there are countless short story competitions out there (see later chapter on same).

In addition, there are all sorts of small press magazines – *Cadenza* and *QWF* spring most readily to mind – that regularly publish short stories. Again, an internet search will reveal many others, I'm sure. While if you are looking to publish online, there are e-magazines popping up left, right and centre. Have a read of what they are publishing already – some of it is total bilge – and try to find one showcasing work you admire.

Whole books have been written on how to write a short story so I will not attempt to cover it all here or this book will end up the size of a house brick, but will try to put it into some sort of nutshell.

I mentioned way back near the beginning that a short story should have a conflict and a moment of change. It is worth repeating again now because it is the one thing you must know if you are going to attempt short fiction and is the most common thing that goes wrong when writers first start out.

A typical example of a non-story goes like this:

A grieving man, Will, stands by the grave of his wife, Margaret. He remembers how they met, what she wore on their wedding day, the birth of their first child, and the pain of watching her die in his arms. He reflects that his life is empty without her and turns and goes sadly home.

This is not a story. It may be a beautiful piece of prose, exquisitely-written, heart-rending and tear-jerking. But a story it ain't.

What would make it a story is if something happened to Will at that graveside to send him home altered – however minutely. Let us suppose he gets talking to another widower who is mourning his own wife or he has an encounter with a child whose grandfather has just died. Perhaps he finds a stray or injured dog that needs his help. Maybe one of the graves has been vandalised and it throws Will into an uncontrollable (and cathartic) rage.

Or – if you have the imagination of a turnip and wish to be seriously unoriginal – he could bump into an apple-cheeked widow whose husband died at the same time as Margaret and they could wander off to the local whist drive together.

Whatever the scenario, if Will goes home with new hope in his heart or his view of life changed in some small way, then what was once merely a description of grief has now become a story.

Remember it doesn't have to be high drama – some very fine and powerful short stories have centred around the slightest shift of perception.

Fay Weldon is brilliant at this – any aspiring short-story writer could do a lot worse than to get hold of her short story collections. I particularly love *Watching Me, Watching You* (Hodder) although any of them are excellent.

Remember that a short story is just that: short. So every word must count. It is not a novel told in a couple of thousand words.

A good short story is a snapshot: it captures a moment in time. It is a thought-provoking, mind-changing polished jewel that leaves one shaken or stirred, delighted or touched. That makes one *think*.

I have never forgotten many of the short stories I studied in English Literature as long ago as my O level days – *Samphire* by Patrick O'Brian stands out, along with *The Rain Horse* by Ted Hughes or the perfectly-judged *The Ice Palace* by Scott Fitzgerald.

Sue Thomas, who was the fiction editor at *Woman* for many years used to say that what she looked for was a story that would bring a "smile to your face and a lump to your throat".

She was talking about magazine fiction where that is certainly a winning combination. I would add to the list for the more general short story. If it angers you, makes you weep or curl your fists in frustration then it has worked. A brilliant story haunts you because in some small way it has spoken to you – whether by striking a chord, or sending a chill, through your heart.

Other Sorts of Writing (the sort I know nothing about)

Writing mottos for Christmas Crackers

Someone must do it. Unfortunately I don't know who.

Writing rhymes for the inside of Greetings Cards

I have only two things to say about this.
1) God save us from another Patience Strong and
2) Lynne Barrett-Lee's account of her experience of being hired by Cardiff WH Smith one February to write Valentine's messages inside cards for those too dumb to think of anything themselves, is enough to put one off

for life. As she said at the time: "I don't think I have ever done anything quite as profoundly excruciating."

Adopting what she referred to as a 'Baden-Powellish kind of strategy', she had prepared herself by penning half a dozen basic templates which she intended to personalise once she had ascertained the loved one's eye colour, favourite things, endearing qualities and so on. Shuddering at the memory, she recalls:

"This produced data of variable poetic quality and left me struggling with such crises as how to find a rhyme for Llanelli RFC, and how to approach a ditty whose subject was called Clive and mostly liked watching old episodes of Star Trek."

Feeling that, as writers, we should rise to every new challenge that comes our way, I have had a go at this myself.

Oh Clive I've just decided – you're not the one for me
You're a pain in the neck
When you watch Star Trek
And Llanelli RFC

It has confirmed my suspicions that I may not be a natural.

Writing Plays

I haven't done this either (are you beginning to wonder why you bought this book?) but I know a man who has.

You will probably never have heard of Steven Todd – unless you live in my home town where everyone has – but he writes fantastic plays under the rather odd name of Ace Books.

Todd (as we all call him) is the total opposite of me. Whereas I am a true Wannabe – wannabe published, wannabe on *Richard & Judy*, wannabe fantastically rich and successful, wannabe famous – Todd is a simply-get-on-and-do-it-be – but preferably for his friends and with his light firmly dimmed under a bushel.

Therefore despite my post-performance squawking about how he should sell/publish/go on a countrywide tour with his plays he typically puts them on for audiences of about 60 people in venues that hold 45. And once they have been met with rapturous applause they are never seen again.

They are none the less valid for that and neither are Todd's excellent tips. I reproduce them here as "Playwrighting for Beginners" but they are applicable to all sorts of writing.

1) Decide on a scenario.
2) Decide, roughly, how many characters you'll need.
3) Think about 'em for a while. Make lists of things you'd like 'em to say.
4) Get some paper and write.

It is, he says, as easy as that.

> Don't stop to re-read. Don't agonise. If it's rubbish no-one need ever see it. Just let your mind relax and your pen go. Don't even worry if you don't understand what it is you are writing – the chances are your subconscious will. Eventually you will produce a rough draft and once you have that things will be a lot easier. Nothing empties the mind faster than a blank page. So get writing and then get re-shaping. You can do it...

Writing for TV

Whole books have been dedicated to this too. A recent one is:

Writing TV Scripts: Successful Writing in Ten Weeks (Studymates Writers Guides) by Steve Wetton.

I have no idea what it's like because I haven't read it yet but Steve is a nice chap so I thought I'd mention it.

Just because I wouldn't know where to begin to write a TV script that needn't necessarily stop you. Sara Lawrence had no idea how they would do it when she and Julie Burchill got a commission to write a one-hour drama for the BBC's *Decades* series together. She didn't let it worry her though.

> Writing for TV and writing with a partner are two things I've never done before, but I like to challenge myself. The thing I thought most about before we started was HOW do you write with someone else? Do you take it in turns to write a sentence, a scene, what?

But in the end they just got on with it.

> We never really discussed the logistics. The day we started we both sat

131

with our laptops opposite each other at the kitchen table, and just cracked on. We chose our title: SCARS & STRIPES, discussed our characters, worked out our basic plot and just let rip. We have great fun when we're writing. The only routine we've stuck to is that we never force it. If we don't feel like writing we don't, and if we come to a natural break and can't think of anything else then we leave it till next time. There's lots of laughing, screaming and yelling and egging each other on and usually lots of cocktails too. It certainly beats working in an office!"

Lovely Raymond Allan who wrote *Some Mothers Do 'Ave 'Em*, advises

> Write about what you know, and situations and characters you're familiar with. You could start with yourself, however uneventful you think your life's been. At 31 I was broke, depressed and couldn't hold a job. How on earth could I write about a character like that? Then I thought of Frank Spencer.

The one piece of advice Ray has never forgotten was written on the door of a BBC Head of Comedy. "Whether he felt this applied to all writers or had just put it up for my benefit I never discovered," he says, but it is an excellent maxim for us all to remember:

The best scripts aren't written– they're re-written!

Writing Film Scripts

Joe Eszterhas, writer of films such as *Basic Instinct*, once sold a four-page outline for a film for $4 million. If this appeals to you, heed the advice he gave in *The Times* in January 2007, on learning about the film industry.

> Hide in a stall in the men's room of the Grille in Beverly Hills any weekday lunch hour, overhearing conversations. At the end of that time, you will have learnt everything you need to know about Hollywood.

But If LA is too far to go, then pop down to your local bookshop. *Story* by Robert McKee (Methuen) is generally considered to be a fairly definitive guide to the principles of screenwriting. You'll be competing with about a million others all chasing the same glories but the rewards, if you make it, are huge.

Joe Eszterhas is also a firm believer in Write What You Know. He began his writing career as a journalist.

"When I was a young reporter," he recalls, "I covered a situation where a gunman was holding his ex-girlfriend hostage. Twenty-five years later, I wrote the story as *Reliable Sources* and sold the script to Paramount for $2 million."

We can all dream…

Wannabe a Restaurant Critic?

This sounds the stuff of fantasies, too, doesn't it? Stuff your face for free a couple of times a week and then get paid to write about it.

Once again, there is a little more to it than might appear. I am fortunate to count among my friends Marina O'Loughlin, restaurant critic for *Metro*. I was very excited the first time I went out to lunch with her as I'd always wanted to see a Food Writer in action, imagining dishes piled high, a lot of swirling and spitting, and fawning waiters rushing to and fro.

It wasn't quite like that. Marina is one of the last two food critics in London who have managed to preserve their anonymity, so she books under a false name and does everything with a minimum of fuss.

She gave me a choice of venues – her only criteria is that the restaurant must be new. I rather fancied the sound of a Portuguese joint until she said the last time she'd been to one she'd been given pig's ear. I don't do peculiar animal parts. I also don't really do Japanese. I have always viewed Sushi as the culinary equivalent of the Emperor's New Clothes – does anyone really like little lumps of cold damp rice with a bit of raw fish on top, or do they just think they should?

But Japanese was what we got as the Portuguese place was full and being anonymous meant obviously that she couldn't pull any strings. So we rolled up at this place called Blossom in Hoxton where I tried pretending I understood the menu and then, having tried to eat something I was supposed to wipe my hands on, and drunk half the finger bowl, decided it was better to let Marina order for me.

Her appraisal of what we ate subsequently appeared in *Metro*, of course. I will quote you an extract here:

Bibimbap (Korean hotpot) lacked clarity – ingredients huddled together into an amorphous, vaguely chillied mass. Tempura soft shell crab roll, beautifully assembled and glistening with tobiko (flying fish roe), featured flaccid crustacean.

Black cod, however, was smokily good, salty and rich with miso. And rice – whether as a base to some silky yellowtail sushi or as a hot side dish – is terrific.

I also wrote about the experience in my newspaper column in the *Isle of Thanet Gazette*. Spot the difference.

All I can tell you is I liked the rice thing with beef bits, the black cod in sticky stuff was totally delicious and the cold pickled cabbage that the Koreans eat for breakfast, wasn't.

You will therefore probably agree that I am not the person to advise you, should you wish to pursue a career as a gastronome. Fortunately Marina, who at the time of writing has just been voted No. 7 in *Olive* Magazine's list of the top 50 decadent foodies of all time, has obliged instead.

So you want to be a restaurant critic? My advice is to get work-experience in restaurants for a minimum of ten years, even if it means doing so without pay. (If the restaurant is good enough, it might!)

Then, mortgage yourself to the hilt and blow the lot travelling the world eating in the likes of El Bulli (weird things made of jelly and foam) or the French Laundry (about a thousand bucks a pop). Ingest everything peculiar you can lay your hands on: testicles in Dalston; duck's blood in Hong Kong; pig's faces in Paris. Only then will the foodie world afford you the smallest degree of credibility.

At last, you can start your own newspaper or magazine – forget any of the established ones, they already have critics in place who will not give up the gig until they expire, strangled by their own expanding girth. It's simple really!

USEFUL THINGS ALONG THE WAY

Whatever sort of writing you're doing, there are certain things that will help. The first of these is:

Friends called Lynne

A Writer needs friends. And very specific sorts of friends, at that. Ideally, you need one from each of four categories of close pal. I am very lucky to have four such friends and as it happens, mine are all called Lynne. To save you confusion, we will call them Lynne the Mentor, Lynne the Novel, Lynne the Spell, and Lynne the Mouth (who might become Lynne the Libel once she's read this).

Lynne the Mentor

Writers are beset with doubt. Some days every sentence you write will look like trite rubbish (maybe because it is).

In order to overcome the horror of reading back your own drivel, to carry you through the humiliation of rejections and the sinking feeling that maybe the reason that X sells a million copies of each of her paperbacks, has a column in a national newspaper and was on Parky last night, is because she can write and you can't, you need someone to tell you that you can do it.

This person – remember – should not be your mum (though she invariably will too) but someone who is some sort of authority on the subject and has preferably been published themselves.

My encouragement came from my aunt, Shelagh, and Lynne Patrick whom I've already mentioned. Shelagh – despite being one who knows her stuff (you may recall she has had several books published) comes into the "Mum" category as does anyone that you're related or married to, so Lynne Patrick it had to be.

She is the one who runs *Real Writers* , an excellent appraisal service, and who looked at my early efforts with a critical eye. She never once told me to retire to a darkened room and put a towel over my head, instead she always found something positive to say and – more importantly – made some constructive suggestion as to what I could do with these early sow's ears.

I credit her entirely with my first sales to magazines – she showed me how to hone and edit my work and taught me which bits wouldn't go down well with the fiction editors. I sent her a bottle of champagne when I sold my first story to *Woman's Realm* (a market that eluded me for a while) and we've been friends ever since.

If you're lucky enough to find someone who has proved they can do it and thinks that you could too, hang on to them. There will be lots of times when you really need someone to tell you you've got talent. (This is especially true if it turns out you haven't.)

Even if you have to pay for it, it is worth getting some professional input on your work. There are some good critiquing services around – although always get a personal recommendation and demand to know their credentials, because there are also plenty of illiterate con-artists ready to make a fast buck.

But the very best thing of all is to make friends with someone a bit further along the writing road than you are, ply them with wine and pick their brains.

Summary: The Mentor: to help you keep the faith.

Lynne the Novel

Once you have entered the giddy world of the published novelist you rapidly need another novelist to spill angst to. This friend has to be chosen very carefully indeed. He or she must have been around the block a few times but not be so much more successful than you that you feel like killing yourself or them.

Lynne Barrett-Lee and I met at a QWF weekend when we were both writing short stories for women's magazines. We both had our early novels published by Transworld, and we have since both been published by Accent Press.

We both started out indecently ambitious, we have both got real. We both have double-barrelled names – what more do you want in the compatibility stakes?

Lynne and I have long, boozy lunches and endless discussions on the minutiae of the novel-writing/book-selling world that would cause anyone else to spontaneously combust of boredom. We also send long, detailed emails to each other cataloguing same.

Lynne likes to imagine us in years to come when, she says, we are going to be two old ladies that lunch, tottering drunkenly around the parties and meetings of the literati banging our sticks at the youth of today, banging on about past glories and kissing all the young men with our hairy chins.

She sees us becoming the two batty old eccentrics of the writing world. I have seen the looks we get sometimes – most people think we already are.

Summary: The fellow novelist: helps keep you sane.

Lynne the Mouth

(Real name Lyn-Marie but let's not get bogged down in trifles) also known as Lynne the Party, Lynne the Drink and Lynne the Holiday.

This good-time Lynne knows nothing about writing and doesn't much care either.

"Never mind all that, love," she yells, when you explain how emotionally wrung out you are by the rigours of re-writing chapter eleven, "get your gob round this!"

Lynne the Mouth opens a bottle of champagne at any excuse and keeps you in the real world by being much more interested in handbags and where everyone's going on Saturday night than your literary pretensions.

She curls up her nose disapprovingly if you say you can't stop for a coffee and thinks you'd be less neurotic if you went to the pub more. She's always up for a good book-launch bash, though.

Summary: The Party Animal: helps give you a sense of perspective.

It is also useful to have a **Lynne the Fan**. She doesn't know anything much about writing either, or books, or anything at all.

But she thinks you – being a writer – or even a Wannabe Writer, must be terribly intelligent and clever beyond belief.

She brags to all her friends about how she knows you, pastes everything you've ever had published into a scrap book, has her picture taken with you and wants your autograph.

Whatever you write, do or say is totally marvellous to her and she keeps your ego pumped to full capacity by carrying your books around with her and reading them aloud on the bus.

Unfortunately I haven't got one of these.

What I do have is **Lynne the Spell**, my friend and *Writing Magazine* colleague Lynne Hackles, also known as Wacky Hacky.

This Lynne understands the vagaries of the writing world and has her own inimitable way of dealing with them.

She doesn't bother with applying logic or offering uplifting homilies. Instead she offers crystals, dream-catchers and spells.

When I was writing my third novel – which is somewhat of a departure from the first two – and fearing nobody would ever want it, she sent me a spell which she claimed had come from an old, dusty leather-bound book handed down through the generations and never known to have failed.

So desperate was I that I actually stopped writing, went out and scoured the local shops for a yellow candle (no other colour would do, declared Wacky), bergamot oil and some gold glitter.

I then laboriously carved the title of the book along the candle (yes I did really) and lit it daily, dropping oil and glitter into the flame as instructed. Later she admitted she had made the whole thing up. And was quite unrepentant.

"It worked, didn't it?" she said.

Summary: The Spell-weaver : Helps you to remember that you're not the only one who's bonkers

There are also the sort of friends you don't need:
- Those that think writing is your little hobby
- Those that think writing is easy
- Those that turn up unannounced with their coffee-face on, expecting you to stop and feed them cake as you're "only writing".

The best advice I can offer if you have friends like these is:
1) Keep the answerphone on
2) Ignore the doorbell
3) Wear pyjamas all day so if they are the determined sort who walk round the back and start peering in the windows, you can pretend you have something catching.

Which reminds me of a wonderful piece of advice for writers everywhere which was recently doing the email circuit:

Always keep several get well cards on the mantelpiece. If unexpected guests arrive, they will think you've been sick and unable to clean.

Writers' Groups

I must admit straight away that I have never belonged to a writers' group. I have, however, visited several to give talks or judge competitions. This is my vague overview of what goes on.

As far as I can gather, The Writers' Group is presided over by someone of a certain age and girth, who wears a sensible skirt and is often called Betty or Doreen.

She is very thick with a bloke called Brian or Stan who has written a History of the Town, and is an expert on pretty much everything. There is usually also someone who once had a travel article published, someone (male) who is writing their memoirs and a very old woman who is now deaf called Sylvia, who sold knitting patterns to *Woman's World* during the war.

There is invariably a pimply young man called Tarquin who is writing a fantasy novel and has been for several years, and often you will find a new member – a young girl who's just joined because her mum thinks she should get out more. She's shy but actually writes rather beautifully but you never find that out because Stan and Brian talk over her.

If you are lucky, the rest are the sort who at least go to the pub afterwards. If you're not, it's instant coffee and Rich Tea biscuits – for which you contribute a pound (Doreen or Betty will keep a record of this in a notebook). There is a definite hierarchy in place which extends from who reads first to who has to wash up the cups and throw the biscuit wrappers away.

Lynne Hackles remembers actually having to audition for a place in her first Writers' Circle back in 1982.

My piece was read and a secret ballot held. I was accepted and informed that I could attend my first meeting.

Rows of seats faced the front where The Founder Member sat at a desk, like a formidable headmistress. She produced a 'clock' around the edges of which were the members' names. The F.M. had supreme control. She moved the finger and if it pointed to your name, you were allowed to read, but, if you had offended her, the finger had a tendency to slip. It whizzed past Dolly's name for nearly two years...

The thought of belonging to a group like this makes my bowels curdle.

But my friend Maureen Devlin will tell me off because she swears by her group – Manchester Writers.

> Tuesday night is Writers' Night – my local group has been meeting every week for nearly thirty years and I hate to miss it. We are a mix of full-time, part-time and occasional writers. Some of us have agents and others have secured publishing deals on their own. Each week someone elects to hold the roster – we make a note of who is there and if they have something to read that week. We are truly democratic about taking turns to read out! We each bring along something we are working on. Just hearing your words out loud is a help in picking up problems – but the rest of the group provides feedback on characterisation, pace, dialogue etc. I've found the group to be enormously helpful – and very supportive. We've all had our ups and downs; and some crushing disappointments which can only really be understood by a fellow writer. We always have a tea break halfway through the evening, and then stroll down to the pub for the last hour for more informal chat...

Another great friend, Trish Maw, describes joining her first writing group as her "Gateway to Heaven," saying, "It was wonderful to discover I was not alone in wanting to write make-believe."

She has now belonged to her current one, Brixham Writers' Group, for 18 years.

> We are all now published writers – it was during my second year as a member that I sold my first story to *Woman's Weekly*. I wouldn't have managed it without the constructive criticism of the Group. We are made up of a mix of novelists, short-story writers and article writers and I think that it's because we meet on a regular basis that we are successful. A typical meeting consists of News (who's sold what and to whom) and then we start reading our current work (we set a homework subject every week and several of us have sold stories from homework) and people working on novels usually read their last week's output. Our criticism is always constructive and we often suggest outlets for stories and articles. Writers' Circles don't work for

everyone but Brixham Writers certainly works for me.

Jacqueline Smith, the Chairman of the National Association of Writers' Groups (NAWG) sees the Writers' Circle as offering "community and friendship within the solitary world of writing".

"Many groups, " she says, "include writers from all walks of life, all levels of experience and all writing genres. Such a cauldron of creativity not only allows you to share your work and hone your skills, but can also provide ideas, constructive feedback and the suggestion of possible markets."

And they should also be "fun", she adds, suggesting that you visit a couple of different ones before you decide which will most suit you.

Libraries and colleges can be a useful source of local information or visit the NAWG website **www.nawg.co.uk** for a list of their affiliated groups.

The association's aim is to support solo writers as well as linking groups so you can join them (I belong) as an individual, too. Mike Wilson, the editor of their regular magazine, *Link*, welcomes contributions from members so this can be a good place to get your first piece of writing published.

And once you start getting published, you can think about joining other organisations.

Writers' Organisations

If you are serious about writing it is a good idea to join at least one organisation. I belong to:

The Society of Authors

This is an excellent outfit that offers advice, help and support to the author – including contract vetting. You also get their quarterly *The Author*, invitations to talks and seminars, discounts on books and a whole lot more.

You can join if you have had either a full-length work published (as long as it is not by the vanity press) or at least a dozen short pieces – such as articles or short stories. In some cases, you may be taken on as an associate member if you are as yet unpublished but have a contract with an agent.

I have found belonging to the SOA totally invaluable – there is always someone on the end of an email to quiz on anything from copyright issues to a clause in a contract and I've made all sorts of great contacts through their events.

If you're eligible to join – go for it
www.societyofauthors.net

And if you're into Romance go for this, too:

The Romantic Novelists' Association

There are two ways you can join. Full Membership of the Association is open to all published writers of romantic novels (this is romantic in its loosest sense – basically if it's got a man and a woman in it and they talk to each other occasionally, you're in) and full-length serials, with either contemporary or historical backgrounds. Once again, if you printed it yourself in your garage or paid a dodgy bloke called Justin £10,000 for five padded-leather bound copies, it doesn't count. We are talking proper publishers.

OR, and this should be very interesting to many a wannabe:

You can become a probationary member within the New Writers Scheme. This is for unpublished authors who can then take part in all RNA activities and also submit a typescript of a full-length romantic novel for appraisal by an experienced, published writer who knows how many novel-writing beans make five.

You get a report covering plotting, characterisation, structure and such like. The reports, "are intended to be honest and constructive – they point out flaws but also indicate where writers need to concentrate their efforts if they want to succeed".

The good news is that if the reader thinks you're any good, they will pass you to another reader and if he or she agrees (yes, there are MEN in the RNA too – Romantic Fiction is not confined to females), then the RNA may decide to support you by submitting your manuscript to a suitable agent or publisher. Successful novelists Marika Cobbold and Donna Hay both started this way.

There is also an associate membership which is open to publishers, editors, literary agents, booksellers and the like – which makes RNA parties a source of rich pickings on the networking front (the canapés are usually quite good too).

For more info visit **www.rna-uk.org**

Women in Journalism

If it's canapés you're after, though, the very best ones of all are served at the WIJ parties where the booze flows very nicely too. Women in Journalism is open to female journalists with at least two years' experience. It offers networking opportunities next to none and fabulous parties.

www.womeninjournalism.co.uk

If you are not a woman you could investigate:

The Media Society

I cannot vouch for their standard of nibbles, or very much else, because I haven't joined myself yet, but they have lots of interesting-looking events listed on their website:

www.themediasociety.co.uk

The Writers' Conference

This can be a wonderful experience for those who write – especially those with bored families or unsupportive spouses who are fed up with you going on about it.

There are all sorts of conferences and residential courses to choose from. If you take my advice and join the RNA you will be able to go to theirs – held over a weekend. And NAWG have an annual one too. I have had a jolly good time at both.

There are other more famous conferences around. I won't name them all here – the internet will throw them up if you are that keen – mainly because one sounds totally ghastly and another certainly was, the only time I ventured to try it.

Like Building Societies, not all writing courses are the same.

Those run by the Arvon Foundation are highly regarded and I know writers who have found them totally life-changing. They have many famous names as tutors and going on an Arvon course can be a unique opportunity to work with a master.

What has always put me off are the rumours of shared bedrooms and bathrooms and having to help with the cooking. I am too old and ugly these days to want to go padding down the corridor with my sponge bag or be anywhere I can't get a ready gin and tonic and have to start chopping vegetables at the end of the day. But if you are made of sterner stuff, then check out

www.arvonfoundation.org – those that have been, wax lyrical.

I am more of a **Writers' Holiday** sort of woman: This happens in Caerleon, in Wales, for five days every July/August and I have been going there as a tutor and/or speaker for several years.

Held in a lovely old university building with (ensuite!) accommodation on campus, this is the one where the alcohol flows, the fun starts, everyone smiles and Lynne Hackles once ate twenty-seven profiteroles. (Be warned: weight gain here is an occupational hazard.)

It was set up by Anne and Gerry Hobbs almost twenty years ago with the aim of helping anyone who really wanted to write to learn how to get published. "I'd been on plenty of writing courses," says Anne "but none provided exactly what I was looking for, so I decided to start one myself."

"It was all about getting the balance right," says Gerry. "We wanted to work a high-powered writing conference around a really good programme of entertainment. It is, after all, a holiday. We want people to relax and enjoy themselves as well as learn."

And learn you will.

The prolific and successful novelist, Susan Moody has been a speaker at Caerleon several times. "All the tutors are top-notch," she says. "Even though I've been a professional novelist for 25 years, I always pick up something new and come away inspired to try my hand at something like travel-writing or short-stories."

Comedy writer Ray Allan (*Some Mothers Do 'Ave 'Em* – remember?) was similarly struck. "I go to lots of Writers' weekends and holidays," he reveals. "But Caerleon is the only one where I've booked up for the following year before I went home."

I don't particularly go to learn anything or be inspired though I invariably do and am. I go for five days of gloriously giggly, girly-student life. From the drunken putting of the world to rights to the hilarious sessions of tinting each others' hair (one year two shower cubicles irrevocably changed colour and Trish Maw banged on my door at 1 a.m. to demand to know why her water glass was purple) to the spontaneous late-night parties in the kitchen.

It is also a chance to flirt outrageously with the Cwmbach Male Voice Choir who always sing on the last night – the whole week is worth it for the privilege of hearing them alone – and to sit up till the early hours and stagger into breakfast looking horrendous. Some years I have taken my laptop and worked furiously while others are on courses; other times, I have taken the time to think and reflect, spent mornings wandering down to the charming village, and afternoons reading books, or drinking wine in the sunshine. (Yes, it is Wales, but it doesn't rain all the time.)

If you fancy a holiday with the chance for lots of writing, try it. Visit **www.writersholiday.net** (and if you're also a railway enthusiast look at Anne and Gerry's latest project **www.railwayholiday.net** too).

Prizes and competitions

Are not to be sniffed at.

Lots of writers who have gone on to great things started out by entering short story competitions.

Kate Atkinson, whose first novel, *Behind the Scenes at the Museum* (Black Swan), was voted a Whitbread Book of the Year, was an early winner of the Ian St James Award.

Alice Jolly and Kate Long were both winners in the *Real Writers* Competition while Carole Matthews' first foray into fiction was by entering a competition run by *Writers' News*.

"Amazingly, I won!" she says. "I spent the prize money on a writing course and on that course the tutor gave me the name of an agent. That agent, Darley Anderson, thankfully took me on and sold my first book *Let's Meet on Platform 8*."

It was a prize that led to publication for Kate Harrison too. The opening to her first novel, *Old School Ties*, came first in a competition at the Winchester Writers' Conference. An editor from Piatkus was the judge and she published the novel 14 months later!

If you fancy your luck, there are literally hundreds of writing competitions to choose from. *Writers' News* is an excellent source of all the current ones, as well as running competitions of its own (a joint subscription will bring you *Writing Magazine* each month, too, and the unrivalled pleasure of being able to read my regular column – see chapter on Useful

Info). The internet will throw up more and magazines such as *The New Writer* (see Useful Info again) lists them too.

If you're going to enter competitions, I suggest entering lots. They are bound to be highly subjective and entering will always be a plunge in the dark.

Who's going to be judging? What will they like? How will your story of a gentle Edwardian Romance stack up against the tale of the Alien with Three Heads? The whole thing can be a very hit and miss affair.

I have taken part in dozens of writing competitions in my time. There are some excellent ones about and some others that are.... not so excellent.

Sometimes I have won, other times I have not even made the shortlist. Sometimes I have had comments written on stories by "judges" who are clearly only barely literate.

That is why I will now give you the opposite advice for competitions to that which I gave you for women's magazines. Unless the competition rules very specifically preclude this, then send the same story out as many times as you like, simultaneously.

These days I am sometimes asked to judge competitions myself. It has been quite an eye-opener.

I don't wish to be mean as we all have to start somewhere and I used to write bilge in the beginning (some would say I still do) but really you would think that adults sensitive and intelligent enough to have writing aspirations would have some sort of grip both on reality and what constitutes entertainment.

That does not mean one's readers have to be rolling about the aisles (tho it would have been welcome relief when reading for one competition where the fifteenth protagonist had just come to a grisly end) but that they should, as I have remarked earlier, be moved in some way.

And while death is all very upsetting if it's just happened to you, endless far-fetched murders, a series of predictable suicides and the interminable and unconvincing droning-on over the loss of a tedious-sounding loved one, does not to a great deal to move *me*.

I once read 37 entries that were all about dying. Mothers, brothers, lovers, stray burglars, the ancient and the tragically young all got to meet their maker. Then there was a nice tale about a cat. "Ah!" I thought. You can guess what happened to that.

Do you think I'm exaggerating? I used to, when I read judges' reports. Surely nobody really wrote in green ink or sent in manuscripts with some of their breakfast attached or photos of themselves on holiday in Scunthorpe?

They do, you know. Some send CVs and flowery binders too. And the poem – give me strength – they wrote when they were thirteen that first got them started.

They also break the rules and send 10,000 words instead of a maximum of 2,000, forget their SAE or write their name all over the manuscript when they've been specifically instructed to put it only on the entry form.

But what all this means is: YOU are in with a very good chance. If you can follow instructions, write half-decently and have a good story to tell, then not only might you win a cash prize or see your work in print for the first time, but by entering competitions regularly, you'll reap other benefits too.

Competitions give you a reason to write and a focus. Writing to a theme and a word count and to a deadline (the closing date) is all good discipline and gives you lots of opportunity to find your own areas of interest and, more importantly, your own voice.

It is also a good feeling to have work out there. To have a reason to wait expectantly for the post. In my competition-entering heyday I would have twenty or thirty pieces of writing out at any one time. If one, disappointingly, came back with a flea in its ear, then there were always plenty out there that might do better the next day.

So if you're writing short stories anyway (or articles, or poetry – there are prizes for those, too) why not send them out to seek their fortune.

Just remember:

Don't write about death unless you have something remarkable to say

Do follow the rules,

Don't be predictable – if I read one more story about an old man who goes back to the café/beach/school he frequented sixty years earlier and finds his first girlfriend there, I shall throw up.

Do be original if the competition has a theme. Years ago I entered a competition run by the Worcester Writers' Circle. Someone – God knows who – had decreed that the theme of the competition should be "The Trouble With Water".

I imagine that they were inundated with tales of floods, tsunamis, burst pipes and luckless individuals lost at sea. And I'm quite sure that the only reason I got a runner-up prize was because my story began:

The trouble with water is that it has no alcohol in it…

The Benefits of Alcohol

If you listen to the right people, you will discover that drinking alcohol is good for you. It is widely recognised that moderate drinkers live longer than the misguided tee-totallers and in my experience they are slightly saner too.

Alcohol (I think we are talking a couple of glasses of red rather than an entire bottle of meths) has a positive effect on the balance of the fats in the blood, increasing the cardioprotective high-density lipoprotein cholesterol (HDL or "good" cholesterol) and reducing the amount of the artery-threatening, low-density lipoprotein cholesterol (LDL).

I learnt all this from reading the lovely Dr Thomas Stuttaford who writes in *The Times* and says heartening things about the benefits of knocking back a good claret in the evenings.

From him I can also tell you that alcohol "alters the platelet adhesiveness". Platelets, as you will know if you took Biology 'O' level like I did (my area of specialisation was the formation of the scab) are the particles in the blood involved in clotting.

"The effect of alcohol is therefore," says Dr Tom, "to reduce its tendency to clot and therefore to cause the thrombi and emboli that lead to strokes and heart attacks."

What this means is that it is a jolly good idea to pour a large glass of wine when you have finished writing for the day, or indeed, when you are halfway through it.

I find a quick snort is very good for reviving flagging spirits and a jaded imagination when you have been writing all afternoon (I have a nice glass of Chablis on the go right now) though a whole bottle may well render your writing gibberish.

No matter, for at least you can re-write it in the morning. That's if your hangover's not too bad*.

*Footnote**: if it is, I recommend the following cure:
1) Open one eye.
2) Take two nurofen plus with a large glass of water and go back to sleep for an hour.
3) Drink lots of tea (I like green with lemon).
4) At lunchtime have a hair of the dog and a bag of kettle chips.
You should then be OK in time for the first drink of the evening.

OCCUPATIONAL HAZARDS

Writers' Bottom

Life would be all very lovely if it could be proved conclusively that the levels of intensive brain power employed in the creative process meant that writing used up 700 calories an hour.

Unfortunately it doesn't. Even if you feel it ought to. You may reach the end of a long stint slaving over a hot keyboard, feeling emotionally wiped out and mentally exhausted, and as though you've run a marathon, only capable of tottering into the kitchen for a large glass of wine and a pizza, but the sad truth is that actually you've sat on your arse all day, the only movement having been the waggling of your typing fingers and you're now well on your way to being the size of a house.

And if you've been cramming in junk food in between chapter headings, you'll soon be the size of two.

If you are one of those irritating individuals who "forget to eat" (grrr) or who naturally weigh seven stone and are fond of saying – cue tinkling laugh – "I find it quite hard to keep the weight on, actually…" you will not, of course, need this chapter.

The rest of us can take a brief pause to imagine giving you a good slap and you can move on to the one about RSI or go and have a Black Forest Gateau.

For ordinary mortals wishing to make it into print, the threat of Writers' Bottom looms large. Or indeed Writers' Stomach – a new phenomenon I had been in denial about until the novelist Margaret Kaine kindly pointed it out to me.

"Sitting so much is deadly for slack muscles," she says, while magazine writer Pam Weaver renamed herself "Pamela Five Bellies" after a year spent writing her first novel.

The thing is, it is very difficult to write in any other way. Although that doesn't stop some trying. "I always used to be a thin person," declares actress and novelist Barbara Ewing, (she still looked pretty good when I last saw her), "and I am not thin now. I am trying to find a standing-up desk."

The lovely Isabel Wolff claims to have writers' waist, legs and underarms as well as bottom. She explains that as well as three huge meals a day, she eats five packets of wine gums and three tubes of Pringles. "The lifestyle of a writer is an utterly unhealthy one."

The trouble is that writing can make you very hungry and because, if it is going well, you don't want to stop and start steaming vegetables, it's very easy to keep having a quick bag of crisps or a couple of Kit-Kats at your computer and suddenly realise that you haven't eaten a proper meal for three days but have consumed 17,483 calories.

The actress and writer Helen Lederer refers to it as 'subliminal grazing' while novelist Kate Harrison says: "I try not to buy anything very fattening as I know I will eat it the moment I get to a sticky point in my writing."

Fiona Walker does forget to eat but we won't slap her. Not only because I loved her from the moment I met her – she is hugely successful but totally un-up-herself (one cannot say the same for the whole of the literary establishment) – but because she makes up for it later.

"One would hope it would lead to a gloriously lean and hungry look," she says," but it actually works the opposite way. Finding myself ravenous after a six-hour writing stint, I'll stuff back all manner of chocs and carbs at my desk for a quick energy fix."

Therein lies the problem. You may be fascinated to know that I, feeling similarly sugar-depleted, have now had a couple of glasses of wine, and almost without noticing it, eaten a packet of Bombay mix (my favourite).

On the face of it, as I didn't have lunch, this is a perfectly reasonable state of affairs, especially since it is also Friday and nearly six p.m.. But a quick inspection of the empty packet reveals they were 524 calories per 100g. And – oh my god – there were two hundred grams of them. Bloody hell.

If I were on a diet – which clearly I am not – I would have eaten my entire day's allowance before dinner. Why?

I should say at this point that it might just be a female thing. Frederick Forsyth tells me he has never heard of Writers' Bottom but says "I've never had it or I'd have noticed," while Mil I-never-consider-my-bottom Millington is adamant that he never snacks but survives on three gallons of tea a day (he's probably too busy going to the loo to eat as well).

So my male readers may now like to skip on to the chapter on the offside rule (see – I do understand it) while we consider what best is to be done with a spreading derrière.

Novelist Hilary Lloyd claims "a dog, preferably long-legged and spirited, is the best cure for Writers' Bum" and Barbara Erskine also cites a long dog walk every morning as a useful way to keep the lard at bay. But this seems a bit drastic.

Personally I would find the downside of dog ownership: (someone else to look after who is needy, dependent, likes licking your face directly after they've been at their genitals and who delivers warm turds that you're going to have to pick up first thing in the morning when you've got a hangover), would somewhat outweigh the advantages. Much easier to have a cat or some goldfish. Though neither will set you on the road to slenderdom.

But there is no doubt that if you take up writing as a serious pastime or, God forbid, as a living, something has to be done. The obvious principle being: if you can't eat less, you've got to move more.

This isn't always easy, either. Mills and Boon Queen, Kate Walker, sees Writers' Bottom as "inevitable".

"I always tell myself that I will get up and go for a walk but if the characters start talking to me I daren't abandon them – I have to get down what they say and the exercise gets abandoned."

Fiona Walker, too, says "I singularly fail to exercise when I'm really into a book. I drink far too much coffee and wine, smoke too much and then wonder why I look like I've just been exhumed when I finally finish the thing."

It is true that all the really slim writers I know seem to exercise madly.

"Fanatically," says Sarah Harrison who also walks a dog, runs, swims, plays tennis, goes to the gym and is learning golf. And I must say she looks fantastic.

Carole Matthews also exercises "like a thing possessed" listing hiking, cycling, yoga and "leaping around my lounge to Davina McCall DVDs" amongst her favourite pursuits.

Novelist Jan Henley plays tennis as well as walking and swimming. Wendy Holden says she views writing as an Olympic sport and trains accordingly. "When I am writing I swim 50 lengths a day and eat soup and smoked mackerel."

Nutritionist Lorna Marchant Dip.ION, BANT would approve. Snacks she recommends for writers fearing for their bottoms and general well-being are:

- Houmous on rice cakes, oat cakes or corn cakes, or raw veg with houmous dip
- Homemade soups, with a pinch of chilli in to boost metabolism. Have as many bowls as you like, also helps with weight loss
- Hot water with a tsp honey and a slice of lemon and large piece of ginger, increases circulation to the brain, stops hunger pangs and speeds metabolism
- Whole hard boiled egg, keeps you full for hours and is a good protein snack
- Slices of cold meat, filled with salad and avocado with a little French dressing and rolled. This is high protein, so keeps you full for hours
- Flaked salmon or tuna and cucumber, rolled in a large lettuce leaf. Eat as many as you like, again high protein and good quality fat
- Vegetable or fruit juices. Beetroot juice with ginger is good as it cleanses the body and boosts metabolism. Also carrot, apple and ginger is beneficial.

Lorna also recommends you:

- Drink lots of water. Writing, concentrating, thinking and sitting can increase the level of toxins in the body. Water will help flush them out
- Drink herbal teas, such as fennel, green tea, peppermint, nettle and detox tea
- Take 1000mg vitamin C, a good B vitamin complex and fish oil to boost brain power
- Avoid coffee, sugary and fatty foods. These prevent the brain and body working properly
- Eat little and often
- For more information visit **www.optnutrition.com**.

Top Diets For Fat Scribes

That all seems fairly straightforward, which is good. I like diets or food plans to have simple instructions (you can't have potatoes, you can have as much wine as you like) that are easy to remember.

My friend Irene used to recommend the yogurt and banana regime which had one simple rule – you could eat as much as you liked of absolutely anything as long as it was plain yoghurt or banana. You were supposed to do it for three days.

Since banana is a diuretic and yoghurt an evacuant (let's not go there) it does work, but by dawn of the second day you are out of your head with the tedium of it and are hallucinating about toast and marmite or anything that isn't bloody yogurt or banana.

If you're like this too, Lynne Hackles has conceived the C plan. On it you can eat anything you like as long as it doesn't begin with that letter. So no Cream, Chocolate, Chips, Crisps, Cake etc. It sounds really good. But it doesn't work. Especially if you pig out on Gateau and French Fries.

Things that do work are cutting out all carbohydrates except wine and chocolate (you've got to be sensible), counting calories (1500 a day max) or not eating in the evenings (at all) – have the last meal mid afternoon at the latest and go for a brisk walk before bed.

But when you are writing a book or a tricky article or anything to a deadline, when your head is already crammed to bursting, I think it is too much to expect oneself to concentrate on not eating as well and your body does need regular sustenance to keep your brain going (fish oils are excellent for this too).

When you are up against it, I would recommend eating whatever you need to eat in the short-term and worrying about the fact that you can't fit into any of your clothes when you've finished.

If this happens to coincide with an important social engagement where you need to cram yourself into a little black number or dress suit two sizes smaller than you are: here are some tried and tested ways to lose weight fast:

Get Food Poisoning. For best effect, go for full-blown salmonella or dysentery so you've got both ends at once and can't even keep fluids down. My most dramatic experience came from a pepperoni pizza in Verona. I was on the bathroom floor for three days and the water bill came to more than the hotel room. I lost half a stone. Another time, I collapsed on a plane and threw up in the *New York Times*. If Italy or America are a bit too far to go, you can probably pick up a dodgy kebab in the High Street.

Fall in Love. This works particularly well with someone who doesn't love you back. Then you can spend hours mooning by the phone waiting for him or her not to call, feeling sick with anxiety and wondering where you're going wrong. Advantages of this plan: you're much too heart-broken to eat. Disadvantages: you're so red and blotchy that nobody will ever want you, looking like that.

Have lots of great sex. (N.B. If you're married, best not to let your husband or wife find out). A good shag uses up lots of calories and increases the endorphins in your body making you naturally high without resorting to chocolate. Points in favour: you spend all your eating-time bonking and when you do come up for air, you don't want to look unalluring by ramming food down your throat. Points against: if you're single, you might fall in love, decide to get married and that will be your sex life gone for ever.

Have a Crisis. (This may follow naturally from above). There are two types of emotional upheaval. The one where you are too traumatised to contemplate food and spend a lot of time staring into space feeling tragic and the sort where only two bottles of wine, half a pound of chocolate, and chips with peanut butter will reach the spot. Make sure you develop the right kind. (N.B. Your partner finding out about the great sex probably comes into the first category but tends to be expensive and upsets the children.)

Get yourself on TV. Following the above, you can go on *Trisha* and bare your soul to the nation. (You might want to consider *Wife Swap* at the same time). Television instantly piles on ten pounds. Once you see the video you'll be so horrified you won't eat for a month.

I offer the above, because let's face it, dieting is very boring.

As we all know, you only get thinner when you eat fewer calories than you use up, so, realistically, to lose a stone you need to live on carrots for a month or spend every spare minute jogging to the gym.

Despite this unassailable fact, new Diet Books continue to be published all the time and we waddle out and buy them. Even though, historically, they usually take 60,000 words to say what you or I could sum up in a paragraph: i.e.

- **The Rosemary Conley Hip and Thigh Diet** – Give up fat and you'll have thinner legs (you might also like to consider starting a multi-million pound exercise-video empire).
- **Dr Atkins New Diet Revolution** – Eat only animal parts and the weight will drop off (you'll also fart a lot, have shocking breath and nobody will want to know you except your butcher).
- **The Hay Diet** – Keep carbohydrates and protein separate (i.e. Give up all your favourite meals and die of boredom).
- **Anything Written by a Celebrity** – Munch weird raw things and forget anything that tastes nice. For Ever. (But you still won't look as good as Geri Halliwell, The Duchess of York or Elizabeth Taylor when they're being thin.) (Or even when they're not.)
- **Various "Eating Plans"** usually beginning "this is NOT a diet book" and then claiming that this way of eating will change your life for ever. (You must drastically reduce your calories.)

Worst of all on the spinning-it-out front, are the tomes that take the quasi-intellectual, psycho-babble route to discovering why you can't fit into your airline seat. Books like: *You're only a fat cow cos really you're a miserable one* (this is not its exact title) that promises a revolutionary approach to getting rid of that wobbly arse for ever. What a con!

Fifteen chapters saying in thirty-seven different ways that the only reason you're always stuffing your face is because you're so unhappy (the author knows because she herself used to weigh twenty-two stone – enough to make anyone pissed off) which is variously the fault of your mother and father (we all know what Philip Larkin had to say about THEM!), your long-forgotten infant school teacher and the first bloke you had a fumble with.

Having taken 70,000 words to establish that you are engulfed in a sea of total and all-consuming wretchedness – hence your need to eat Mars Bar sandwiches on the hour – it then, on the final page, tells you to go into therapy and join Weight Watchers!

If anything's going to send one rushing for double pizza and a bottle of red then it's flogging out forty quid an hour to sit on someone else's sofa bleating about your childhood while they cross-examine you.

And, frankly, Weight Watchers – with its emphasis on ritual humiliation to keep you on the straight and narrow and or its own incomprehensible points system – wouldn't be for me either.

What we all know, what every diet book boils down to in the end is:

- If what goes in is greater than what goes out you get fat
- If what goes in equals what goes out, you stay the same (this may equal above)
- If what goes in is less than the sum of what goes out you get thin (hurrah!).

Though maybe not "hurrah" for long, because the moment you start eating anything at all that you like, you'll be waddling again.

Many a book has been written about how, when you drastically reduce your calories, your body thinks it's starving (and so do you!) and your metabolism slows down so it can start conserving fat. Then, the minute you start collapsing with malnutrition and fall on a doughnut, it packs it away in a nice wobbly layer on your bum before you can say GI index!

This is why dieting is pointless and also why some time ago I had the brilliant idea of writing an eating book of my very own.

It was to be called *Bugger The Diet and Everything Else That Life's Too Short For* and contained chapters such as:

- Why Chocolate is Good for You
- Fourteen Units Is Not Enough
- The Beauty of a Tent

I was very excited about this, having visions of myself on *Parkinson* and *The Jonathan Ross show* with a string of BTD merchandise including mugs, T-towels and deep-fat fryers, the best thing being that, since the whole premise of the book was to be 'why bother, you'll only put it back on,' I could remain my usual gross self while doing it.

In a state of eager anticipation I sent the opening chapters off to The Fearsome One. She didn't call.

When I could stand it no longer (after about two days) I called her. She did not sound overwhelmed.

"Hmmn," she said fiercely. "All very amusing but it's not a book. Reads more like a series of articles. Pitch it to one of the Sunday supplements."

I grizzled a bit but she is not a woman to be trifled with. "Couldn't you just try a few publishers?" I whined. "No," she said.

Now it so happens I was in touch with a publisher or two myself at the time – gathering pearls of wisdom for my *Writing Magazine* column – and, feeling misunderstood, and knowing I was sitting on a work of genius, I mentioned it to one of them.

"Would you like to see it?" I ventured, after extolling its virtues.

He, probably thinking it the quickest way to get me out of his hair, said he would. This was very daring – some may say foolhardy – of me as if The Fearsome One had found out, she would have felled me with one glint of her evil eyes at ten paces. (In fact if you have heard that I am no more, and all proceeds from this book are going to the *Fund for the Impoverished Children of Impoverished Authors Who Never Made It and Are Now Dead*, she probably has.)

But I figured I would deal with that when and if Mr Publisher showed an interest, and was already planning a complicated tale by which we had happened to bump into each other at some glittering literati party that I had just happened to be invited to, whereupon he had happened to say: "Hey, you don't happen to know anyone who's written any good non-diet books lately?" – when his letter arrived.

"Dear Jane," it said, "this is all very amusing but does not read much like a book – have you thought of submitting it to a Sunday supplement as a series of articles?"

TIP forty three – if you are lucky enough to get an agent do not think you know best. You don't – he or she does.

Still, nothing is ever wasted – remember the chapter Waste Not, Want Not? I posted an extract from it on my website **www.janewenham-jones.com/buggerdiet.htm** (do feel free to buy a few more books while you're there) and I shall now paste in another one.

If you are like magazine short-story writer Sue Hougton who has gone from a size 12 to a size 16 in two years and says "I just KNOW it's from sitting at the PC," you may find it helpful.

But guys – if you are still with us – look away now. If Richard Morrison in *The Times* is to be believed, you simply don't want to know...

Hiding the podgy bits

It would be much more useful if instead of all this endless literature on "How to be thin," which, as we've discovered , involves too much self-sacrifice and tedious practices like staying sober, someone wrote a book called "*How to Look*

Thin", because with a few tips up your sleeve, or more pertinently, wrapped tightly round your bulging stomach, you can give the impression of being a whole lot more sylph-like than you really are.

Most of us are at that in-between stage between nicely-rounded and totally gross, at a weight where you can dress cleverly – well-cut black or oversized shirt – and cause others to trill "You fat?? Don't be silly……" or just stick on any old jogging bottoms and T-shirt and let the truth hang out. (Experiencing that moment where, when you fish gently with close friends – by sighing, pointing to your stomach and murmuring, "Of course really I need to lose half a stone…"– they just smile sympathetically and pat your arm.)

People are always telling me I've lost weight (or showing by their sorrowful expression that they think I've piled it on). In reality, aside from the natural variations brought on by a hard weekend on the Chablis and Kettle crisps, my weight is relatively constant (if a stone more than it should be) but I have learnt that posture and well-chosen attire are everything.

Try this simple test: Take your own BEFORE and AFTER pictures

Stand sideways in front of a full length mirror wearing a pair of white leggings and your saggiest bra. Pull the leggings up round your navel, droop your shoulders, lower your chin and thrust your stomach forward. There!

Don't you exactly resemble the BEFORE photo in an ad for that must-have contraption that will sort out your stomach muscles and turn you into Pamela Anderson in exchange for a mere ten minutes a day and £29.99? Hideous, isn't it?

Complete the experience and make yourself feel totally and thoroughly revolted by repeating with the waistband of the leggings beneath the roll of your gut and use a small mirror to view your vast behind.

Now, throw those nasty garments in the bin and put on your thrust-em-up-and-out wonder bra and a pair of support tights, or better still a corset, with something well-cut in black and a pair of high heels. Head up, stand straight and – see? A world of difference. Half the people you see who look good are probably holding themselves together by other means.

I once walked into a party and saw a good friend in a red, glittery number, teetering on a pair of stilettos. She looked fantastic and about three stone lighter than she had at lunchtime.

"Where's your stomach gone?" I shrieked subtly , having seen her at large in the playground only hours earlier. She smiled secretively.

"I'm wearing one of those squash-it-all-in things," she confided. "If the poppers give way, it's every man for himself…"

I went and bought one myself and can advise, it you want to do the same, to be careful.

Check where the flattened flesh is ending up! Some of the lesser examples of the all-in-one "body-shaper" send all the spare blubber into a nasty bulge that pops out under your arms or half way down your thighs.

A good rule of thumb is that if you can't breathe or sit down and going to the loo is out of the question, then it's probably working. N.B. This is not the time to rush into things with a new conquest. You'll probably knock him out when he tries to undress you.

Play it cool, pretend you never do that sort of thing on the first night (how ever much of an old slapper you are normally) and tell him you're off on holiday for a fortnight. Then have a St Tropez tan (always good for the illusion of shapeliness) and wear something slimming when he takes you out three weeks later.

Hopefully, he'll have been so drunk when he picked you up that he won't really remember what you looked like or that you're now several inches bigger all over. If he does, blame it on all the paella you've been stuffing and remind him what size Marilyn Monroe was.

Taken from *Bugger the Diet and Everything Else Life's Too Short For* and printed for the first time by kind permission of the author (that's me).

N.B.: If you would like to read the entire work, please write to your favourite publisher demanding they offer a six figure sum, or lobby your MP.

Repetitive Strain Injury

One of my favourite-ever letters to my *Writing Magazine* column was sent by Phyll Handley from Worcester.

She wrote:

I have been writing for some time now and the more fellow scribes I get to know, the more I realise what a hazardous business it is. Every writer I meet seems to have something wrong with them. If it's not repetitive strain injury from all the typing, it's writers' back from sitting still too long. Then there's writers' shoulder, writers' stiff aching neck, writers' knees, writers' wrist and writers' headache. And finally it seems, writers' tears from a broken heart over all those rejections. I am beginning to wonder why all these outwardly normal-looking people want to become writers at all. Can you explain it to me? And will I end up the same way?

It made me laugh, because at the time I had a bad neck and Lynne Hackles had been emailing me about a whole new slant on writers' bottom – hers had a cyst on it! (Caused, she is sure, from all that sitting).

But it's not funny really. Unfortunately it's true that writers can be prone to all sorts of odd afflictions and it is widely recognised that spending half one's life hunched over a computer or notepad is not the healthiest of pursuits.

Repetitive Strain Injury primarily affects the muscles, tendons and nerves of the neck and upper limbs, and symptoms can include varying degrees of aches, pain, numbness, swelling, tingling, cramp, reduction in mobility and weakness. And it affects a lot of writers.

Freya North developed such bad RSI that she had to have thrice-weekly physiotherapy and now wears a splint on her right arm when she works.

Lesley Horton trapped the brachial nerve in her shoulder through being hunched at the computer and had to take four months off.

Carole Matthews has "chronic neck and shoulder problems" for which she has weekly massage and manipulation treatments and also has a tendency to develop "painful nodules" on her finger joints,

So will you end up an old crock too? Not if you're careful.

Alex, the wonderful woman who comes round to give my own stiff muscles a good seeing-to, says that writers should get up from the desk every half an hour and move about, taking the opportunity to rotate their head and shoulders, look at other things to refocus their eyes and perhaps do a few stretches and some deep breathing.

I am fortunate in having the concentration span of a gnat so this is no problem for me. I usually forget the stretches but I am always leaping from my chair to do something that suddenly seems much more pressing than composing the next sentence. (I make about two dozen cups of my green-tea-with-lemon in the average day, and sometimes have to fetch chocolate too.)

But if you are the sort of writer who gets absorbed for a ten-hour-stretch (grrr) you would do well to heed her advice.

I would also add from my own experience that the right chair is essential. I now have one of those kneel-on affairs. They may look peculiar and be the subject of some very rude jokes but they have rendered all back pain a thing of the past.

It is also crucial to ensure that if you are writing onto a computer, your screen is the right height. Position the monitor so that you can keep your head erect and look straight ahead at the text (see my excellent and informative diagram below). If you find you are looking up or down, your neck, back and shoulders will suffer. If you haven't got a monitor shelf, some thick books or telephone directories will do the job just as well.

Karen Howeld, a children's writer and journalist, has suffered various back problems and was advised by her chiropractor to change the height of her screen in this way. She says: "My back and neck have improved loads since. I've realised that, previously, more than a couple of hours at the screen left me with headaches or a stiff back. I feel about 2ins taller and less like a hunchback now..."

Some writers swear by gel-filled wrist rests. I haven't tried these yet but I do find I need to push the keyboard far enough back so that I can rest my arms on the table while I'm typing.

Novelist Margaret Kaine also recommends a 'rolling footrest', explaining that by resting your feet on something you can rock back and forth while sitting at the computer, you keep the circulation moving and avoid the risk of cramp or stiffness.

And several writing friends suggested a natural ergonomic keyboard when I woke up with a painful wrist and hand some months ago.

I went for treatment with both a chiropractor and a lovely lady called Linzi Grogan **www.bridgewaterretreat.co.uk** who offers all sorts of complementary therapies, and it gradually got better, but I am convinced that the keyboard is what has kept it strong since.

It's really a case of personal preference and whatever is comfortable for you but don't underestimate the risks.

Linzi explained to me that when one carries out any one activity – with repetitive moves – for more than twenty minutes, the collagen in the body starts to set in that position.

Then a substance called fascia, which is a connective tissue that goes right throughout the body, becomes tight and dehydrated, which causes pain and discomfort.

Linzi compared it to a wrung out dishcloth that has dried out while all twisted. The blood and oxygen supply can't run through the tissues freely. This is why massage is so helpful – it loosens those areas and allows blood and oxygen to flow through them again.

Other treatments might include osteopathy or physiotherapy along with rest, the use of heat and cold, medication and exercises. It will obviously depend on the individual and exact diagnosis of the problem. But as Linzi says: "Prevention is better than cure. Maintaining good health means taking positive steps to minimise the risk of injuries developing."

Her recommendations are as follows:

1) Make sure the monitor is correctly positioned at eye-level. Screen distance should be arms' length, the chair back should support spinal curves, chair height should be adjustable and the chair should be tilted to bring the pelvis forward. Feet should be flat on the floor.

2) Consider getting an ergonomic keyboard and mouse. Try accessing the settings to slow down the mouse and reduce muscle tension in your hands. Learn keyboard shortcuts to minimise mouse use.

3) General stress and poor overall health are all contributing factors to RSI so stick to a healthy diet and reasonable alcohol consumption**. Drink

Author's footnote** Linzi Grogan had actually added: "Not Jane's idea of reasonable," to this sentence. But I deleted it.

two litres of water a day and take regular exercise. Smoking also restricts circulation so is a further risk factor.

4) Think about your posture. Body management through Pilates, Yoga and Tai Chi are all good for relaxation, focus, flexibility and core strength.

For further information, AbilityNet is a registered charity dealing with computing and disability, and offers independent advice on avoiding RSI. Visit **www.abilitynet.co.uk**

Jealousy

Jealousy is not very attractive but it is perfectly natural. In case you are trying to get published and are madly, savagely jealous of others who have already been successful, I will – in the hope of making you feel better – admit right away that I have been there too.

In fact when my first novel was being rejected by the world and his wife, I got to the point where I could hardly bear to go into a bookshop. And I found it really difficult being around other authors who were terribly excited by their first book deal.

I remember a newly-published novelist, around this time, saying that she hoped I'd have "a magical Christmas".

"How can I?" I nearly shrieked, "when nobody wants my book? It's all right for YOU…"

She was just being kind of course but it is a sad fact that some writers soon forget how awful they felt when they were still trying to make it themselves.

I know of one in particular who will witter away endlessly about how wonderfully well her latest book is doing, quite oblivious to the misery of the desperate wannabe standing next to her who's just had her manuscript returned – again.

I do try to be sensitive but I am ashamed to say I've done it too. I remember moaning on about the problems of not being in a three-for-two deal, without considering how my listener, who would have been grateful to see herself in print at all, might be feeling.

"Hmm. I'd like to have your problems," she said, bringing me up short.

The thing is, the goal posts do change. And published authors can get jealous too.

"A novelist would have to be made of stone not to feel the occasional pang," says Sarah Harrison. "She got paid for all that money for *that*? Etc. But you can only give it your best shot."

For me it is not so much the money I might envy (although it would be very nice) but the marketing and promotions. If you'd asked me ten years ago, I would have said that just holding my own book in my hands would have been enough. Now I dream of being in ALL the shops and on the supermarket shelves, as Book of the Week, Read of the Month and ultimately on the best-seller lists.

But I tell myself you can go on for ever. For I imagine that once an author has reached this happy state of affairs, all they long for is to sell the film rights.

So if you are the jealous type, there is plenty of scope to get irked by what's going on with other people because there's always going to someone higher up the food chain. However successful you are.

"I'm completely bitter and twisted about not thinking of *The Da Vinci Code* before Dan Brown," quips Carole Matthews. "JK Rowling? One hit wonder!"

"It's really dangerous to focus on other people," agrees Kate Harrison. "The best advice I was given is that you're only really in competition with yourself – to write the best book you can. The rest you have no control over."

It is also worth remembering that for everyone ahead of you along the path to published bliss there will be others further behind. You might be jealous of someone because their novel has been published, without realising how much you are envied by others for having sold some articles.

And even if you have yet to see a thing in print, others might wish they had your time and opportunities to try.

So it is best to listen to nice, sensible people like Adele Parks who says: "Jealousy? What's the point? People can buy more than one book, it's not like I'm building houses. My view is the more decent writers there are out there the better it is for everyone: readers, writers, mankind." (She does however admit she hates it "when terrible books are successful".)

Or Frederick Forsyth, who declares "I am delighted to see a new writer crack it with a bestseller. The thing about writing is that there is room for everyone… and more next year."

If you are not able to be this generous-hearted may I suggest:

• A punch-bag

- A packet of plasticine and a shiny new pin
- Photographs on your darts board.

Or best of all: a steely determination that you will do it too.

Snobbery

If you sell to the women's magazine market or decide to try your hand at a novel for Harlequin Mills & Boon, you will inevitably come up against the snobs.

You might do anyway – I've been asked if I've ever thought about writing "a proper book" and I know several writers of Chick Lit who say others have a tendency to turn up their nose.

It is totally beyond me to understand why. This sort of attitude is born of sheer ignorance.

Pretentious individuals who sneer at popular, accessible fiction usually take the line that they "wouldn't want to" write such stuff themselves. The truth is that they couldn't.

As Jenny Haddon, a past chair of the Romantic Novelists' Association, wisely points out: "Easy reading is hard writing."

Mills & Boon Romances are notoriously tricky to perfect. Jenny has published well over forty of them – under the pen name of Sophie Weston – and knows plenty about negative attitudes.

She gets them "all the time", she says. But her books have been translated into twenty-four languages and are sold all over the world. So she's doing something right.

And if further proof were needed, novelist Eileen Ramsey has a lovely story to tell. Asked to give a talk on "The Romantic Novel" at the Edinburgh Book Festival, Eileen prepared a session called "The Genre that Dare not Speak its Name".

She took in a pile of books – a mixture of classics and modern romances – covered in brown paper and read a short extract from each of them. They included:

Anna Karenina – Leo Tolstoy,
A Tale of Two Cities – Charles Dickens
The Flight of the Heron – DK Broster

Emma – Jane Austen
The Cinderella Factor – Sophie Weston.

The audience was asked to guess their identity.

The results, she says, were "amazing" with hardly anyone getting it right and with one member of the audience – a Russian student at Edinburgh University being convinced that the passage from the Sophie Weston Mills & Boon novel was from Tolstoy's *Anna Karenina*.

Eileen says: "Now I haven't read the book in Russian and the girl hadn't read it in English but there are great passages of slushy writing in Anna Karenina – together with wonderful writing, – and I had read a beautifully-written piece from that particular M&B. *The Cinderella Factor* knocks all criticism of that genre on its feeble little head."

Kate Walker would applaud. Kate has written more than fifty romances for Harlequin Mills & Boon and says writing them is harder than her MA thesis ever was.

"It's the restricted word count, the parameters that confine the subject of the stories, the fact that there are so many of them, that mean you need to develop your own voice as strongly as possible so that readers notice you and come back again and again for your books."

Kate wishes she had a £1 for every time someone's been disparaging.

"I've had people tell me that they are going to 'knock out' a M&B and so make a fortune. They ask me if I am still 'churning out' those 'smutty books' or those 'soppy love stories' or tell me that they know the books are written by a computer – one with heroes' and heroines' names programmed into it with jobs, character descriptions, settings etc. – and you just press a button and the computer does a random selection and prints out the result…"

Kate says she does sometimes get angry "not only on behalf of the authors… but for the millions and millions of women who are dismissed so insultingly because they enjoy light, easy-reading romances – usually in amongst plenty of other reading as well. Women who range from age 15 – 95 who have all sorts of education levels, career levels, jobs, nationalities. Many women with high qualifications read romance for relaxation."

So how does she deal with it?

"Sometimes I point to the market research that shows that, somewhere in the world, one of these books is bought every 2 minutes. Sometimes I list the 40+ countries and dozens of languages my books are published in. Or perhaps the hundreds of thousands – *millions* – of copies I've sold all over the world in my 20 years writing for Harlequin Mills and Boon."

"But mostly, honestly – I'm really just laughing all the way to the bank. I couldn't earn this sort of money if I'd stayed as a librarian and I'm enjoying every single minute of it…"

My own favourite response to such critics is to suggest they have a go themselves. Many a respected novelist will admit to having tried and failed to write a category romance and you will find, if you dig deep enough and the other is honest enough, that quite often those most vociferous about magazine fiction being worthless are those who've had at least one story turned down.

And did they then realise how much imagination, discipline and editing skill it really requires? No – they usually explain that their offering was "too clever" or "too literary" for the editor to appreciate.

But overall I don't know what is more galling really – to find that someone thinks you write garbage or that they believe they could write it too. I remember sitting next to a gynaecologist once, who, upon hearing I wrote magazine stories, said "Oh, that would be a good idea for my wife – she needs something to do."

Hmm, I thought, get her to run off one of your hysterectomies then.

Stress

Being a writer might sound like an easy option – all that sitting on your backside all day, working at your own pace – but it does have its areas of angst. Some common causes of stress can be as follows:

- You have to do 'a proper job' all day and are too totally knackered in the evenings to write more than a paragraph.
- Your partner or spouse doesn't understand why you want to.
- They also don't understand why you never listen and spend a lot of time staring at them with a funny look on your face.
- Whenever you get shot of them and the muse is flowing, the children interrupt.
- Your writing keeps getting rejected.
- You don't know where your next fiver's coming from.
- You've put on weight.
- You're smoking too much.

- You haven't got many friends left.
- Those you have got keep saying: ha, ha, ha, haven't you got that book published yet?
- Your in-laws are coming to stay.
- They will say it too.
- You have a commission for an article due to be delivered on Friday afternoon and everyone you need to interview has already left for the weekend.
- There is also a power cut and you can't use your computer.
- And you hadn't saved the last edit.
- You've got a contract and the deadline is tomorrow.
- You haven't got a contract.

As we all know, stress is very bad for you indeed and will kill you off much quicker than any amount of fried food and drunken debauchery. So you need to develop some strategies to keep it at bay.

May I suggest ten top stress-busters:

1) A brisk walk or run. Exercise releases endorphins: the feel-good chemicals in the brain.
2) So does sex and chocolate.
3) Epsom salts – not what your great-grandmother used to do with them but in your bath. Linzi Grogan (her of the RSI advice) put me on to these and they work a treat. Get them in quantity from the chemist or on the internet, put between 500g and a 1kg into your bath water and lie in it for at least twenty minutes. The magnesium helps relax tense muscles, eliminate toxins and improves the circulation. Add a few drops of lavender oil, light a candle and take a glass of wine in there too and really feel the difference. You'll be so totally chilled out, you'll be asleep on the sofa later.
4) A good book – preferably something totally different from anything you're attempting to write yourself.
5) A good romance. The BBC4 television series: *"Reader I Married Him"* showed that reading romantic fiction lowered stress levels.
6) A real romance (see no.2).
7) A cat – stroking one lowers stress levels too.
8) A good writing friend to moan to.

9) A good non-writing friend to get drunk with.

10) A crossword or sudoku.

If all else fails, I find three days holed up in a luxury hotel, on my own, staying in bed with my laptop, watching daytime television, ordering room service and having the odd facial usually does the trick.

N.B.: For domestic purposes, this is called 'research'.

On Being Vile to Live With

Personally, of course, I am a very lovely person to share a house with but some other writers aren't.

"I am impossible to live with when I'm writing," says Jeffrey Archer.

"Difficult," says Judy Astley. "I get tense and tetchy around deadline time when I panic that I'm late and know it's all My Own Fault. And I hate it when I'm just well into a chapter and my husband comes and asks things like 'Did you ring the plumber?'"

Frederick Forsyth says his wife describes him as "not so much difficult as absent. Miles away in another world."

Daniel Blythe explains: " The thing about writers is we find it very hard to switch off. My wife has a "traditional" job, and it's one which sometimes involves bringing work home, but even then it's physically there for her to deal with. My "bringing work home" manifests itself as "think time", which I need to have whenever I need it – this can lead to long silences on journeys and during weekends. Non-writers find this hard to understand."

Bernardine Kennedy agrees. "Oh yes! I HATE being disturbed when I'm concentrating! Non-writers don't understand that staring into space or playing solitaire is a big part of the thought process. 'But you're only playing cards' is the single sentence most likely to send me to the knife drawer."

It might also send you to Holloway or Wormwood Scrubs so it is best to restrict your expressions of displeasure to sulking, sighing and walking around with a face on. If your partner has already cornered the market in all these and has started negotiations over who gets custody of the cat then it is probably best to embark on some damage limitation (having to move out/ get counselling/ comfort the children will really hold the writing up).

Only you know what your loved one might fall for but these can all work:

- Announce that you are dedicating the book to your amazing girlfriend, wonderful husband, gorgeous fiancé etc.
- Write them a card – thanking them for all their support and offering forgiveness for the fact that it is entirely their fault you have now forgotten the ending you'd planned for chapter seven.
- Promise all sorts of special meals / dinners out / exotic holidays when you have finished the article / serial / novel / trilogy. You don't have to stick to it – they'll be so thoroughly fed up with you by then, they won't even want to be in the same room.
- Send flowers.
- Buy champagne.
- Bring home chocolates and don't eat them all yourself.

And finally, I suppose, spare them a thought:

Alice Jolly recalls how when she was writing her first novel she used to wander around the house saying, "I don't think there is anything worse in the world than writing your first novel."

One day she heard her husband reply under his breath. 'Perhaps living with someone who is writing their first novel?'

OTHER THINGS TO CONSIDER

Sex

I feel silly writing sex.

In my early days as a novelist I avoided people doing it at all. If they absolutely had to, then I'd get them started, close the bedroom door and then cut hastily to the next morning.

Or, as I said on *Ready, Steady, Cook*, when asked about such things by Ainsley (with whom I'd be willing to do all sorts of things – mmmn) I go straight to the post-coital fag. (Causing Sally Zigmond to email me with the reprimand: 'you can't say "post-coital" on daytime television – my mother watches that!')

I got a bit better with my next book *Perfect Alibis* – you can't really write an entire book about adultery without someone performing at some point – but it doesn't come as naturally to me as it does to some.

The only time I ever tried to create something truly "erotic", the magazine I was writing it for gave up on my descriptions of passion and wrote in the final scene themselves. (Cue simultaneous orgasms and the immortal line: "the ball of his thumb found her clitoris").

I blushed when I read it. I am not good with squelchy body parts. The first and only time I ever saw a porn film I felt so queasy I had to go into another room for a bit of a lie down.

So I am of the "less is more" school of thought when it comes to writing sex but, as I firmly believe that we writers have to stick together, I always buy friends' erotic novels in order to support them, even if ultimately they end up as door stops.

One friend I can read is Fiona Curnow. Fiona writes so beautifully that even when she is being her alter-ego Maria Lyonesse (*Lust Under Leo* and *The Taste of Temptation* both X-Libris) she retains her page-turning quality and does not make one feel as if one is sitting through a biology lesson (although I still get slightly light-headed at times).

Asked for some tips on writing a great sex scene (no good looking to me, obviously) she offers the following pointers (no pun intended):

Believe in what you're writing 110%. If you don't find it arousing, neither will your reader. Remember that your character has to be aroused in her head as well as lower down and we have to believe that she is. You are not aiming to write a medical textbook but to create an atmosphere that will arouse your reader – they have to feel what's going on. Writing erotica will arouse you, too. If it doesn't, you're not doing it properly!

"Don't over-poeticize the shenanigans," adds Freya North. "It reads as far more sexy if a cock is a cock and not a 'throbbing member' and boobs aren't 'heaving bosoms'. And whatever you do, DON'T censor a sex scene while you're writing it because you worry about who'll be reading it. Imagining your parents or your next-door-neighbours reading it – that's the fastest way for a writer to lose their mojo..."

Freya has a theory that the secret of writing good sex "possibly has to do with not getting much oneself!" which, she says, leaves the hapless author "wishing to live (and shag) vicariously through one's characters!"

She sportingly shares this experience with us:

"I was pregnant whilst writing my 4th novel, *Fen*. I was RAMPANT. My editor (who is far from prudish) actually wrote 'yuk' and 'too much information' and 'urgh' in red pen in the margins!"

Freya takes a fairly earthy approach in general. "Make it rude and squelchy," she says. "Close your eyes and fantasise..."

I am also grateful to author and journalist Emily Dubberley, who is a bit of a sexpert – **www.cliterati.com** is her brainchild – who offers, from the website's guidelines, this additional tip for the men:

"Women are unlikely to be moved into paroxysms of pleasure if you dress the women in your story in 'red crotchless panties'. Who wears those things? We've never yet met a woman who professes anything other than loathing for them – silk knickers or no knickers are way sexier."

So now you know, guys. But whatever your gender, for the ultimate summing-up, I shall leave you with the words of Susan Lewis, the author of over 20 best-selling novels, many of which have a raunchy streak :

"You should write sex as you would do it: wholeheartedly, full-bloodedly and don't stop until you've reached a spectacular climax."

Money

One of the early questions for my *Writing Magazine* column was from a woman called Margaret Chambers who had been offered a redundancy package. She wondered if she should take it and try to make a go of being a full-time writer.

I answered Margaret the only way I realistically could, by saying: Ask yourself this question: if I earn nothing at all from writing for the coming twelve months, can I survive? If the answer is no, then don't do it!

I got letters afterwards, telling me off for how negative I'd been but I still stand by my advice.

Writing is a fickle game. You may earn a great deal of money from it, you may earn none. And just because the dosh pours in one year, it does not mean it will do so the next. There have been times when I've had an exhilarating run of selling every article and short story I've sent out, getting booked to speak at conferences, receiving advances on books, getting generous PLR payments and selling rights abroad. Out comes the champagne and the dreams about getting a house-keeper.

Then nothing at all happens for six months and I count myself lucky to earn £10 for sharing my feeble jokes with the Young Wives Club (they were eighty if they were a day) or to get £50 from a small-circulation mag that can barely afford to pay me at all.

As author and journalist Michael Bywater says, only be a writer if "you haven't noticed that one of the things which really, really helps make life go smoothly is a reasonable income, regularly received".

Which is why – when asked in an interview for my hottest writing tip – I once said: "Marry someone rich!!"

It raised a laugh but there was more than a grain of truth to it. Making a fortune from writing is a wonderful bonus if it happens, but is not something to bank on. Especially literally.

Surveys by the Society of Authors show that an alarming proportion of their members earn less than £10,000 per year from writing alone which is probably why so many of them have more than one string to their bow. (When Miles Kington sent his contribution for this book he described himself as a "humorous writer, broadcaster and *Independent* daily columnist, also double bass player for hire.")

Many writers also teach, give talks or have part-time work editing or reading. There have been months when I have earned more from after-dinner speaking than I have from sitting at my computer.

Having said all that, some people have huge success from their earliest endeavours and make a very comfortable living indeed. Who knows, you might be one of them. But until you've got the contract in your hand the best advice anyone can give you is: keep buying that lottery ticket.

For even when you do have a contract, your financial worries may not be over. An advance of, say, £20,000 (and many are an awful lot less than that) may sound OK but consider how it is paid out.

Typically, this would be for a two-book deal and you might receive £5000 upon signature of the contract, another £5k when the first book is published, a third payment on delivery of the second manuscript and the final amount when the second tome hits the shops. This entire process could take two years and suddenly it's not very much money at all!

Ah, but what about all the royalties when your books start selling well? Unfortunately it is only those authors at the very top of the tree who reap the serious money.

Literary agent Jonathan Lloyd gave an excellent talk at a Society of Authors event a couple of years ago in which he quoted some statistics that showed how the big brand-name authors were getting bigger but at the expense of almost everyone else. This, he says, "reflects the increasing power of the supermarkets who tend to concentrate on the top authors".

At the time, the top-selling 25 authors had increased their sales on average by 28%; the next 25 were holding their own but with no increase; the next 25 had sales down by 10% and the next 25 had sales down by 25%.

"Depressing but that's life," he says. "The rich are getting richer and the poor are going bust. An exaggeration but not far from the truth."

Let's not get too depressed, though. As Jonathan also says, unknown authors can come from nowhere and hit the best-seller lists, either suddenly and dramatically by being *Richard & Judy* picks or over time, by gathering word of mouth momentum. What I find exciting in the book industry is that anything really is possible and nobody can foretell exactly where the next fortune will be made.

But whether you are one of the lucky ones out choosing the new yacht or are just scraping by on bread and marg, one thing you can be sure of: your bank balance will suddenly become a source of fascination.

"Etiquette about discussing personal finances goes out of the window when someone finds out you write books," says Dorothy Koomson. "They assume you're a millionaire and that it's more than OK to ask how much you earn. Most people don't realise that the majority of authors have to work one or two other jobs and write in their spare time. And that it's just plain rude to ask how much someone earns."

It is indeed, yet it happens often. Nobody would dream of asking a plumber or a solicitor but we writers are fair game.

Novelist Santa Montefiore, whose seven novels have sold over two millions copies, says it happens to her all the time.

"I constantly find myself sitting next to arrogant city blokes who consider my trade home-spun, like knitting socks for the local charity shop or something. They sniff in a rather patronising way and ask how I manage to pay the bills with such a sweet little hobby. I think the answer is to rise above their rudeness and reply 'because I'm very good at it!'"

"I think," says author Daniel Blythe, "that people are fascinated because of the aura of glamour around novelists." (Cue for hollow laugh while I reflect on my equally hollow eyes, unbrushed hair and crumpled pyjama bottoms – the deadline on this book is looming large.)

Dan puts it down to lurid headlines about 6-figure advances. "Well, we all get 6-figure advances," he says firmly. "It just depends where you put the decimal point..."

I like this and am going to announce to the next person who asks that I am a sixer myself. Which might have silenced the dinner companion who once asked pointedly: "Are you rich?"

And the countless others who try to be subtle by saying: "Do you make a living out of it?" ("Sadly not," I am tempted to reply. "Any chance of a loan?") My mate Lynne Barrett-Lee does just this: "I quote endless gobbets of depressing financial statistics at them and drone about my hourly rate working out at about 50 pence."

But the best riposte I've heard so far comes from novelist Sarah Duncan who, upon being asked how much she earns, answers sweetly: "enough to feed my lingerie habit."

Smoking

Several agents and publishers I've spoken to have said there's nothing worse than opening a manuscript that smells like an old ashtray.

I have given up and so should you.

Handbags

If you don't smoke it will be one less thing to put in your handbag.

A recent article in *The Times* explained that the reason designer bags are getting bigger and bigger is that we all carry around much more than we once did. (The average weight of a handbag in the UK is now 3 ½ lbs.)

If you are a writer you end up carrying even more junk around than usual.

In addition to tissues, make-up, keys, money, phone, hairbrush, and mineral water, you'll want space for a notebook, several pens – you'll add a new one each time you leave the house because you've become so neurotic about going out without one – a dictaphone, a camera, the book you're reading and another notebook in case you lose the first one.

This makes the whole handbag business even more annoying than before. For the thing I've never understood about women who carry lots of different bags is how they find time to keep unpacking and refilling them.

I have quite a few handbags but can't be fussed to keep changing their contents around so I'm rarely colour-co-ordinated, carry about seventeen pens and haven't investigated the three inches of fluff at the bottom of my current one since 2003.

The offside rule

This is a non-discriminatory, equal opportunities handbook so for those of you who thought I was getting a bit girly back there I will now devote as much space as I did to handbags to the finer points of football.

Personally I think this "interfering with play" business is a free kick too far. I see nothing wrong with a bit of goal-hanging, or – when I am playing with my son, who is a lot better than me – tripping your opponent up and sitting on him.

When I was a teenager I fancied George Best but overall, I would say that rugby players score more highly on the shaggablility scale than footballers.

And Victoria Beckham is probably a perfectly nice girl, but she's far too thin and ought to smile more.

Copyright

New writers often seem to get very steamed up about copyright but there is really no need. Nobody is really very likely to want to pinch your writing and pass it off as their own. Other writers will be producing their own and if publishers want it, they'll pay for it.

It is worth remembering anyway that there is no copyright on titles, none on pseudonyms and none on basic ideas or the bare bones of a plot.

Obviously you need to establish that you wrote it and when, but typing © followed by your name and the year at the end of any work you send out should be sufficient safeguard.

If you are concerned, however, you can deposit a copy of your manuscript with your bank or solicitor and obtain a dated receipt, or adopt the simpler method of posting a copy to yourself in a sealed package (which must remain sealed) and using the date of postage as proof of the work's date of origin.

Alternatively you could write something like this on the bottom of every piece of work:

> These series of hints to budding writers are copyright Miles Kington, in all parts of the known universe, in all formats, in all media, in all colours, in all languages, and if you reprint them without permission you will get a mysterious wasting disease for which there is no known cure. Except, perhaps, money.

Or you could decide not to. I laughed when Miles sent the above to me. But if you do do it, someone else might think you're nuts.

AT THE END...

What to Do When You've Finished

So, you've finished your story, your article or – if you really are a glutton for punishment – your full-length manuscript. What now?

Well, first, obviously, particularly if it's the latter, you whoop and congratulate yourself and pour a large drink and very probably collapse in a heap.

But once you've done that, I'm afraid, the hard work begins.

Now, before you have any thought of sending your magnum opus out anywhere to seek its fortune, you must go through it all again, cutting and inserting, honing and shaping and polishing it to within an inch of its life.

But if you want a few days off first, now's your chance.

Creative writing tutor Catherine Merriman suggests putting work aside, for at least a week and preferably longer, before looking at it with a fresh eye, and always reading it aloud – from a print-out, not the computer screen.

I know this is excellent advice even if a nuisance to stick to. I am usually too impatient to leave work lying fallow in a drawer but there is no doubt that if you do, the dodgy bits will leap out and hit you between the eyes when you next pick it up.

And it is an odd thing that one spots all sorts of errors on the printed page that can be missed in a dozen readings from the monitor.

However, Bernard Knight, author of more than a dozen murder mysteries (The Crowner John Series, Pocket Books) says: "I write everything on screen, edit on screen, then e-mail it to my publisher. So I don't see anything on paper until I get the proofs."

He would be skinned alive by The Fearsome One.

She is very hot on printing out and always knows if I try to cut corners. It was her other complaint when I sent her the sub-standard opening chapters for which I got a good roasting.

"You didn't print them out before editing, did you?" she demanded. She was right, I hadn't. When I did, it made all the difference.

I do read my work aloud – inside my head – constantly. It is the only way to check for fluency and rhythm. If you find you are stumbling over sentences or not having enough breath to get to the end of one – something needs looking at.

Every writer I know writes and re-writes, fiddles and tweaks and goes over and over the manuscript endlessly – it is the only way. Alice Jolly says she re-wrote her most recent book 17 times and many a novel changes radically in the months between completion of its first draft to the end product sitting on the shop shelves.

For me, the editing process is the most enjoyable bit of all. The stressful, frightening stage is over – the story is down, the first draft complete – now I can spend happy hours ensuring it is the very best I can make it.

And how does one do that?

It is a matter of making sure the prose is sharp and – in the case of a novel – the story flows. You are looking to make it shine. These are the sorts of things you should be checking for:

- Unnecessary words or dull, superfluous detail
- Repetition
- Places where you have stated the obvious e.g. : 'He yelled loudly' or 'She whispered quietly'
- Overuse of adjectives and adverbs
- Grammatical errors – especially it's/its, who's/whose etc
- Spelling mistakes – especially those that spellcheck won't notice – see above
- Typos – we all make them
- Overuse of clichés (N.B. These give some creative writing tutors the vapours but I don't think one need be too neurotic. We all use them sometimes, and in dialogue they are often part of common usage . E.g. I see nothing wrong with a mother saying of a child "he's usually as good as gold." Or telling a friend: "he marched in here with a face like thunder." Beware of it them in general description though. Clouds like cotton wool, anything that's "as white as snow" or a girl with "hair like silk" can get a bit tedious.
- Paragraphing – as a general rule short is better than long
- In dialogue check it's clear who's speaking

- On the structural front, keep it tight. Does everything you tell your reader either move the plot along, or, in the case of non-fiction, add to and hold their interest? In other words – the acid test of any good book – are they going to want to turn the page?
- Does the book start in the right place? Does your beginning have impact? Does it grab the reader from the off?

I have a post-it note – rather faded and curling now – stuck on my monitor shelf with The Fearsome One's instructions to me on the writing of *One Glass Is Never Enough*. It reads:

1) Plot rounded?
2) Who / What / Where / Why / When?
3) Five senses?

I keep it there as my personal checklist. Am I fleshing the story out? Looking after the sub-plots? Making sure plenty happens?

Have I explained all the five Ws? And can my reader clearly imagine the sight, taste, sound, smell and feel of everything I'm describing?

Ask yourself these questions, too.

This is a chance to read through your very own book with fresh eyes, as if for the first time. To read it as a reader would, except with a fat red pen in your hand – marking anything that interrupts the flow, that seems clumsy or unclear, or that you suddenly realise you've already said a couple of chapters ago.

This is your chance to turn competent writing into something exceptional – to polish those grey pebbles until they become diamonds and you become excited and proud and think: Gosh – I wrote that!

It's an exciting thing to do and that's why it's so pleasurable.

The next bit isn't.

The Dreaded Synopsis.

Yes, I'm afraid you do need one.

Three chapters and a synopsis is what most publishers will want to see in the first instance so you may as well get down to writing one as soon as you are happy with everything else.

What exactly is it? A synopsis is, as editor Carolyn Caughey from Hodder puts it so succinctly: "a summary to tell an editor what is in the book".

It should be short – Carolyn recommends 2 pages max, double-spaced – to the point and be interesting enough to have whoever's reading it eagerly reaching for your manuscript.

For some reason, the thought of writing a synopsis fills many writers with dread and I must admit my own heart sinks too.

Carole Matthews, who's currently writing her eleventh novel still describes it as "a horrible process".

She says: "I'd rather write a 100,000 word book and that's what I normally do! Only when I've finished the entire novel do I feel that I can write a decent synopsis."

But "unfortunately," continues Carole, "the synopsis is king these days. It's your marketing tool and, along with your covering letter, it should be as perfect as possible!"

Don't panic just yet. Sherise Hobbs, a fiction editor at Headline recommends keeping it short too but counsels: "The most important thing is that it's very clear, so that the reader can quickly process the information. The synopsis should give a brief resumé of the plot, including the ending."

Carole Matthews mentions endings, too. "Please don't be tempted to write 'Ha, ha! To find out what happens you'll have to request the whole manuscript," she says. "Unbelievably, writers do this and, more believably, publishers don't bother."

Broo Doherty, a partner in the literary agency, Wade and Doherty explains: "The function of a synopsis is to show that the novel has a structure – a beginning, a middle and an end. "Don't over-complicate," she warns. "Keep it short and sweet and remember to make it sound like something YOU would want to read."

I think this is a good point. The piece of advice I always remember, given to me by another literary agent, Lizzy Kremer, when I was writing my first novel, was to imagine that I worked in a library and needed to know both what a book was about and what sort of book it was, in order to recommend it to a borrower. "Don't write a cover blurb," she said. "Just describe the story."

All of which illustrates that agents, like the rest of us, can beg to differ.

Merric Davidson dislikes "great long outlines" and says he actually prefers "jacket-flap blurbs".

"All I want is a trigger to make me go to the manuscript. Once there, I'll hardly ever refer to the synopsis."

So the best thing is to see what the agent or publisher you are targeting (we will come on to this shortly) is actually asking for, and if that is a "one-page synopsis" then keep it to one page.

However long it is, do make sure you have clearly identified your reader in your own mind, so if you're aiming at the female-in-her-forties market for example, or men over sixty whose only interest is fishing, make sure it sounds an intriguing read for that profile.

Agent Simon Trewin suggests that you get someone else to write it for you (sounds like an excellent idea to me!). "A member of your writing group perhaps," he says. "They may see elements of your novel that you've missed – the writer can have blind spots." Simon also recommends reading other examples of synopses and points to Amazon as a good place to start.

On the face of it, writing a page or so describing the action in one's own book sounds easy, but it obviously isn't, as whole books have been written on the subject.

The best-known is *How to Write and Sell a Synopsis* by Stella Whitelaw (Allison and Busby) which I haven't read myself (the very title makes me twitch) but have heard good reports of.

The agent Carole Blake also gives sensible tips in her excellent *From Pitch to Publication* which I do have on my shelf and can recommend.

But in case you're now feeling totally daunted, I will leave you with the words of Sherise Hobbs, the kind of decision-maker you're going to need to impress.

She sums up by saying: "Although it's useful to provide a good synopsis, the editor is primarily concerned with reading a sample of the novel itself. For example, I will generally only look at a synopsis if I'm already hooked by the partial."

In order to be helpful and to show I do not always get it right either (agent Jane Judd's tips for a good synopsis include "don't use full caps for characters' names as if it were a film script" which I always used to do, because I thought it looked cool) I have been searching my hard drive for an example of a synopsis to share with you. The one I wrote for *Perfect Alibis* bears no resemblance at all to the final book, which is proof, if proof were needed, that there's not much point in writing one (unless it's for your eyes only) until you have finished.

So here is the one I wrote for the first version of *Raising the Roof* and is a reasonable summing up of what goes on in the book although the How-to-Write-a-Bestseller course got dumped along the way.

You will also see that I hadn't then had the benefit of Carolyn Caughey's advice "I want to know who dunnit – a synopsis isn't a teaser" because I don't actually explain how everything works out in the end. I also haven't included any mention of who my heroine ends up with. But hey – now you can get a copy and enjoy finding out…

BUILDING BLOCKS
(Later re-titled Raising the Roof) by Jane Wenham-Jones

A SYNOPSIS

After ten years with husband Martin, who leaves her for a blonde bimbo called Sharon, Cari – aged thirty-two – is single again. She has no money, a batty mother, a manically-depressed sister and a friend called Nigel – a dodgy builder who wants to get his leg over.

Cari wants fame, fortune and a grand passion. She plans to achieve this by writing a ground-breaking, best-selling diet book, becoming stick-thin herself and finding love along the way.

In the meantime, she drinks too much, gets involved in an ill-advised property deal with Nigel and becomes a quasi-builder while her sister Juliette has psychotic episodes, her friend Louise has a disastrous affair and her mother drives everyone mad.

The property venture does not go well. Cari is left with a half-converted house, a squatting drug addict, irate council officials and an unamused bank manager. As things hit rock-bottom she accompanies her friend Henry to a regional gathering of supermarket managers and makes a contact that will change her life.

But not before she is packed off to Cornwall on a *How to write a Best-seller* course – a present from her well-meaning mother. Her failed writing progresses no further but she does meet Guy with whom she spends a wild passionate weekend, discovering the hitherto uncharted territory of the female orgasm and imagining she has found her true love.

Back home, reality grabs her by the throat as the bank closes in, the marital home comes under threat, and Guy under her own roof is not quite the catch she thought he was. After various ghastly goings-on, Cari hits rock bottom, depressed by the temporary nature of passion, the loss of her sister's sanity and the lack of loss of her own fat stores.

She throws Guy out and finds herself all alone. Nigel has been hauled up by the VAT inspectors, Louise is in trauma, Juliette is in hospital again and there are bailiffs at the door. Martin, returning briefly, only makes matters worse.

However, by a strange and wonderful twist of fate, the property deal comes right after all and Cari is able not only to save her own day but Nigel's as well. And then the icing on the cake – love pops up from the most unexpected quarter…

Finding an Agent (how not to)

The trick with this chapter is to do as I say, not what I did.

I did it wrong and didn't have an agent for my first two novels. I have one now as you know, and there is no doubt that having an agent is a GOOD THING (even if, in my case, she's the scary sort who tells me to talk less and write more and doesn't always want to listen to my fifteen-point career plan for the second time in a week).

Agents deal with all the tedious bits like the money and the contracts; they can sell your books abroad which I, for one, wouldn't have the first clue about, and, most importantly, they can wax lyrical to prospective publishers about how wonderfully you write, with a greater ring of authority than if you say it yourself, or get your mum to.

As literary agent Broo Doherty of Wade and Doherty puts it, an agent can "manipulate and manoeuvre their way round a publishing company on your behalf" while Merric Davidson says simply: "an author is a creator. An agent looks after business."

So how do you get one? With difficulty, I would have to say.

Or at least it was hard for me. Several agents offered to represent me once I was published – they are a bit like buses – but in the beginning, they did not exactly fall at my feet.

To give hope to any of you who are beginning to despair of ever seeing your book in print and as a cautionary tale to those who are just starting out, I will tell you what happened.

Being an optimist at heart, I started off by looking on the bright side. I'd heard the tales of how hard it was to secure an agent, how it was easier, indeed, to get a publishing deal, so elusive and picky were this rare and precious breed, but I didn't believe it .

It was a bit like all that logic-defying business with camels and eyes of needles – how could it be true? Surely, I thought, if you have something publishable, then an agent will recognise that and be only too glad to step in there for you.

Naïvely, my reasoning went like this: I'd had a fair few stories and articles published, and I thought my book – what there was of it at the time – was readable. I thought, if I was determined enough, someone, somewhere would take me on.

But just in case – despite my positive thinking – they didn't come flocking, I thought I'd start early.

I wrote my first-ever letter to an agent when my novel was still "in progress". The lucky chap was Merric Davidson, now with the MBA agency, who I'd come across in his role as editor of *The New Writer*. (Remember I said he had a sexy voice? I do like a nice voice…)

I did mention in my letter that the novel was unfinished (just not that there were still another eighty thousand words to go) and I see now – with the benefit of hindsight – how very kind was his response.

"Lively," he said. "Modern," he added. "Witty, well-written…" and "No-I-don't-want-it," he finished. But in such a nice way I was left convinced someone else would.

I hoped that someone would be Jonathan Lloyd. He was Wendy Holden's agent. I'd seen his name briefly when I first read about her success but it didn't really register until it popped up again.

After Wendy's diary piece in *The Times,* telling the story of the writing and selling of *Simply Divine* the paper had several letters from disgruntled wannabes for whom the novel-writing experience had been very different.

The Times responded by presenting three agents – Caroline Dawnay, Simon Trewin and Jonathan Lloyd – with the opening chapters of a novel from each of four wannabe writers. The result made a gripping article which I immediately cut out.

I was particularly attracted by Mr Lloyd's grumpier observations:

"Comedy, groan…"

"Typeface is too small and single-spacing unacceptable, especially to people of my age…"

"Where is the story?"

"I'm not sure where I'm going and I'm afraid I don't care..."

He was the one, I decided, to target. Inspired by Wendy, I was now typing away every spare minute and my manuscript was growing. I wrote to Jonathan when it was about 10,000 words long.

My letter began like this:

Dear Jonathan Lloyd

I hope this typeface is big enough for you...

I enclosed a brief outline of what the book was about, explaining it wasn't finished but could be very quickly (I still had a lot to learn about novel-writing!) and although I wouldn't dare describe it as a comedy, it *was* amusing in places...

Three days later I got a reply. He said he didn't really like reading unfinished work (by the time he'd finished dealing with me he'd be positively allergic to it) and was a bit wary of "writers who write about writers" (my heroine, Cari, was writing a diet book in her spare time) but ended, excitingly, with the words:

"Anyway, let's see (since I loved your covering letter)."

Hurrah!

Naturally, I rushed the first three chapters to the post office. Well actually I sent the first six, on the basis that they were all short and I am one of those people – if you give me an inch...

(N.B.: I hope you are still holding onto the instruction I gave you at the beginning of this chapter – none of this is to be tried at home.)

I scattered the covering letter with smiley faces ☺ and ended it: "*Will I be sending you roses and declarations of undying love? Or popping down to Woolworths for a packet of plasticine and some shiny new pins...?*

He sent me a great reply.

"*So far so good. I can't commit yet but am happy to see another batch of chapters (so hold the plasticine and pins)."*

He also asked how many chapters I had completed altogether.

Not wishing to put him off, I tripled the true figure and told him I was going on holiday for a fortnight but would send them when I got back.

Fifteen days later in a state of nervous collapse from lack of sleep and staring at a computer screen for sixteen hours a day, I lugged my Jiffy bag to the Post Office.

Jonathan again replied quickly. He liked these too. And would read "the rest". Oh my God.

After a brief celebratory getting-slaughtered, I slaved over a hot keyboard for what seemed like months and probably was. Every now and again I would send Jonathan another packet of chapters and he would reply – sometimes including little pointers for me – "*the first quarter seems to have set up the main characters well and I imagine that the next batch will pick up the pace – i.e. from a walk/trot to a trot/canter...*"

In other words: get on with the story! I did my best. Jonathan was brilliant at replying quickly but if ever he didn't, I would fall into a panic that he had gone off the book and wouldn't want to read any more. Then I would have to find out (I can't believe I had the audacity to do this but I did).

I wasn't on email in those days so I would fax him instead. To save him time I would send him a reply-sheet with tick boxes:

To: Jane
From: Jonathan

1) Yes I received it ☐

   No I didn't ☐

2) Yes, I've read it ☐

No I haven't! Have you any idea how many things
   Managing Directors of Leading Literary Agencies actually
   have to *do*? ☐

3) Yes it was terrific. I can't wait for my next package ☺ ☐

   No, it's in the bin ☹ ☐

Best wishes/Now for God's sake leave me alone (please delete as applicable)
Jonathan

And, bless him, he would send them back, writing encouraging things like: *"The character – if not the liver – of the heroine is emerging well "* and scrawling *"Don't worry"* across the bottom of the page.

But worry I did. I was in a high anxiety state the whole time, hardly daring to believe my luck at having an agent reading my manuscript and terrified that that luck would run out.

And run out it did. Patience has never been one of my virtues and I did not know then what I know now about polishing and honing, writing and re-writing. I also, looking back, knew bugger-all about plotting. Desperate to get to the end of the book I wrote at very high speed and whizzed off all the remaining chapters together with a whole list of possible titles (I knew the working title of *Building Blocks* wouldn't do ultimately) and an outline for Book Two, drew a few jolly cartoons on the letter with as many witticisms as I could muster and sat back and waited.

And waited.

It seemed like a lifetime of waiting but looking back at the correspondence now I see that it was in fact only 18 days. (Which is nothing. Please do not run away with the idea it is OK to hassle an agent after less than three weeks. It isn't. They get hundreds of submissions and you may have to wait months. So ignore what I did. Miraculously, every agent I have ever had dealings with is still speaking to me – I would like it to stay that way.)

Anyway, it was the longest I'd ever had to wait for a response from Jonathan and dread, as they say, gripped my heart. I figured that if he'd liked the rest it would have taken no time at all to say so in a sentence. Explaining why he didn't was bound to be more time-consuming – especially since he knew enough about me now to realise I might come and stake out his doorstep.

I left him a phone message – telling him I was beginning to have nightmares – and on Day 19 I sent him a fax entitled "Quietly Dying".

I explained my state of mind, apologised for being a bloody nuisance and the fact that I'd never got the hang of this playing-it-cool lark and went back to the tick boxes for the nitty-gritty:

1) Have you read it?

Yes ☐

No ☐

2) Overall, would you sum up the situation as one of

Plasticine ☐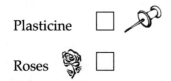

Roses ☐

And then he phoned me up and admitted that he didn't much like the end at all and that now he'd had a chance to really think about it, he wasn't over-sure about the middle either…

He was very nice. He said I had talent. He said on the roses/plasticine front it was a 65/35% situation with roses in the lead. But although he'd enjoyed the chapters with the tension mounting over the unpaid bills and problems with the house, he'd got a bit bogged down when my heroine had gone on her writing course and stayed up all night, afraid of a spider. He thought it needed a lot more work.

He suggested he gave it to another agent he worked with, who was very hot on the chick lit market, to see what she thought. I agreed to sit on my hands for three weeks while she read it.

I caved in after two and a half and sent a fax. In return he sent a copy of the other agent's report. She absolutely hated it.

Jonathan pointed out how very tough and competitive the market was and how many publishers were reducing the number of titles they published. He offered me the names of other agents to see if they would differ but said he thought it would be "very difficult" to get me a deal on this book. He suggested I put it to one side now and started again with another idea. He said he'd be happy to read a synopsis…

I was distraught and horrified at the idea of shelving a whole manuscript. After I'd finished wailing and spent an afternoon on the brandy for my post-traumatic stress, I waited till I knew his assistant would have gone home and he'd have to answer his own phone, and called him.

"Very difficult," I said, was not the same as "impossible". I reminded him how much he'd once liked the beginning. I offered to rewrite the middle and do something drastic to the end. I generally ranted on like Julie Walters in *Educating Rita* just before she tears her essay up.

And while I was re-writing it, I said, I'd take him up on the offer of the list of the other agents just in case he was still going to be a miserable old sod about it when I'd finished.

Jonathan, who, you will agree by now, probably deserves the Nobel Prize for Tolerance, said OK.

So that was what I did. The very next day I started work on the list of changes and additions he'd suggested and I spent the next three months giving the whole manuscript a face-lift and overhaul.

In the meantime, I did send the first version to a few other agents – just to see if they'd snap it up. They didn't. Though I collected some encouraging comments about my writing style and Carole Blake ended her letter by saying: "I'm sure you'll get this published", which was heartening.

While I was re-writing it I used to send Jonathan the odd note with the odd drawing like this one:

Just in case he was missing me and I sometimes phoned him up when I was three sheets to the wind (Dutch courage) just to make sure he was still looking forward to the re-write, or sent a quick note through the post.

It is to his credit that he didn't take the opportunity to emigrate.

Instead, come April 1999, he read the new manuscript which even I could see was a vast improvement on the old.

Not quite an improvement enough, though, as Jonathan gave me a few more suggestions for small changes which I duly carried out. It was in July that a very exciting letter arrived.

He'd had lunch with an editor at Harper Collins and given her my manuscript. "Be patient," the missive ended, "and I'll let you know what happens."

Even I sat on my hands this time, and as it happened, I didn't have to sit on them long. A mere two days later he sent through what he called a "gentle rejection." The editor thought my "voice and style were 'lovely' and the characters "good" but she didn't go much on the storyline. "Don't despair," wrote Jonathan. "I will now try another publishing house." He didn't tell me which one, probably afraid I'd follow the Chief Executive home and hold him hostage, so again all I could do was wait.

This took a lot longer – it was the end of September before news came. The second publisher said no, too.

This time the editor rather liked my storyline – thought it was "original" but she wasn't keen on my heroine, finding her "too sharp-edged".

I could cope with that – after all, there were many more publishers to try yet, weren't there? Apparently not.

"I suggest that you do put this to one side now," wrote Jonathan. "We can always resurrect it later. Perhaps you would now like to think about the next idea. Send me some sample chapters…"

This was a bombshell. I was used to the magazine market where I kept sending out stories until someone, somewhere, bought them. Where I sold everything, eventually, however long it took. Where I never, ever, just gave up.

"It's different for books," said Jonathan.

Apparently both publishers had said they'd be happy to look at another manuscript from me; Jonathan's feeling was that I should get on and write it.

If you told me this story now, I would tell you to count yourself very fortunate. I would point out that lots of writers don't get their very first book published and that having a top agent and two big publishers willing to look at your second attempt is an excellent position to be in.

But it didn't feel like that at the time. It felt like the end of the world. I can see now that I'd lost all sense of proportion but I still wasn't ready to give up.

When I was a child, my riding instructress had one big rule. When you fell off your horse – which I did frequently – you got straight back on.

So the very same day, I stopped snivelling and went back to my battered *Writers Handbook* and composed a witty and pithy fax explaining how brilliant I was (though by now the jokes were wearing a bit thin, even on me) and whizzed it off to another great name in the world of agents.

And Hallelujah! He faxed straight back. "I would love to read your manuscript," he said. "Tomorrow would be nice!"

Phew! I spent all afternoon kicking the printer and rushed a fresh pristine copy down to the post office at 5.29 p.m.. He was a man of his word. He read it the next night. And two days later back it thumped onto my doormat. *Your writing has a lot going for it,* he declared. *However I think the main problems with this novel are…..* They ran to three sides of A4.

"Why don't you just stick to those magazine stories?" asked my husband kindly while I tried hard not to stab him. "You're good at those…"

But I wanted to be good at this, too, so out went more letters, emails, faxes, sample chapters, synopses, whole manuscripts, part manuscripts and feeble jokes and back came the responses.

After a few months I made a detailed analysis of the list of objections in case I needed to consider yet another re-write. These were the conclusions of my study:

The heroine was both too weak and too assertive. She was unbelievably naïve and also hard-nosed. There was an abundance of her mother in evidence and also not enough. The plot-line was both highly original and old hat. It had a strong beginning and a slow start. The ending was unusual and predictable. My favourite sub-plot needed to stay in and be taken out.

73% of agents thought I was amusing, 47% would be willing to read my second novel if I didn't place this one, 18% suggested I try other agents. 1% offered to meet me for lunch. 100% were saying NO.

I was supposed to be writing the opening chapters of a second book but it wasn't going well. I showed a couple of them to Jonathan Lloyd and he was decidedly underwhelmed. I wasn't surprised – they didn't really grab me either. I was still obsessed with *Building Blocks.* I was losing heart as more and more agents told me the Chick Lit market was overcrowded and/or on the way out, but I was determined not to give up totally until there wasn't a literary stone unturned.

So on I went, but it was hard. It became a case of waiting for the post not to come. I would look with one eye through the glass of our inner door praying not to see a Jiffy bag which meant the manuscript had come back – again.

Good news, I assumed, would be in the shape of a small envelope or a phone call. Once my heart leapt and pounded when a letter with the right London postmark arrived. It was a leaflet advertising books.

"What is wrong with me?" I wailed to a writing friend – who'd got an agent at her third try and was now basking in the glow of her first two-book deal.

"Nothing, probably," she replied. "I really don't know why," she added casually, "you don't just send it out to some publishers direct…"

I remembered a publisher I'd read an interview with. He sounded fun. I was now on email which made things quicker and also meant I could act on impulse.

I typed *Remember Me?* in the subject line.

We met at a party, I continued. *I captivated you with my wit and charm and you said when I had finished my novel I simply must send it to you…"*

That must have been some party, came the reply. *I don't remember you at all. But I like your style. Do send me your manuscript…*

He didn't buy it but he said all the things I needed to hear. You have TALENT he said. A HIGHLY ORIGINAL VOICE! "Have you tried approaching an agent?" he asked.

But I was already emailing the next publisher. The same line worked again. I changed tack when I went on to target a female editor but I kept it jokey.

Francesca Liversidge from Transworld replied in six minutes. "Anyone that can make me chuckle on a Monday morning gets my vote," she wrote. "Please do let me see your manuscript."

And three weeks later she bought it…

Finding an Agent (the right way)

So let's get this clear. That was the story of how I became deranged. This is how YOU should go about things instead.

It is possible, as I have shown, to sell your novel or non-fiction book without an agent but I don't recommend it.

It is, as Jonathan Lloyd says, "a jungle out there".

And let us not forget that I would not have sold my book if I hadn't had his advice or done all that rewriting under his guidance. Which is why I shall be forever grateful. Jonathan was incredibly generous with his time, very kind and patient and did, as he has succinctly put it since, read my manuscript "about four f***ing times". Thank you Jonathan xxxx

An agent, as Jane Judd (who is one herself) explains, can "provide emotional support, relatively unbiased feedback and knowledge of the market and publishers." He or she is someone who will also "take the flak and argue your side of any problems with the publisher and offer help and advice on your next move".

So before you go any other route, you should give finding one your very best shot.

Where do you start?

Do some detective work to find out who represent the writers that most resemble what you are doing in terms of style or genre, ask questions of any published novelist you meet and speak to other wannabes to find out who is currently being kindest to those still being rejected.

Keep an eye on the press, too. Long before I ever sent out my manuscript, I used to scour writing magazines and the literary sections of newspapers for interviews with agents and publishers, squirreling away any cuttings that included words of wisdom and usefulnames.

These all stayed in a file marked "One day…"

Even if you haven't started writing your potential best-seller yet, keep alert for contacts.

If anybody ever tells you who their agent is, remember the name. If a novelist you admire thanks his or her agent in the acknowledgements (they often do) write it down.

If an agent comes to give a talk anywhere within a hundred mile radius of where you live, get there. If it's a really big name, travel further.

For I always think: "I read you/met you/saw you/heard you" is a much more flattering opener in your letter of introduction than "Dear Blah-blah, I picked you with a pin from *The Writer's Handbook…*"

Agents are human too and everyone likes to feel they have been specially chosen for a reason, and haven't just formed part of an alphabetical list you're working through.

So the more you find out about whoever you're targeting the better. "I'm not interested in personal flattery," says Jane Judd. "But it's always nice to have someone say they are a fan of one of your authors. It shows they have done some research, too."

You'll find a lot of such information in *The Writer's Handbook* or the *Writers' and Artists' Yearbook*. Go through either with a highlighter pen. Check for those that do actually handle the sort of thing you've written – many will specifically say no to children's books or Science Fiction, for example – and put a big ring round any who positively welcome unsolicited manuscripts or first novels.

Sometimes gut feelings work as well as anything, so if a particular name leaps off the page at you – give it a whirl.

Do follow the instructions they give, e.g. "Send a query letter in the first instance" or "no phone calls." The Fearsome One says it drives her mad when it is very clearly stated in *The Writer's Handbook* what she requires and "people still don't follow it".

"It is NOT," she says sternly, "a good indication of how they are going to be as an author."

Some agents will want only to see a synopsis and covering letter to start with. Others will invite sample chapters straightaway.

In both cases, your covering letter is of paramount importance – it needs to clearly describe the sort of book you have written and any relevant information about yourself. A "writealike" can be also be useful – indicating that your offering is similar to a Joanna Trollope, say, or a certain title (I used to describe *Raising the Roof* as "*Real Women* meets *Rising Damp*" – not an entirely accurate description but it gave agents an idea). The letter will be the first thing the agent picks up and all agree it speaks multitudes.

"A poorly-written letter doesn't bode well for the accompanying manuscript," says Grainne Fox, from the famous Ed Victor agency. "If the author can't string words together to write a coherent letter it always puts me off before I even get to the submission itself."

All the agents I spoke to had their pet irritations – The Fearsome One had a pageful!

Jane Judd dislikes being addressed as "Jane," while Merric Davidson is put off by approaches like: "this will make both our fortunes/this would make a very good film/friends have said this is the funniest book they have ever read/why this script is so much better than Bridget Jones."

Merric's advice is to keep it simple and "put all the work into the synopsis". Broo Doherty loathes jokes in a submission, and The Fearsome One agrees. "If you were going for a job interview, you wouldn't expect to joke your way into it," she says briskly.

Simon Trewin doesn't mind the odd quip – I know from experience – but has his own list of things that annoy.

He is put off by the letter smelling of cigarette smoke or it being handwritten and says it should not be overlong. "Authors should be able to condense what they have to say into one page. Otherwise what hope is there for the manuscript?"

And, talking of the manuscript, if it's dog-eared that does not inspire confidence, he says. "It shows it's obviously done the rounds."

The Fearsome One gets cross when manuscripts aren't laid out properly, are presented as a mocked-up novel or are in a font that's too small. "People don't seem to realise we spend all day reading and we need a decent-sized typeface!"

They may also not realise the sheer volume of submissions agents are getting.

Broo Doherty and her business partner Robin Wade get 5,000 manuscripts a year sent to them; Simon Trewin gets 6,000. As Caroline Dawnay, an agent at PFD with Simon, said in the article in *The Times* I mentioned earlier: " One is always looking for a reason *not* to take someone on."

So try not to give an agent that reason before you start.

- Don't send the whole manuscript unless you've been specifically asked for it.
- Make sure your letter is grammatically sound and that you have spelled the agent's name correctly.
- Lay the manuscript out properly – double-spaced, indented paragraphs etc.
- Don't write your acknowledgements and dedication at this point. It just makes you look a prat.
- Don't send manuscripts that stink of old ashtrays.
- Be patient.

The last one is a toughie. Waiting for verdicts from agents, or any decision-maker, is very hard. Especially when all your hopes and dreams hang on them.

As Kate Harrison says: "I totally understand why they can't drop everything and read mine first but it's still hard to think of anything else while you wait..." while Lesley Horton describes it as "like waiting for A level results".

There is nothing for it but to hang in there – if you hassle you will only get up your agent's nose. Simon Trewin cites those who phone up an hour after the post's arrived, to ask him if he's read their offering yet, on his list of least-appealing potential clients and I would add that if you do phone – about anything – be very polite to whoever answers.

Some of the bigger agents will have assistants and it is worth remembering that they have quite a lot of clout, too. One assistant – we shall call her Violet – who works in a very big agency, had this to say:

> People should treat the assistants with FAR more respect! They really seem to believe that every agent spends his days poring over their piles and piles of unsolicited manuscripts when often the reality is that an agent will only see an unsolicted submission if his assistant tells him to. So it is totally absurd for people to ring up and haughtily demand to speak only to the agent. You simply will not get through if we don't like the sound of you. To be rude to an assistant is serious folly – your submission will very likely end up back in the post to you without being opened. When people are very polite and/or grateful to me personally, they'll get a lot more out of the whole experience. We are effectively trained readers, and if they make us feel valued for our opinion, the chances are that we'll give a few pointers on where they are going wrong.

So now you know.

The Fearsome One has more dos and don'ts:

- Don't staple the Jiffy bag – otherwise one can rip one's fingers opening it.
- Do send an SAE and check that that the manuscript will actually fit into it.

- Do put enough postage on the manuscript – you wouldn't believe how many we receive with postage owing – I don't accept them now.
- Don't send glamour photos of yourself.

"But what REALLY makes me mad," she says, "is someone sending me a novel before they've even bothered to finish it. A novel is a work of art. You wouldn't dream of sending a half-finished painting to the Royal Academy, would you?"

(Good thing I didn't send mine to her all those years ago.)

"And it makes me INCANDESCENT," she goes on, if PEOPLE DON'T EDIT ON PAPER. I interrupted her tirade at this point (a lesser woman might not have dared) as we've been through all this already.

Fearing for her blood pressure, I turned to things she did like. "I love it," she said wistfully, "when a manuscript is beautifully presented, on good paper, properly laid out, paragraphs indented. When I can see the author has taken the time and trouble to edit it properly. I know straight away when an author has done that – you can tell instantly."

One of her authors is Debby Holt. "I read the first page of her manuscript and thought 'this is it'". Debby, she says, "worked like stink" to polish it. The resulting novel *The Ex-wife's Survival Guide* (Pocket Books) sold "fantastically well" and her second one, *Annie May's Black Book* (Pocket Books) is set to be even more successful. "This proves," says The Fearsome One, humour fully restored " that good writers do get discovered."

Jane Judd agrees. She tells how she found both Jill Mansell and Manda Scott on her slush pile while Jonathan Lloyd sums up:

"I always believe the goodies win in the end and that real talent will out."

I would agree with him, but if it's all taking too long for you and you feel all else has failed, you could always try sending direct to a publisher…

A Word About Publishers

The most useful thing I can say to you about publishers is: GET REAL.

Publishers are not locked in a conspiracy against you, they are not going to steal your ideas, they do not have a policy of only taking on celebrities, they will not reject a brilliant manuscript for any reason other than actually it wasn't that brilliant and they do, generally (famous exceptions aside) know a good thing when they see it. Or one of them will, eventually, anyway.

Also publishers do not close their lists. However many books they publish already, if a fresh new voice turns up or an amazingly original idea (if there are any left) they are all going to be scrambling for it.

If you get a letter telling you their lists are closed, you can safely assume that they were about as interested in your first three chapters as I would be in shagging John Prescott and are rather hoping you will now go off somewhere and keep ferrets instead.

The truth is that publishers are ordinary, often likeable, people working in a business that exists to make money. A shame yes, a shame that they aren't a philanthropic, benevolent charity there to bring joy to every illiterate half-wit who thinks he can knock off a best-seller because his life has been so fascinating, but they are not.

Unfortunately for all of us, they have sales targets and turnovers to consider and for every commissioning editor who loves a new author with a passion, there is a marketing man, a publicist, an accountant, a sales director and a heap of shareholders who are only prepared to see that author taken on if they can be sure his or her book will make a few bucks. It's called The Real World.

This is not to say you won't be that lucky one who makes it – there are over 8–10,000 new books published every month of the year – but it is as well to face facts.

Alan Samson, head of Weidenfeld & Nicolson, part of the Orion Publishing Group, gets 3000 proposals a year to look at – about sixty a week. That's just from agents. The company as a whole gets more than 5000 unsolicited manuscripts a year of which about 500 land on Alan's desk (where, remember there are already three thousand teetering there).

Unlike some publishers, Alan does look at them. Even though he describes many of them as "absolutely terrible, totally unpublishable" and says with feeling: "It seems as though in every street in Britain someone is writing a book and I do wish they'd stop."

The main problem, he says, is people who have no real passion for writing but are just after the financial reward. Once again we are talking those who think, that because they've got a vague interest in writing and once won the school essay prize, they can knock out a best-seller. As Alan puts it: "We're a nation of gardeners but I wouldn't expect anyone else to pay to look at my roses."

Before you start fashioning a small plasticine model of Alan and sticking pins in it, read on. He says he still takes unsolicited manuscripts seriously.

Indeed, he publishes two or three books a year that have come from the slush pile – often in the areas of humour or travel.

Looking at unsolicited manuscripts he believes is something publishers "should do", mentioning in passing that Margaret Drabble's first novel came from the slush pile as did Iain Banks's. I can add here that I know the brilliant Minette Walters did, too. (It's my book so I can be as subjective as I like!)

But as you will gather from the above figures, for you to have any hope of similar success, you are going to need to stand out in a big way. And stand out fast.

Francesca Liversidge at Transworld gives a manuscript thirty pages to grab her. "It if doesn't," she says, "I usually skip to halfway to see if there's any improvement." I would suspect this is more than a lot of readers would do and you must remember that Francesca is a publishing director with a big job and has an assistant to vet everything first. You've already got past one hurdle if you reach her (or, you could say, several since Transworld's company policy is not to accept anything unsolicited) so, as a general rule, I'd say you've got to do that grabbing a lot sooner.

Sherise Hobbs, a fiction editor at Headline, says she looks for "an opening paragraph that hooks me immediately. If I haven't been engaged by the first few pages it's a bad sign."

Suzanne Baboneau, publishing director at Simon and Schuster, also looks for an arresting first paragraph. She also asks herself if there is a "clear sense of direction, good title, sense of the market and – most importantly – can the author write!"

"Is it pacily written?" asks Susan Opie, editorial director at Harper Collins. "Are the characters immediately interesting? Do I care about them enough to read more? Or does it feel like a dozen others I've read this month…"

Carolyn Caughey, an editorial director at Hodder & Stoughton, simply goes for "compulsive readability" which, she is the first to admit, is difficult to quantify. But it shouldn't be.

We've all read books we literally couldn't bear to put down – so ask yourself, is yours like that? If in doubt, test it out on someone else – an avid reader whose opinion you trust (not your mum, remember, and probably not your partner either) and see what they think.

Even if you are lucky enough to grab your editor by the throat the book still has to pass muster with Publicity, Marketing and Sales – all the other people I mentioned earlier. Every book is bought by committee these days – usually at weekly Acquisitions Meetings after projected sales figures and forecasts various have been assembled. (I well remember pacing the floor in a state of high neurosis the day I knew Transworld were deliberating on mine.)

It is knowing this that makes many an embittered wannabe complain that you only get published these days if you are famous/a celebrity/blonde and gorgeous/know the chairman of the company/have slept with same. This is complete rubbish.

Nobody had ever heard of me when I got my first two-book deal and other totally unknown authors are taken on all the time.

"Only the book matters," says Alan Samson. When I spoke to him, Weidenfeld & Nicolson had recently taken on a book called *Salmon Fishing in the Yemen*. Its author Paul Torday is retired and in his late fifties. "It's a great title and a great book," says Alan. "And no-one here said: 'What a shame it's not by a blonde woman.'"

Alan was also in the process of taking on another book by an author of retirement age, who was an East End midwife. "It makes a refreshing change to read books by older people," he says. "Promotability has many heads."

Francesca Liversidge admits it is easier to get the attention of the sales, marketing and publicity departments if an author has some sort of notoriety or fame but says that first : "I have to love their work. Absolutely."

"The bottom line," says Susan Opie, "is you can get away with a less than good book once but if the hype isn't matched by the content then you're unlikely to manage it twice. Publishers are happy to take the risk for a real celebrity in whom there is a genuine interest. But overall we're looking to build the careers of writers, as that's what readers seem to want – and for that you need the right content. The rest is a bonus."

Sherise Hobbs is only interested in "the novel itself". Overall, so is Carolyn Caughey, although she points out: "What will get a novelist somewhere sometimes is their "real" life – not necessarily as a celebrity, but perhaps as a cop for a police story, a lifestyle guru for a lifestyle story. Or indeed an unmarried urban 25-year old with a job in advertising and a boyfriend in television for chick lit. But THEN we really have to love their work. Non-fiction is different – a person with a great story to tell can be matched up with a ghost writer if potential sales are high enough."

"It's all about communication," says Alan Samson. "Not only in the written word but the spoken, too. "It's important that an author can shape up well in interviews, for example. Being articulate is much more important than being pretty…"

So there you go – don't despair that you look like the back of a bus. Have you got the gift of the gab? Let's say you have. And a great story, a gripping first paragraph, tantalising plot and page-turning quality to die for.

So you go through *The Writer's Handbook* or *Writers' and Artists' Yearbook* with your highlighter pen in hand – making sure that your targeted publishers do actually publish your sort of stuff (no point sending your Aga Saga to a small niche outfit that only publishes books about Scientology) and you find that all the publishers most suited to your particular work of genius don't take unsolicited manuscripts. What do you do now?

I am a firm believer that you don't get anywhere without taking the odd risk and that rules are made to be broken but you have to do it carefully or you will just hack everyone off before you've even started.

They may not thank me for saying this, but the truth is that even publishers who have a stringent policy of "no unsolicited manuscripts" are still in the business to capture the next big thing. If you target the right person, say the right things in the right way, and politely ask if you might send in your manuscript, they will probably say yes – just in case it's as good as you say it is.

When I started approaching publishers by a variety of means – mostly email – all replied and not a single one refused to look at my book.

I sold my first two novels to a publisher who doesn't officially take unsolicited manuscripts but, as you will know if you read the previous chapter (I do hope you're concentrating and not jumping about all over the place), I did email and get permission to submit first.

Hodder editor Carolyn Caughy says: "We don't accept unsolicited scripts at all. Unagented authors sometimes contact us after a personal meeting or via a personal recommendation, perhaps from an existing author, but in that case we regard it as a solicited script."

Where can you contrive to meet these publishers personally? Well, I met Carolyn at a Romantic Novelists Association bash so if you're writing contemporary fiction in which someone at least vaguely has an interest in someone else, you could do worse than to join yourself, as I have explained earlier.

The Society of Authors, too, is another good stamping ground for authors, agents, publishers and the like (for details of both see chapter on Writers' Organisations).

But however you make your initial contact, above all remember that if you send your book direct to a publisher and they read it then they are doing you a favour – not the other way round.

If they take you on and your book sells a million copies and makes them a packet, then might be the time to start expecting a bit of a say in things, but right now, a publisher owes you nothing. If you are a wannabe and start throwing your weight around, you will do yourself no good at all.

A few dos and don'ts:

Make sure you're targeting the right person. Don't send the book out into a void. Addressing it simply to "Harper Collins" or "The ABC Publishing Company" is a sure way of it getting only a cursory glance – if you're lucky.

It's a good idea to check the person listed in *The Writer's Handbook* is still actually there – a polite call to the switchboard number should confirm this. Spell their name right. Make sure they publish what you are offering. Alan Samson says he often gets sent stuff that is totally inappropriate. "We don't do business books, we don't do touchy-feely therapy books, yet we get sent them all the time – and from agents too!"

Don't be too clever. It's best not to attempt to be funny either (unless you are very confident that you genuinely are) and if you're going to try a spot of sucking-up, don't make it obvious.

I can tell you now that all the publishers I spoke to agreed that flattery will get you precisely nowhere. "Flattery just annoys me," says Carolyn Caughey.

Alan Samson agrees personal flattery is "counterproductive" but says some knowledge of the company and what they publish is good. "If an author wrote to say they'd enjoyed certain of our books that would show they'd done their research which can only help."

For those of you who are now disappointed, Susan Opie from Harper Collins is prepared to give flattery a test-drive.

"Will it get you anywhere? I'd like to say not but if anyone would like to try sending large, expensive gifts, preferably of the chocolate variety, we could see if that's true…" (I trust, Susan, when the sackloads arrive you will send some this way).

Write a sensible covering letter, sticking to the point – what the book is about, what genre it's in, any particular marketing hooks it's got, some brief facts about yourself.

Don't make things up – Francesca Liversidge says it particularly annoys her when prospective authors imply that she requested to see something (I'm not surprised – it's a totally ridiculous thing to do) – or deliver it yourself, dressed as a chicken with a rose between your teeth. Yes, it may get someone's attention but won't mean they like your book any better. Susanne Baboneau's areas of irritation also include: authors demanding to see an editor or hassling them with phone calls. "Never be too pushy," she counsels. "Let the material speak for itself." But show you CARE, urges Alan Samson. "What is really irritating is when someone says: I've written the beginning of six novels and I don't care which one you publish. Perhaps I can come in and we can kick around a few ideas… Well, we have our own ideas, thank-you, why would we want yours? We don't want a smorgasbord of ideas – we want some Passion!"

Don't throw a strop when they turn it down. That's simply stupid and you run the risk of going straight in the bin next time (when, who knows, you might have hit lucky – lots of authors get published on their third or fourth novel rather than the first). Sounds obvious, but amazingly, some rejected wannabes do then write in with abuse.

Francesca Liversidge says she gets "the odd threatening letter" – one does wonder what the author in question thought THAT would achieve – while Alan Samson tells wonderful tales of wannabe authors who have put a hairpin or similar on page 250 and then written indignantly to complain, when the manuscript has been rejected, that they know it wasn't read all the way through because their marker is still in place.

Again – no point making a fuss. It may not have been read in its entirety but think about it. If a reader doesn't read all the way to the end it's because they thought the beginning was crap. Live with it.

As Alan says: "You wouldn't need to recite the whole of Hamlet to show if you had any acting ability. I've been in this business a long time – the first couple of pages tells me if it's any good."

Suzanne Baboneau agrees. "You know immediately if something ain't going to work."

Keep the faith. Remember every publisher longs to discover the next best-seller – they want to find the jewel in their slushpile just as much as you want to be it.

And while nobody can deny it is very hard to get published these days, Carolyn Caughey surprisingly says "it is probably easier to get a first novel accepted than it used to be." She takes the view that things are toughest for those already published. "It's harder to make a comeback after a setback, now," she explains. "Our customers read the figures on what the last one sold and if it's bad news it's all but impossible to get them to take another chance."

Sherise Hobbs points out that while more and more books being published means more competition, the "huge consumer appetite for books" is also a great opportunity for publishers. They are, she says, "always on the lookout for that exciting new voice to launch. When these do come along, competition among publishers is intense."

Suzanne Baboneau, who says about 50% of the manuscripts Simon and Schuster gets are unsolicited, ends on an upbeat note:

"Yes, the market is crowded, the pressure from the trade ever greater, but the good will always out."

It's a fine mantra to hold on to so if you've got as far as writing a whole book, and editing it and polishing it and you're sure it's the very best you can do, and you think that best is pretty good, then you may as well try your hardest to sell it to someone.

You only need one publisher to love it – and that, after all, is what they're there for. Francesca Liversidge sums up: "After 27 years in this business I still love it to bits. Nothing beats the excitement of discovering a wonderful new talent or one of our authors breaking through."

Publishers rely on writers to make their living. They are on our side, not against us. But there is a small thing worth remembering: we do have to be able to write!

Rejections and How to Deal with Them

Let us assume you can write, and write well. You will still get rejections. I particularly like the analogy novelist Daniel Blythe draws on the subject:

Sending your stuff out to publishers is a lot like asking girls to sleep with you. Most of them will stalk haughtily away, laugh, or possibly even slap you, but it's worth it for the one who says yes. A writer's career is entirely based around attempting to improve the shag-to-slap ratio.

If you start your writing career by writing short stories or pitching articles it does at least give you some practice in having to take it on the chin. Rejections are one of the occupational hazards of being that sort of writer and even the most successful scribes chalk them up more often than you might imagine.

Della Galton has sold over 500 stories, written a dozen serials for the women's magazines and published a novel. "Rejections? I get hundreds, of course – part of the job," she says matter-of-factly. Although she wasn't always so sanguine.

Once she had eleven short story rejections on the same day that a completed serial was turned down and says, "I cried buckets."

But the next month she saw more sales than she'd ever had in a four-week period and has since sold ten of those eleven stories.

Proving that – in the world of short stories at least – just because the first editor doesn't want it, it doesn't mean it's no good.

Let us imagine you submit a 1000 word story about an Art teacher and a dog called Daisy. These are the things you can't possibly know: the editor has very recently bought two other stories about teachers. The editor is allergic to dogs. She has a good store of 1000 word stories – what she really wants now is 2000 words for her double-page slot. Her husband left her last week for a woman called Daisy. And the Art teacher at her primary school emotionally scarred her for life by pouring scorn on her still life of a milk bottle and two tomatoes...

Which is why when you get a piece of work rejected you should consider any criticism that has been made, deciding if you think it is valid and worth acting on and then **send it out again**! If you're not in it, you can't win it, as they used to say about the lottery (proving that some people get in print for merely stating the obvious). You only ever need one editor or agent to say YES and you've made it.

Obviously you do have to keep a tab on what they *are* saying. If seven different agents say the ending to your novel is weak or the middle sags then it probably does. On the other hand if only one publisher says he found your heroine irritating and everyone else seems to love her, then stick to your guns, leave the heroine exactly as she is and keep searching for someone to take her on.

As novelist Lisa Jewell sensibly says: "Play the numbers game. Send your manuscript to as many agents as possible. It doesn't matter if thirty agents reject your submission. You only need one agent to like it. Prepare yourself for rejection. All the best people get rejected. Take it as part of the unique experience of being a writer."

And I would say be realistic about those rejections, too. Don't start asking "why?" or trying to get into correspondence over them. All you will do is waste the rejecter's time and irritate them for the next time you want to send something in.

Don't read too much into anyone being nice to you, either. When agents send your manuscript back saying "I didn't absolutely fall in love with it…" that means they don't want it. It does not mean they can be persuaded to change their minds. Of course it is nice if they are kind people who find something positive to say, but at the end of the day, a no is a no.

And at least a blunt one cannot be misinterpreted. Much as I wasn't overly thrilled at the time, I have a grudging admiration for the agent who once wrote to me:

"I'm afraid I don't like these chapters enough to feel I can encourage you. I found them derivative and not terribly funny."

It's because you are bound to get some like this that I always urge writers to have loads of work out at any one time and, if approaching agents or publishers, to send several query letters simultaneously.

That way you've always got a ray of hope left when the first rejections come, although I should probably also tell you that The Fearsome One takes the view that if you are submitting to more than one agency at a time it is COURTEOUS (the capitals are hers) to mention this.

The late fantasy writer David Gemmell, who was always very kind to me when I was starting out, used to amuse audiences by reading out extracts from some of the more scathing rejections that he had had in his early days. E.g. *"You mention in your resume that you are working as a lorry driver's mate for Pepsi Cola. This is an occupation not without merit. Good luck with it."*

I never knew if they were real or not but he made them sound hilarious.

Which is why, even if you feel like screwing them up and hurling them against the wall, it is worth keeping all the letters you get.

The most blistering rejection I ever received brought tears to my eyes. It used words like "unfunny" (what, me??) "tedious" and "dull". I thought briefly of throwing myself under a bus but instead swore that one day, when the same novel was published (*Raising the Roof,* Bantam, in case by some oversight you've never bought it) I would read it aloud to a group of writers and laugh about it. It took nearly four years to realise that ambition but it was a very sweet moment when it came.

Just so you can feel comforted by the fact that you can get a rejection this bad and still get published in the end, I will give you the edited highlights here:

"the manuscript lacks originality"
"the story isn't sufficiently compelling"
"the characters fall easily into stereotypes"
"the novel struggles to find its pace"
"I found her, as a narrator, quite dull"
"The heroine… doesn't seem very bright or funny, just a bit whiney…"
"The humour isn't handled very well"
"Her gags are predictable"

This was all in the one letter. You can imagine it took several drinks to overcome.

But just so you don't think it's not worth buying to see for yourself: here are some nice things other agents said:

"I did enjoy this"
"you have a very original voice"
"you write well"
"I like the energy and humour of your writing but … "(there is always a BUT) and

"You have a great voice and lots of energy and capacity to keep the story developing and moving along strongly. The characters bounce off each other well and there's a lightness of touch which is absolutely what's needed for this kind of story. Clever you. But here's the rub…"

There is always going to be one of those after praise like that, too.

All you can do is keep your fingers crossed and your spirits up. Brace yourself for most to say No but remember that sooner or later someone might say –

210

Ten top things to do when you get a rejection

1) Eat chocolate.
2) Get drunk.
3) Throw the rejection letter on the fire.
4) Keep the rejection letter – swearing hysterically that one day you will read it aloud as an after-dinner speech when your manuscript is on the best-seller lists and the short-sighted agent or publisher who couldn't see they were sitting on a work of genius is washed up and poverty-stricken.
5) Bore your friends with tales of how many times Harry Potter got turned down and keep muttering: this is what happened to the Beatles.
6) Re-read something you've written before that was published to remind yourself that you can do it. (If you haven't had anything published before, re-read something you're proud of. Or ask your mum to.)
7) Affect a hollow laugh and say things like: "you can't win 'em all" or "I didn't want to be with a great big publisher anyway…"
8) Be realistic. Remember that rejections are all part of being a writer.
9) Send the same piece out again the very same day (check you haven't spilled your wine and chocolate on it first).
10) Have another drink.

Keeping the Faith and Keeping your chin up

I've always thought it would be a very good idea if someone published a directory in which you could look up any successful book from the last twenty years and see how many times it was rejected before a publisher took it on and how many other books its author had written previously that never made it into print.

This could be a great source of comfort to those whose literary attempts have been turned down and could remind us all that the next book we write might be The One.

For remember that relatively few authors, in the whole scheme of things, hit first time lucky.

Alice Jolly's first novel has never been published. "It came very close," she explains. "Editors were full of praise for it but marketing people described it as 'too small'. But I got my second and third novels published and am working on a fourth."

Agent Carole Blake in her book *From Pitch to Publication* has spoken of the countless rejections and "four years of hard slog" it took to sell Barbara Erskine's first novel, *Lady of Hay* (Harper Collins). That book has now sold well over a million copies and Barbara has written eight best-selling novels since.

Carolyn Graham, the author behind the hugely successful *Midsomer Murders* series, describes a "rambling Gothic horror" that is still in her garden shed and novelist Daniel Blythe says: "I think we all have our embarrassing bottom-drawer novel. Mine was ghastly."

Kate Walker, who, you may remember, has published over 50 books for Harlequin Mills & Boon, got there on her third attempt: the first two novels were turned down.

More famously, *Lord of the Rings* was rejected a number of times and as I've said already but it's worth saying again, so was Harry Potter – an "I turned down the Beatles" decision for a few poor souls in publishing.

And comedy writer Ray Allen recalls:

"My first attempt at a television comedy script was rejected by a producer with the advice: 'To be a comedy writer you need three things, talent, a sense of humour and an ear for dialogue. Unfortunately, you don't appear to have any of these. Give up!'

Luckily for us he didn't.

His second script was *Some Mothers Do 'Ave 'Em*, which he wrote when "he stopped crying ". He says now: "So my advice is to take advice, but not all of it!"

So, summing up, you may as well toughen up now and learn how to keep positive for this is not a game for those who easily fall by the wayside. "I wrote at least a million words before I got published," says Rebecca Tope, the author of 12 crime novels, and even once they are in print, not all authors have a smooth ride.

The prolific novelist Susan Lewis faced a setback after years of success. "You've heard the countless stories of authors whose books were turned down by 20 publishers before finally hitting the shelves? In my case it was my 20th book that was turned down and it's never seen the light of day." She describes it as "quite a blow" but says philosophically: "I'm sure I was wrong and my publisher was right." She has since written another book *A French Affair* (Arrow) and says, "So now we're both happy."

Novelist Tamara McKinley is happy too but she's also had her ups and downs.

"I learned very early on that writers have to become thick-skinned," she says. "Getting published is the goal, but that is only the start of a very long journey." Tamara's first two thrillers were published but the next three were turned down and, thoroughly depressed, she was on the point of giving up.

"Then I thought about a story I had written back in the days when I was still struggling to be published, and thought that as I had little to lose, I'd give it a try." This was turned down too at first – but *Matilda's Last Waltz* (Piatkus) has since been translated into sixteen languages and sold over a million copies world-wide.

After six more sagas set in Australia, she decided to move on "to grow and stretch my ability" and wrote *Lands Beyond the Sea* (Hodder) for a new publisher. "There is life after rejection," she says "and it's very sweet."

Victoria Connelly has seen how success can spring from unexpected quarters too.

After a stream of what she describes as "very nice rejections" from UK publishers, she had all but given up hope of her novel, *Flights of Angels*, ever being published, when her agent told her that Germany was interested. A bidding war followed and a lucrative book deal. German publishers Heyne launched Victoria's novel as a lead title and it sold 20,000 copies in the first three weeks. Since then there's been a book club edition and they've bought her second book, too.

"It's really been the most exciting and unexpected experience," enthuses Victoria. "It's proved that there's a whole world of book-loving countries out there and you shouldn't give up hope if you don't succeed with your first round of submissions."

You have to listen to the voice in your head and do what you know is right," adds Tamara McKinley. "Have faith in your ability to tell stories, and never, never give up. Grit your teeth and prove to yourself and others that you were right all along."

They are stirring words but I know how very upsetting and disheartening it is if you have sent your book out to every agent and publisher in the land and everyone has give you a resounding thumbs down.

There is no quick fix but don't jump off a cliff just yet. All is not lost.

Firstly, you can always write another book – don't forget all those above who didn't get there the first time of trying – and secondly, if you're really determined to do something with your first effort, there are still a couple of avenues open to you.

E-publishing

Kate Johnson is the author of thirteen e-books and novellas, including the Sophie Green Mysteries from Samhain Publishing, and, writing as Cat Marsters, erotic romance from Ellora's Cave and Changeling Press.

She explains the process by comparing e-books to downloadable music files. In the same way that you might download a track straight onto your computer rather than buying a CD, so, instead of buying a paperback, you download a text file directly from the publisher.

"The submissions process for e-publishing is pretty similar to submitting your manuscript to a print publisher," she says. "You get your manuscript in the best possible state, research your publishers, then send it out. The biggest differences are that you send it by email—thereby saving what can be huge amounts of postage, particularly internationally—and that most, if not all, e-publishers accept unagented submissions."

Kate tells me that the author signs a contract as they would with a traditional publishing house but that royalties are much more generous at 30–40% of the cover price.

"E-books are released simultaneously all over the world. Anyone with an internet connection can access the publisher's website, and anyone with a credit card can buy your book. There's no postage, and no wait for shipping: the download is more or less instantaneous. You'll have readers all over the English-speaking world, and beyond: I've had fanmail from Finland and Pakistan."

On the downside, Kate says, you have to do a lot of the promotional work yourself and you'll be chained to your computer as almost all of this will be online.

It's time-consuming for another reason, too. "Every time someone asks you what you do for a living, you have to spend half an hour explaining what e-publishing actually is, and that just because you can't hold the book in your hand, it doesn't mean it's not a real book."

You'll be in good company if you give it a whirl. Stephen King tried it with his e-story *Riding the Bullet* and more than 200,000 customers on

Barnesandnoble.com requested free copies when the company held a 24–hour promotion.

"One day," said a spokeswoman, "there's going to be a time when every book in print will be available in digital format."

Let's hope they keep the paper versions too – it's bad enough sitting in front of a computer all day without having to take one to bed.

Self-publishing

Self-publishing has never been more respectable. Over the last few years, books that were initially self-published have become word-of-mouth phenomenons, won prizes or been taken on by one of the big boys.

The wonderful Asian writer, Preethi Nair, is a shining example of what can be achieved with flair and determination. Preethi trudged around every bookshop in London asking them to stock her first, self-published, novel – *Gypsy Masala* – adopting a separate persona to do her own PR. The result was some incredible sales, a three-book deal from Harper Collins and a BBC adaptation – so never think it can't be done.

However, we have to face facts. Despite the occasional fairytale ending, the reality is that there are a whole heap of shiny new tomes from mainstream publishers already jostling for space on the shelves and – let's be honest here – a lot of self-published books are total bilge.

But if you really believe in your book and have exhausted all mainstream possibilities, then you go for it.

I can't begin to attempt to tell you how to go about it here – for a start I've no experience of it – but the internet is, predictably, the source of a huge amount of information and dozens of books have been written on the subject. To get you started, *Writing Magazine* has published a couple of guides to the whole process and I had a quick shimmy through them for you.

I can tell you that the two biggest advertisers in there were Matador **www.troubador.co.uk/matador** and Halftitle **www.halftitle.co.uk**. Both have comprehensive and professional-looking websites and seem to know what they are talking about. Matador offers both a free guide to self-publishing and a sample copy of one of their books.

I would guess that buying in the right expertise is pretty much like buying anything else – you'll need to speak to several different outfits, get prices and follow your instincts. But if your instincts are strong, follow them.

It paid off when the established children's author, Jill Paton Walsh, followed hers and self-published *Knowledge of Angels* (now Black Swan) – she was short-listed for the 1994 Booker Prize – and if you enjoyed the film *Cold Mountain* you might like to know that the book by Charles Frazier was self-published too and spent over a year on *The New York Times* Bestseller List.

Closer to home, short-story writer Ruth Cocks from Selsey undertook a huge project when she decided to self-publish a book to raise funds for various sea-faring charities, including the Selsey RNLI. *Voices from the Sea* is a remarkable collection of true stories from fishermen, lifeboat crew, divers and coastguards – all sorts of people with experiences at sea.

It took Ruth sixteen months of interviews and then another nine months to edit the 1,200,000 words and 1,400 photos she'd gathered before she single-handedly arranged the typesetting and printing. She describes it as a "mammoth task" but to date sales of the book have raised nearly £20,000 (see **www.voicesfromthesea.net** to find out more or to buy a copy yourself) and Ruth is "over the moon." As well she might be.

Ruth has donated all her profits to charity but do note that this was a money-making venture. She paid a unit price of £X for the production of each book and sold them at £2X with the difference coming her way. This is the main idea of SELF- publishing which is not to be confused with any other sort where you are expected to shell out for the pleasure of seeing your work in print and not make a bean back, namely:

Vanity Publishing

The clue is in the name. This is for sad losers. Forget it.

Deals and How to Celebrate

I don't think I have ever felt such pure, unadulterated joy as I did when I sold my first novel. As I wrote at the time: imagine all the orgasms you've ever had, a bottle of Bollinger and a packet of Kettle Chips – it's better than that.

Kate Harrison describes getting her first deal as "like drinking champagne without the hangover, all fizzy inside."

Mine wasn't *like* drinking champagne, it *was* drinking it – I was slaughtered for about a week – and I expect I did get a hangover but I was too happy to care. For months afterwards, whenever anything went wrong and I was feeling tense or grouchy, I would suddenly think: but my book is going to be published, and hug myself instead.

When you get your first deal, hang on to that huggy feeling for as long as you can. You'll have things to worry about again, soon enough. I have heard several authors say that the best time in a writer's career are the months between getting the deal and the book actually coming out – often about a year of them, in fact. It goes really quickly because there's lots going on – edits, copy edits, page proofs to check, cover designs to look at and launch parties to plan…

Launch Parties

Whether or not your publisher puts on a launch for you, contributes towards it or you do it all yourself, make sure you throw the biggest bash you can afford.

You have achieved something amazing and it deserves to be celebrated. Buy a wonderful outfit, gather up as many of your friends as you can find (the more the merrier – they'll all feel duty-bound to buy a book) make sure the books themselves are piled high, get the booze flowing and have a ball.

A small word of advice for the amply-built – despite all I said earlier this is one occasion where you might like to consider losing some weight first. Suddenly all sorts of photographers will be popping up and the sort who work for local papers are often notorious for using a wide-angled lens and bringing out one's inner grossness.

I intended to diet for six weeks before my first launch party so I could waft about looking suitably stunning and about-to-be-famous, but somehow I forgot and was so excited I kept eating peanuts.

Which was unfortunate, considering my choice of slinky, clinging, so-expensive-it-still-makes-me-light-headed-to-think-about-it, rubber-look dress, which, by the time the fateful evening came, I could only just waddle in.

It was still one of the best nights of my life, proving you do not have to be thin to have fun. Photographs show me clutching a huge glass of champagne and bearing a strong resemblance to a black pudding.

WHICH IS ONLY THE BEGINNING...

Fantasies and Myths

When I was consumed with longing to get a book published, I never really thought beyond that. I sort of assumed, if I turned my attention there at all, that the book would be automatically stocked by all the bookshops and then shoppers would wander into them and buy it.

In moments of fantasy, I might imagine this happening in such quantity that I would shoot up the best-sellers lists, become Book of the Month and get my own window display. Ha ha.

I had no idea that there were up to 10,000 new books a month published and that bookshops picked and chose the ones they were prepared to stock, or that any promotions were paid for.

I didn't realise that if there was only one copy of your book, spine out, under W (down in that dim corner where the cobwebs lurk) that its chances of it being sold to a passing browser were zilch.

It hadn't occurred to me that only the select few get into the supermarkets or get displayed at airports or on stations. I didn't realise that Word-of-Mouth is everything and that as a brand new author that nobody has heard of, the best thing you can do is to make sure as many people as possible hear of you pretty quickly.

I have, as they say, learnt on the job.

Back to Earth – The Grim Reality of Sales

When I first met Sara-Jade Piper she was working as part of the central buying team at Waterstones Head Office, selecting new titles, and organising promotions for all stores.

You would be surprised at how many issues they consider when deciding which books to stock.

"For new titles, you look at many different factors," says Sara-Jade. "Some are no-brainers. The latest Grisham, Keyes, Jamie Oliver – regardless of the details, you are going to buy it."

But for less-well-known authors there are various other considerations.

Does the author have a track record? What is his or her sales history on previous titles? For a paperback edition, how did the hardback go? How much publicity/press/TV exposure is the author and publisher planning? Has the book has been shortlisted for a prize?

Has the author been courted by the publishers and is there a buzz already surrounding the book?

All these factors can be discussed, says Sara-Jade, "before you even see a copy of the book."

The bookstore is also of course concerned with the bottom line – what margin they are getting from the publisher and what promotions they are willing to pay for – but this is something the author has no control over.

It makes a big difference, though, if you are what they call "Front of Store or "Face out in Section". As Sara-Jade says, "It will cost your publisher money – but your sales will increase hugely if customers can find your book first in sea of 100,000 others."

A lot of this is luck of the draw – it will depend on how big a marketing budget your publishers have allocated you, which in turn depends on how high they rate the chances of your success. Nothing you can do about that – save try and convince them you are star material – and it's disappointing if you only appear in a handful of shops in very small quantities, but you'll have to live with it. And hope.

Sara-Jade does however make the following suggestions to give yourself the best possible chance:

"Go into your local bookshop and make friends (but don't become a stalker) with the booksellers. Offer yourself for meet-the-author events, sign some copies, ask the booksellers if they've read your book, and don't be scared to ask for feedback. Their recommendations to customers are worth their weight in gold. They will champion your book in a way that money just cannot buy".

This is all good advice but you may need to do other things too. The most useful one would be to get yourself on *Richard & Judy*.

Richard & Judy

In the old days when bookshops were quiet, fusty places run by bald men with thick glasses, and all the books were arranged alphabetically, your newly-published writer had a fairly limited set of dreams. They could hope to get some good reviews, to gradually build a readership, to one day hit the best-seller lists by word of mouth or by being shortlisted for a prize.

Then, when the net book agreement went and bookshops started sporting sofas and coffee shops, it was, as we've discovered, about being in a three-for-two deal, hoping your publisher would shell out for you to be Book of the Week and that the buyer for Tesco's or Asda's would take a shine to your cover.

"If you're not in Smith's Travel and at least one supermarket," I remember a well-known author saying, some years ago, "you might as well pack up and go home."

But now there is just the one fantasy that every writer with any sense shares – the catch-all, umbrella dream that will bring all of the above and more in one fell swoop – and that is to be chosen by *Richard & Judy*.

Or more accurately, by Amanda Ross, Head of Cactus TV, the company that produces the show, and the force behind the *Richard & Judy* Book Club.

Hailed as the most powerful person in publishing today, she is the one all the publishers and agents want to befriend. The one that authors weave a daydream around – the sort where they just happen to be passing by as she falls into a lake or out of a tree and they are able to stop and save her life. Or the one where they get her car out of a snowstorm by fashioning a new fan belt out of a pair of tights or rescue her favourite dog from a rabbit hole.

So naturally when I got the opportunity to interview her in person for this book, I leapt at it like a tramp on a kipper.

"I wanted to see how scary you were," I told her. She cackled. In my mind she'd been a peroxide ice queen, all cold glamour, scarlet lipstick and killer heels. The reality was softer, friendlier and decidedly down to earth. She'd just been clearing up dog sick, after Poppet, her Tibetan terrier had heralded my arrival by throwing up on the carpet. "Oh yes," she said, gesturing around. "I'm very scary and cool – my office is a pit."

Her office is nice, actually – homely and full of books – and not the high-tech chrome and glass affair I'd been expecting from one who exerts such a staggering influence over the publishing industry.

Between January 2004 and May 2006 the *Richard & Judy* Book Club featured thirty books. During that time readers went out and bought 8.3 million copies of them at a cost of £55 million pounds. One in every four of the top 100 books sold in the UK in 2006 was recommended by the show. Since its inception, the Book Club has made at least eight of the authors chosen into millionaires and books that are showcased routinely go straight to the top of the best-seller charts.

"One publisher told me if I could just choose two books from them a year, one in the Summer Read and one in the Best Read then their annual turnover would be complete," says Amanda calmly.

Blimey! No wonder they all get cross with her when the lists are announced and their favourites aren't on them. Or that's what I'd read anyway. "Is it true?" I ask Amanda. "Of course it is," she says.

So when she first conceived the idea of the Book Club did she have any idea what sort of dynamite she was sitting on?

She shakes her head. "Probably completely the opposite. When we first gave the idea to Channel Four they didn't want to do it, because they thought books hadn't worked on telly before. They agreed we could try but said: on your head be it."

And on her head it was. The outcome has been truly remarkable. It seems as though every agent and publisher I've spoken to while writing this book has mentioned the *Richard & Judy* phenomenon in some context or other. Publisher Alan Samson described it simply as "a great force for good".

For an author it can be totally life-changing. Joseph O' Connor's *The Star of the Sea* (Vintage) had sold just 4,000 copies when Amanda picked it for the Book Club in 2004 – sales have since risen to well over a million. Do the sums yourself.

But it's not all about money. Dorothy Koomson, whose third novel *My Best Friend's Girl* (Sphere) was selected as a Summer Read in 2006, describes being chosen as "one of the sweetest, most fulfilling feelings in the world".

"For me, the best thing about *Richard & Judy* wasn't the increase in sales," she says, "although I'm grateful for it, don't get me wrong. It was the fact that it was recognition for something I love doing. Writing is hard work, I cry, don't sleep and fret over every book, but I do love it. It brings me immense joy and deep satisfaction. And the fact that people I've watched on the television since I was in my teens were going to talk about it... Wow. Even now, that still makes me go, 'wow.'"

Martin Davies, author of *The Conjuror's Bird* (Hodder) which was chosen for the Best Read in January 2006 doesn't harp on about sales either. "Of course it's fantastic publicity," he says. "It means that you can go into pretty much any bookshop and see your book within ten seconds of walking in. But what I got from it was more than that. It was the encouragement on a personal level from Amanda and the Cactus TV people. Them choosing the book and really having faith in it."

His sales did get a boost, however, even though he received what Amanda describes as "the worst review ever" at the hands of Tony Robinson. "Richard and Judy and I loved that book," she says, "but what Tony said did it a lot of damage."

It has still sold in excess of 150,000 copies. Nick Sayers, Martin Davies' editor at Hodder, describes it as "faultlessly written – a warm and generous book" and says that despite Tony Robinson's disappointing reaction, the book certainly benefited from the exposure it got.

Martin himself is philosophical about his book being "savaged".

"It was good TV and it's probably good for the audience to look at that sort of thing and think: oh, it's not just a cosy club with people being told to say nice things." He has nothing but praise for the whole programme. "I was enormously impressed that they thought to make popular TV out of books and then that they had the courage to stick in some pretty challenging choices. Picking my book was a risk because it was completely unknown. I'll always be grateful for that. Amanda Ross is a star."

And so to the million dollar question that's on everyone's lips: what makes a *Richard & Judy* book? Dorothy Koomson's editor, Joanne Dickinson, feels that *My Best Friend's Girl*, got there because it is "intelligent, well-written fiction, incredibly moving, unafraid to tackle strong subjects, with characters that you're really engaged with from page one." Plenty of readers have clearly agreed with her – at the time of writing, the novel's been on the best-seller lists for over six months and has sold 500,000 copies.

Amanda said at the time it was chosen that it was "definitely the best chick lit" she'd read, a genre she admits she finds "difficult". So what does she like best? What makes the perfect *Richard & Judy* book?

"There isn't a perfect book," she insists. "Every one is completely different and does different things for me. Or if there is, each one is perfect in its own right. *Cloud Atlas* is perfect because it's a work of genius by someone who should have been more widely known than he was before and it's probably one of the best books ever – that's why it won the Booker Prize. *Moondust* was perfect for me because the discussion was so interesting, because you thought: oh-my-god I did not know that about those astronauts; it made my hair stand on end. *Labyrinth* was perfect because it was the kind of thing you can't put down. *The Farm* was perfect because if was a snapshot of history…"

I told Amanda that I knew a writer who had given up writing chick lit in order to work on "a big fat book" – one conceived with the sole aim of getting into the *Richard & Judy* Book Club. Did she think it could be done that consciously?

"Well, if she knows how to do that, then she's a genius," she said immediately. "I don't think anybody can guess what's going to be in a *Richard & Judy* book, including me, until I actually read one that is. And certainly don't make it a fat book," she adds. "Fat is not good; thin is better. I'm asking people to read eight books in eight weeks and they can't all be weighty tomes."

When I persisted in trying to get Amanda to define the archetypal Book Club read (I'd like to write one too!) she explained something interesting:

"One defining thing is, I'll never, ever choose a book that's the same as one I've done before. I never want to do *The Lovely Bones* again, ever. And this last year obviously *Labyrinth* was a massive success so publishers are saying: here's another *Labyrinth*. But I'm never going to do another one! You can't have the same sort of book twice because people remember the last one. They don't want to read it again."

OK, so what do they all have in common in very general terms? Emotional truth perhaps?

"Takeaway and sofa chat," says Amanda. For the uninitiated, we are not talking pizza-to-go, but the lasting effect a book has on its reader – its thought-provoking, haunting quality – and what gets said about it.

As each book is presented on *Richard & Judy*, a short film is shown of the author talking about his or her novel and then Richard and Judy discuss its themes and appeal with a couple of celebrity guests – all sitting on the sofa, of course. "This is the most important thing," says Amanda. "It doesn't matter how much I've loved a book, if it doesn't make good sofa chat, then it isn't going to work."

I am fascinated to know what sort of lengths people will go to, to get their books on the show. "Do people send you things or camp on the doorstep?" I ask, secretly wondering if there is any mileage in filling her office with flowers or sending round a crate of champagne.

"I get a lot of letters," she says. "Often from people who've met me briefly and now expect me to pick their book. It's not like that," she says firmly. "There's so much riding on it. I'm not going to pick someone's book just because I know them or like them and I'm certainly not going to pick someone's book who thinks I should pick them because I met them once in 1976."

She is generally sympathetic to the plight of the unknown writer, though. "With 10,000 new books a month, how can anybody possibly punch through – the way the bookshops are run now they don't leave things in the shops long enough – you only get a few weeks which is silly because it doesn't allow time for the word of mouth to take hold." She tries to help the unpublished, too.

She showed me a letter she had received that was rolled up inside a cardboard cut-out of a cactus. "People are quite creative in how they send letters. I'll have to reply to this as she's made so much effort and that's really, really nice."

The "How To Get Published" competition the show ran with Macmillan received 46,000 entries. They had to hire trailers to store them all in and on the last day alone three post office vans turned up filled with packages. Amanda hired in extra staff and teams of readers to make sure that they were all looked at.

But she's also a realist. "There are only a certain number of people that can break through in any industry," she points out. "How many actors are there that are on the breadline? They are trying really, really hard to do it and it's never going to happen for them because there is only one Kate Winslet or one Maggie Smith or whatever and there's only room in the market for a few people to break through. And unfortunately that's true in publishing but I think I am trying to help other people make it and not just the obvious ones who are going to get big marketing spends anyway."

She says she knows quickly if what she is reading is good, often opening a book at random and reading the first sentences that catch her eye. Sometimes it draws her in – "I immediately care about the characters I'm reading about" while at other time it's "complete drivel".

She adored *The Time Traveller's Wife* (Jonathan Cape) but hated *Marley and Me* (Hodder). "The last three chapters are all about poo," she complains. "All about the dog's bowel movements. It was too much for me and I'm a dog-lover." We both pull faces at each other.

"So how does it feel," I ask, when we've unscrewed our noses, "to be the most powerful person in publishing?" Amanda pulls another face. "Very bizarre", she says. "It's bizarre to be the most powerful person in an industry that you cannot make a single penny out of." (She is prevented by Ofcom from gaining in any way from the massive book sales she creates.)

"It's weird when publishers think they can be rude to me or try and to bully me. I can't be bothered with it. When shops are critical or book-buyers are sniffy about my choices and stuff like that I just think: you're making money out of this! I don't know what your problem is."

It seems weird to me, too – you'd think they'd be showering her with adoration and lavish gifts. In fact I would have thought every author in the land would – where else could you go straight up the bestseller lists and make a packet almost overnight?

However, before we all get too carried away, let's remind ourselves of those 100,000 plus new books published each year.

The odds of yours or mine becoming one of only 16 *Richard & Judy* choices are probably somewhat longer than those of contracting Lassa Fever or bumping into Terry Wogan in Asda.

You therefore have to be prepared to take other steps to secure fame and fortune. You have to get out there and put yourself about.

Putting it About – The Art of Exposing Oneself

There are quite a lot of things you can do to get your book and yourself noticed. Unfortunately I have run out of room to give you all the gory details here – you will have to wait for the sequel – but they include, in addition to the book signings and author events already suggested, giving talks and after dinner-speeches, putting on workshops, going on the radio and TV, getting yourself in the tabloids (if you know anyone high-profile now is the time to start an affair) and carrying out publicity stunts.

I have done quite a lot of all of this (except the affair) with varying degrees of success and/or lying-awake-at-four-in-the-morning-cringiness.

But there's no time or space left to tell you about it now. If you're interested to know what really goes on behind the scenes of *Ready, Steady, Cook* or what happened when I met Tania, the-woman-who-has-shagged-a-hundred-men then buy another copy of this book (or a copy at all if you've been a cheapskate and borrowed it from someone). When I've sold a million copies, I'm going to write the next one: *Wannabe a Media Tart?*

If I only sell five, it will be called *Wannabe Poor?*

I will however, just before I go, give you my words of wisdom on book-signings:

Book Signings

"Get three friends to stand in line – the British will always join a queue…"

This is probably the best piece of advice I have ever received on the subject of "The Book-Signing" – that much-chronicled ritual humiliation that has even the most famous scribes offering their own most toe-curling memory of sitting in a wide space, behind a teetering tower of books, being studiously ignored.

But it only works if you have those friends to call on. In your home town, you can give a pal fifty quid and four different wigs and tell him or her to come in and out all morning, but what to do if you're not known in the area at all?

Then your only hope is that Mother's Day, Christmas or St Valentine's is around the corner and most of the shoppers are male.

Men, as we know, are notoriously bad at present-buying and easy to persuade that this year's must-have is a novel signed by the author.

Last Christmas Eve I sold twenty books in as many minutes to desperate husbands with a haunted look in their eye who knew the hours were running out and all they'd managed so far was the same Body Shop basket they'd got her last year.

Otherwise there's nothing for it but to make eye-contact and strike up conversation in your jolliest tones so that the hapless shopper cannot escape.

Handing out bookmarks can work well (as well as loving a queue the British also like a freebie) along with a cheery description of the book, hoping it is the sort that appeals. It doesn't always.

"This is a good book," I once said boldly to a stern-looking woman hovering by the best-sellers. She regarded me suspiciously. "What's it about?"

"Infidelity," I explained brightly, expanding as she stared at me blankly, "lots of fun, sexy, racy, all about what women get up to when the old man's not there…"

"I don't like that sort of thing," she said firmly. "Well, never mind," says

I, hurriedly changing tack, "cos really it's more of a romance – a love story in fact."

She was still unimpressed. "Don't like them either."

"What do you like?" I asked, as she tried to edge away and I prepared to highlight the sub-plot involving much adventure and intrigue in best thriller tradition and wondering if I could get away with describing it as a detective story. "Blood and guts," she said.

If people do home straight in on you, you can safely assume they think you're staff and want to ask where the Harry Potters are, but just occasionally they really have come to see you.

This can be awkward, too. At my last signing session a smiling chap arrived who looked vaguely familiar. "How are you?" he asked warmly, going on to enquire after my sister, husband and son, and to remind me of the helpful advice I'd given him last time we'd met. I didn't have a clue who he was.

Which I was getting away with nicely until he picked up a book and handed it to me for signature. "Can you put my name in it?" he asked.

For a long moment I sat, pen hovering, my mind blank. "Just remind me which way you spell it," I said at last, pleased by this stroke of genius. He looked at me strangely. "You know," I trilled desperately, "there are so many variations these days, I always check…"

He frowned. "B – O – B," he said.

Do You Need a Website?

If you're going to be a writer, it's a good idea. When you become a published author you can publicise your books, in the meantime you can publicise yourself.

I resisted having one for years since it seemed a rather self-absorbed, inflated-idea-of-own-importance thing to do (and I am more than capable of that without the help of the internet, believe me) but when my third book was coming out it felt – in some symbolic way – that the time had come. (I.e. I got fed up with people saying: "Why haven't you got a website? Here's mine" and thought I might be missing out.)

I soon found that creating a website is nearly as taxing as writing a book. "Have you got plenty of pictures?" asked Andy Harcombe, the brave and patient soul who designed mine.

I did have lots of pictures but...

Obviously it was probably best to draw a veil over the photo that appeared with the ill-advised interview in *The Star* (although I didn't – see it on my site – I am wearing a red feather boa and showing too much cleavage) and the one where I'm waving five packets of Trojan condoms could also fail to hit the right note.

Holding one's own books can appear a bit prissy and the one looking like a horse next to Edwina Curry might show one has mixed with the famous but was also an alarming shade of orange (these St Tropez tans are not all they're cooked up to be).

Can I also advise against photographs taken too long ago? You may meet someone who's seen you online.

"Oh," they will say, "you don't look like your photo," their faces showing they mean you look like your grandparent and that nothing had prepared them for your multiple chins.

And what do you *say*? Does anyone really want to know you have fourteen goldfish and a Shetland pony? Or the fact that one of your greater achievements was forcing someone to marry you?

Fortunately, Andy was extremely tolerant in the face of my dithering and general ineptitude, patiently setting up pages one day and taking them down the next, thus deleting the joke that seemed very funny after three glasses of Pinot Grigio but not quite so hilarious the next morning.

He did clever things like set up a shop where you can click on the covers of my books and zoom straight through to Amazon; and I did lots of irritating ones like constantly changing my mind over which photos were the least gross and wiping the diary page every time I tried to update it.

But together, eventually, we somehow produced **www.janewenham-jones.com**, giving me what I wanted most of all – a dinky little counter so I can see how many surfers have a look. My initial worry that this would be three (including my mum and two sisters) was unfounded when I had 1218 hits in my first week (a reflection I am sure, of my widespread fame and innate charm and nothing to do with the fact that I emailed everyone in my address book).

What you are supposed to have is a blog. I understand the trick is to include lots of salacious sexual details until you have millions of eager blog-readers logging on each day to see who you've shagged next until a publishing house emails to say could they turn it into a novel and an agent pops up with offers for the screen rights.

This may sound like the stuff dreams are made of but this is pretty much what happened to Mil Millington (not the shagging but the interest in his website) when *Things My Girlfriend And I Have Argued About* **www.thingsmygirlfriendandihavearguedabout.com** led to a newspaper column and his first novel of the same title (Phoenix Press).

And it took just a few weeks of blog-writing for Judith O'Reilly's *Wife of the North* – an account of adjusting to life in deepest Northumberland after moving from London – to be spotted by an agent. She has since landed a £70,000 deal with Viking Penguin.

So blogging could be worth a try. You might be discovered, too.

In the meantime, remember that journalists and commissioning editors often use websites to check out contributors – so it can be very handy to have one if you are intending pitching ideas to magazines and newspapers. Here are some website suggestions:

- Have links to any pieces of work that have been published. If these are in well-known publications, so much the better, but include the piece you wrote for *My Teapot* or *Nobody's-Heard-of-It Monthly* too. We all have to start somewhere.
- If nothing's published yet, post up something great that should have been.
- Include photos of yourself looking writerly.
- Try looking mysterious/gorgeous/sexy too.
- Ask all your friends with websites to put a link to yours on theirs (and return the favour of course).
- Start a blog and tell the world everything that happens to you.
- If nothing happens – make it up. You wannabe a writer, don't you?

Useful Info

Because I am all heart, I have listed below some of the websites I have suggested throughout this book and some other books and sites you might find helpful.

Useful Organisations to join
The Society of Authors **www.societyofauthors.net**
The Romantic Novelists Society **www.rna-uk.org**
Women in Journalism **www.womeninjournalism.co.uk**
The Media Society **www.themediasociety.co.uk**
The National Association of Writers' Groups **www.nawg.co.uk**.

Health
Complementary Therapies **www.bridgewaterretreat.co.uk**
Nutritional Advice (sensible) **www.optnutrition.com**
Diet advice (daft) **www.janewenham-jones.com/buggerdiet.htm**
RSI **www.abilitynet.co.uk**

Life Style
Life Coaching **www.anotherjourneybegins.com**
My friend Lesley's jewellery **www.coburgcrafts.co.uk**

Holidays and Writing Courses
www.arvonfoundation.org
www.writersholiday.net
www.writersconference.co.uk
www.real-writers.com
www.writersnews.co.uk/homestudy

Self-Publishing
www.troubador.co.uk/matador
www.halftitle.co.uk

Journalism
www.nctj.com

Research
www.expertsources.com

ME
www.janewenham-jones.com
Bring on those counter clicks

Magazines
Writers' News/Writing Magazine
www.writersnews.co.uk
The New Writer
www.thenewwriter.com

Books you must own
This one – obviously. (And why not buy one for a friend while you're at it? Ideal Christmas Gift etc.)

The Writer's Handbook and/or **Writers' and Artists' Yearbook** – invaluable information for every kind of writer

Other Books Worth Reading
Bestseller by Celia Brayfield
Comprehensive and readable. A bit more highbrow than this one (not difficult)
On Writing by Stephen King
Yes, THE Stephen King – it's a great book – full of wisdom
Pitch to Publication by Carole Blake
Useful advice from an agent
Any Novel by Jane Wenham-Jones
One Glass Is Never Enough
Perfect Alibis
Raising the Roof
– you might not learn anything but I could do with the sales

Thank you! ☺

STILL WANNABE A WRITER?

A Funny Game To Be In

So summing up, if you are a writer you are likely to be:
Broke
Bonkers
Bad-tempered
Unfit

With a Fat Bottom
Disgruntled family
And a lot of time on your own

You may feel:
Stressed
Exhausted
Disappointed
And begin to wonder what on earth you do it for

But when that acceptance comes and someone says

You'll know...

Wannabe a Writer?

What the experts say:

Starving in a garret is for Victorian junk fiction. Keep an income until you hit the incoming breaker and ride it to the shore. Then do it again. Then burn the old career. You have just become a novelist who can pay the rent.
Frederick Forsyth – Novelist

Convince me.
Jonathan Lloyd – Literary agent

Keep your paragraphs short, three sentences maximum. Always remember the five senses: What things feel like, taste like, smell like, sound like and look like. It immediately lifts a scene. Finally, use colour: "a man riding down a lane on a horse" is a dull sentence. How much more exciting: a man in a red coat, riding down a green, grassy lane, on a grey horse.
Jilly Cooper – Novelist

Go for it! You'll need faith in your abilities, a thick skin, a lot of luck, perseverance, the ability to take (objective) criticism without flinching, some good stories to tell…and friends to see you through the tough times!
Ian Rankin – Novelist

Establish first whether this is a passion or whether this is because you, mistakenly, think it's an easy way to make loads of money. If it is a passion of yours then you should follow your dream and never give up. But find a voice you're comfortable with.
Francesca Liversidge – Publishing Director, Transworld Publishers

Live a bit. Die a bit. Then you're ready.
Adele Parks – Novelist

Good idea! It's far better than working.
Richard Morrison – Journalist

Writing is damned hard work; getting published is harder still. And don't imagine that when you've done the first draft, that it's ready for publication. Just get on with it.

Jeffrey Archer – Novelist

You have to be fit. Fit so that you can work the long hours writing whilst still holding down a full time job, which will be the beginning of your career. Fit, so that your brain works and you can consistently come up with ingenious, innovative plots over and over again. Fit, so that you can cope with the long hours of gruelling, uncomfortable travel on promotional tours. Fit so that at the end of that arduous travel, you can smile and give witty and charming answers whilst being asked inane questions.

Jane Gregory – Literary agent

Read as many books as possible, keep a diary to get into the habit of writing and ENJOY writing – it's supposed to be fun.

Jacqueline Wilson – Children's author and Children's Laureate 2005–2007

If you're the type of person who enjoys solitude, anguish and anxiety – it's the ideal job.

Ariel Leve – Journalist

A fondly remembered conversation with a would-be writer.
W–W: I want to write a book.
Me: What's it about?
W–W: Er – no – I just want to write a book.

Mavis Cheek – Novelist

If you want to be a writer – write. Don't talk about it, bore your friends and family with it, or – heaven forfend – approach publishers about it without having written something. Don't wait for the muse to descend. Sometimes that just isn't going to happen. Learn your craft and then when you do get a fabulous idea you'll have the wherewithal to make something of it.

Susan Opie – Editorial Director, Harper Collins Publishers

Have big tits and get a ghost-writer.
Michael Buerk – Writer, journalist and broadcaster

Listen to advice (but only from people who know what they are talking about). Ignore your Aunty Mabel who says you are brilliant. Listen to any editor or agent or booksellers… don't necessarily take the advice but at least think about it.
Barbara Erskine – Novelist and short-story writer

Research is key. Will what you are writing appeal to people? It's a business, a retail business – and your book has to sell and appeal to more people than your immediate family and friends. Be advised by the editors you contact, and take all criticism as constructive. If your mum loves your book, but the 50 publishers you sent it to say otherwise – be open to the fact that possibly you need to work on it some more. Why not post the first chapter and a synopsis on one of these new-fangled blog-type websites and see what feedback you get? Also, enter every writing competition you can, online and in magazines. Check out the books section on the BBC website for starters. The more experience you get of writing the better.
Finally, there is a misguided belief that everyone has a book in them. Be warned – you may have a book in you, but before you put pen to paper or finger to keyboard think carefully. Would anyone other than you want to read it?
Sara-Jade Piper – Book-buyer

You mean: "I want to be a writer". Definitely try. You probably won't succeed, but that won't eat at you later; what will eat at you is not trying, then wondering what might have happened if only you had.
Mil Millington – Author

Don't wait. I wish I'd started years ago.
Margaret Kaine – Author

Get yourself an agent.
Eileen Ramsey – Novelist

If you are serious about getting a book deal, you need a Prada-clad American literary agent with the manners of an alley cat and the morals of Tanya Turner from *Footballers Wives*. Scares the shit out of English publishers and comes in handy for premiere party invitations and weekending in the Hamptons (no! not South or Little Hampton, darling!).
Keith Barker-Main – Author and columnist

Don't give up the Day Job.
Simon Trewin – Literary agent

Only do it if you feel you would be wretchedly unhappy with a great big gaping hole in your life without it. Do it for the sake of it, not for expectations of any financial reward. Don't believe what your friends and family say about your work.
Caroline Graham – Novelist and playwright

Writers write – just put it down on paper.
Alan Samson – Publisher, Weidenfeld & Nicolson

If you don't *have* to write, don't. There are far too many books out there anyway. If you *do* have to, never give up. Persistence and confidence (even if misplaced) are half the battle.
Catherine Merriman – Novelist and creative writing tutor

If you know what you're doing is good, keep on doing it. If you keep on banging on doors long enough, one day some bastard will open one.
Tamara McKinley – Novelist

I used to think there was some kind of magical "thing" that writers knew, but if there is I've never found it. Just hard work, determination and a thick enough skin to take the knocks.
Teresa Ashby – Short-story writer

How old are you? If you're young then I'd say have a go, but remember you do need a certain talent. I would have liked to be a footballer player or a rock musician but.... If you're forty or fifty and still aren't a writer, there's probably a good reason why not but that shouldn't stop you giving it a try.
Robert Crampton – Journalist

If you want to write on a specific subject and you don't know enough about it, find out! Fact and fiction are inexorably linked and the latter without the former will not produce a convincing story line, unless it is pure fantasy.
Liz Smith – Fiction Editor, My Weekly

At last you can make use of everything that has ever happened to you – the good and the bad.
Carole Stone – Author and networker

Get on with it then!
Karen Howeld – Journalist and writer

Read a lot. Sounds obvious, doesn't it? However, you cannot imagine how many would-be writers don't actually read very good writing! You should also read Stephen King's book *On Writing* and polish your own style (i.e. having read his book don't set out to be Stephen King) before sending it to an agent. A good agent can spot talent (as it is so rare!) and coax a novel out of someone who has written a brilliant short story for example. But we aren't alchemists. I can't do anything with your work until you write the damn thing, or make sure that the version I read is the very best you have in you. Harsh perhaps, but true, very true.
Grainne Fox – Literary agent

Work at it with all your heart, but never give up the day job until you have a publishing deal you can live on!
Sherise Hobbs – Fiction Editor, Headline

You need determination, not genius. Keep on writing and sending it off, though the latter is getting more difficult these days as most publishers will only accept work through an agent – and an agent usually doesn't want unpublished authors, so it's a vicious circle. Try submitting to new author competitions, you may strike lucky.
Bernard Knight – Novelist

You'll need courage, stamina, the hide of a rhinoceros. You'll have to be brave to send your creation out into the cold hard world of publishing and risk getting it sent right back to you – but if you never take that risk then you'll never have any chance of success.

Be genuine and don't try to copy the big sellers out now. Publishers are looking for the original, new voices, not pale copies of the big stars who have gone before. Your individuality and your individual voice is what will make you unique.

You'll need to learn to take criticism – so always remember you can't please everyone all of the time. Learn to distinguish between criticism and constructive criticism. Even with an editor, it is always *your* book. Feedback is a gift, so study it, even when it hurts. Take a deep breath, try to read it calmly and see if you can agree with it, learn from it.

What is it that Jack London said – 'You can't wait for inspiration. You have to go after it with a club'.
Kate Walker – Novelist

Am assuming here that the person has talent and ambition? In which case, I would wish them well. If not, then I'd do likewise, and also smile sweetly and ask them not to send me their manuscript to critique.
Lynne Barrett-Lee – Novelist

The old adage about inspiration (1%) and perspiration (99%) is SO TRUE... make that 0.1% inspiration. Take joy in what you are trying to do. As someone wise once said, all art should be 'self-delighting'.
Amanda Brookfield – Novelist

So you wannabe a writer. Sure, vanity and a desire to earn a fast buck for doing what appears to be very little in the way of hard graft are fair enough reasons for booting up – many a writer now in print was fuelled, at least in part, by just those transient motives when he or she started out. But when the nights grow cold and the rejection slips pile up, the guys and gals who more often than not make the breakthrough into print are those who would rather write than do anything else.

Once, not so long ago, the late Bernice Rubens asked a class of wannabes if they were prepared to live a large part of their lives enclosed in 'secondary reality', by which she meant alone in the back room with just you, a typewriter and the work in progress. An odd little shiver ran through the group as the implications of Ms Rubens' question struck home and a strange silence fell over all those who until that moment hadn't quite figured out what 'being a writer' really meant.
Hugh C. Rae/Jessica Stirling – Novelist

I always think the first 2,000 words of a novel are a doddle. It's the last 98,000 that are the bugger.
Catherine Jones – Novelist and Chair of Romantic Novelists' Association

You'll never know if you're any good until you try.
Melanie Whitehouse – Journalist, writer and editor

Everyone who wants to be a writer can be a writer. But what you do have to consider is whether you are writing for your own pleasure or because you want someone else to read it. If writing for publication in print – books, articles, scripts – decide who your target reader might be and study the most professional way to reach your market. Thorough preparation in that area will save you hours of heartache.
Judy Piatkus – Publisher, Piatkus Books

BE PROFESSIONAL – URGHHHH! But it does make a difference.
Teresa Chris – Literary agent

Do it!
Elizabeth Buchan – Novelist

Just start writing a journal. Do it for twenty minutes a day to begin with. Write about anything. If you get stuck just describe what you see around you. You may be surprised by where this takes you. Don't sell out. Write what you really want to write. If you do that then you will get some personal satisfaction from what you are doing – even if you never get published.
Alice Jolly – Novelist and creative writing tutor

Write about something you feel really passionate about; write about something that moves you – and make sure it's a really good story.
Maeve Haran – Novelist and journalist

Nobody has ever regretted time and energy spent in creating something new. Whatever happens, give it your best shot, be persistent, believe in yourself. But don't expect instant success. Like any skill it takes practice to do it well. Writing and being published are not the same thing – there are many other outlets for your stories or articles than the printed word. It is

extremely unusual to make serious money from writing, so if that's your motivation, forget it. Real writers do it because they can't help it.
Rebecca Tope – Novelist

What have you got to say? I have never been very interested in writing as just a job/end in itself/ticket to a free lunch. For an old fogey like me, I'm afraid writing is about fighting for something, be it a cause or simply the truth as you understand it.
Mick Hume – Journalist

It's a great job but don't make the mistake of thinking it's going to be easy.
Carole Matthews – Novelist

Stop talking about it and get on with it.
Daniel Blythe – Novelist

Be honest, can you write? If you can't there is no point carrying on. If you think you can (and others do too) find out what your market is and develop your own voice. Above all develop a thick skin and be prepared for lots of rejection. If you work hard enough, are persistent enough, and are lucky enough, you will succeed.
Julia Williams – Novelist

Don't be precious about your work. A successful novel is about you and your writing, but it's also about your agent, your editor, your copy editor and everyone else involved in producing that book. Agents and editors know what they're doing and if they want changes, make them.
Lesley Horton – Novelist

So you wannabe a writer? My best advice is to read, read, read and start with us – you'll be glad you did!
Hilary Bowman – Editor of *Writing Magazine*

Have a go, but question yourself as to what best would suit you in terms of genre, i.e. be true to yourself rather than jump on any commercial bandwagon that isn't your style. Ask yourself if you have the discipline to start and sustain an entire book (the synopsis is the "easy" part), and are prepared to shut yourself away to write. However good your agent or your publisher, no one can write the book for you. And can you do it again? And again? Be aware of the marketplace, which authors are working. And don't give up the day job!

Suzanne Baboneau – Publishing Director, Simon and Schuster

When people tell me that they want to be a writer, I slip them a tenner and say: "Do us a favour – there are too many of us already – just go and do something else instead, and here's a small inducement." If they keep the money and go away, but don't give up writing, and don't give the money back, I know they are born to be writers.

Miles Kington – Writer, broadcaster and columnist

STORY FIRST – STORY FIRST – STORY FIRST – STORY FIRST
Oh, and did I mention? STORY FIRST.

Sarah Harrison – Novelist and author of *How to Write a Blockbuster*

How thick is your skin?

Sue Moorcroft – Novelist and creative writing tutor

Every now and then someone tells me that they've got a great idea for a plot. But I don't think it's the great idea that's the thing – though it helps – it's actually getting the book down on paper – finishing it, making it into a coherent form, making it live. Also, if you're going to be a writer, you have to be able to work day to day on your own. Would you be happy with this? And you have to be able to withstand a lot of knocks – and sometimes quite public knocks. However successful you are, someone will reject your work/ give you a bad review at some time. I can't really see why anyone would choose to write unless they loved the actual writing, but I'm sure there are other writers who would disagree with me about this.

Judith Lennox – Novelist

Use your imagination and let it flow. Don't get too hung up on the minutiae of the manuscript. A rollicking good read will rise above the typos and occasional grammar/punctuation errors. Do it but remember that the likes of J.K. Rowling and Stephen King are the exception rather than the rule. If it's big bucks you're after then look for something else to do! Be professional!

Bernardine Kennedy – Novelist

So do I, mate.
Chris d'Lacey – Children's author

Never iron when you can write.
Lynne Hackles – Writer and creative writing tutor

Persist. And don't forget a big part of writing is rewriting. It's not glamorous and many people hate it but it's this one thing that often sets apart the professionals from the also-rans. Learn to be really tough about your own work: hone it, polish it, cut out any flab. Agents and editors will be tough when they read it, so the tougher you are before you send it to them the better.
Claire Calman – Novelist

Don't take the whole process too seriously. Don't take yourself too seriously. Maintain a normal life. Don't call yourself a writer until you get a book deal, Keep your head out of your bum at all times. That way, if you don't get a book deal you won't feel like a failure. It will just be an experiment that didn't work out. Pat yourself on the back for having the discipline and chutzpah to write a whole book. Then move on.
Lisa Jewell – Novelist

Ask yourself why you want to be a writer and what you have to say that will give people a reason to fork out good money for it. Research the market and read as much as possible, and work out why some books succeed and others don't. Find good characters and let them go.
Jane Judd – Literary agent

Keep going and even if everything is pants, don't stop writing. Grab every opportunity offered to you, even if you think it's too big a mountain to climb.
Pam Weaver – Novelist and short-story writer

Stay determined and don't let the bastards grind you down. Go for it.
Jan Henley – Freelance writer

Get an agent. Research the industry well and know where your book would fit in. And understand that writing is hard work – but that seeing your book on the shelves makes it all worthwhile.

Joanne Dickinson – Editorial Director, Sphere Books

Writer's bottom comes from sitting too long and glooming away, but if you're writing well the wiggles of joy work it off. You can tell who's a good writer and who's a bum one just by looking at their back view. That's my theory anyhow!

Biddy Nelson – Short-story writer

People who are going to be writers don't advertise the fact – such is the writers temperament that they tend just to get on with it quietly, almost secretively.

Isabel Wolff – Journalist and author

Take a long, cold shower. Dry yourself in front of a fire with a copy of *Madame Bovary* or *Anna Karenina* and if after reading both tomes, you say to yourself "this is a mug's game" – become a writer.

Jonny Geller – Literary agent and author

Want it enough. Find something that you know about and use it as a setting so you don't have to worry about authenticity. Then think up a really good story with characters you like or respect. And keep going!!!!!

Kate Fforde – Novelist

I'd say you're barking up the wrong tree. You should be telling me "I want to write" not "I wannabe be a writer". The latter suggests desire for an imagined lifestyle (often remote from reality), the former suggests total commitment to the craft.

Freya North – Novelist

If writing is what you really want to do, learn your craft by going to classes and NEVER give up!

June Tate – Novelist

Work out how many words you can write in an average hour so you have an instant easy way to work out how long a project will take you/how much you should charge for it. And if you get commissioned to write a book, don't start it – and certainly don't submit it – until you've got the contract sorted. Try to avoid selling 'all rights' if you possibly can – there's money to be made out there in international deals. And if you're a student, get involved with student press – it's a great way to get clippings and contacts.

Emily Dubberley – Writer and journalist

Why?

Margaret Penfold – Novelist

Try all forms of writing to find out what suits you. Your first choice might be wrong. I wanted to be a serious writer and spent fifteen years submitting about forty television dramas, without selling one. I also failed at novels, short stories and poetry. Eventually, in desperation, I finally tried comedy, and within six months was earning a living from it.

Raymond Allan – Script writer, *Some Mothers Do 'Ave 'Em*

You won't know whether you can do it until you sit down and do it – so stop talking about it and write it instead.

Caroline Caughey – Editorial Director, Hodder and Stoughton

I would say: try, try, try to write even just one sentence every day even when things are at their most difficult. Somehow this keeps your brain and your sub-conscious mulling over everything that you are working on and thinking about, even though you don't realise it.

Barbara Ewing – Novelist and actor

Start Writing. Send work off to agents. Don't be put off by rejection.

Jill Mansell – Novelist

Don't give up your day job, identify your market and read everything there is to read within that genre. Never say: I don't read because I don't want another author to influence my writing. Be aware of what is being published at the moment and identify where you want to be placed within the market. And then it's simply a case of dedication and determination.

Broo Doherty – Literary agent

Where's your notebook?
Penny Alexander – Writer

Therapy's cheaper.
Zoë Sharp – Photojournalist and author

Do it. Again and again and again if necessary. A born writer can't give up, even if he/she wants to at times.
Jane Bidder – Novelist

You are a writer if you write. So write.
Dorothy Koomson – Novelist and journalist

Write what you truly enjoy writing however bonkers or off the wall you suspect it is. Take time to learn your craft and don't give up.
Cari Crook – Writer, creative writing tutor and editor.

Make sure you want to write for its own sake – not because you think it's glamorous or easy, because it very rarely is. If you love writing, then publication and good reviews are the (unquestionably delicious) icing on the cake but the joy of telling stories will sustain you during the tough times. If you want a quick buck or fame, I'd suggest *Big Brother* over novel-writing every time.
Kate Harrison – Novelist, script writer and journalist.

Why be a Writer?
Because you can't think of anything else to do.
Because the only fully-functional body-parts you possess are your arse and your typing fingers.
Because you haven't noticed that one of the things which really, really helps make life go smoothly is a reasonable income, regularly received.
Because you have the social graces of a squid and the world has rejected you.
Because your motto is "It's not what I do that counts, it's what I say."
Because you did something awful in a previous life.
Michael Bywater – Author and journalist

Write, write and then write some more.
Lesley Gleeson – Writer, creative writing tutor and ex-literary agent

Get on with it. Bury that worm of self-doubt in the garden and pick up your pencil.
Hilary Lloyd – Novelist and short-story writer

DON'T! But if they keep on insisting I ask them why aren't they sitting down and writing.
Patrika Salmon, Writer and journalist, *Writer's News*

Write about what you know. Don't think about getting the work published or you'll be inhibited, write it for yourself or your grandchildren and be as flamboyant and true to yourself as possible. Get it written then get it right, i.e. don't go back time and again to polish or you'll never finish it. Just get it done then go back and play around with it, which for me is the really fun bit. Have confidence and belief in yourself, you only need one agent and one publisher so never give up. Read the best writers while you write, you never know, their genius might rub off on you.
Santa Montefiore – Novelist

You can be one, if you've got the determination to do a day job and then go home and write all night. To shut yourself off from friends and family. To wait months for a reply from an agent, only to be turned down. You can find fame quicker and easier by thinking up something to get yourself in the *Guinness Book of Records*.
Lesley Pearse – Novelist

Don't try to write someone else's book. Emulation and publishers' guidelines are all very well but they can fog you up if you stick with them too long. Mine your own being.
Most of us start writing because we love reading. Emulation goes with the territory. But you have to emulate your admired authors' spirit – not their structure, not their plot, above all, not their voice.
More and more publishers produce guidelines, particularly for commercial fiction. (They're supposed to reflect reader preferences and expectations.) Creative writing courses proliferate. So do How To books, some of them very detailed – and *very* prescriptive. Agents have their own ideas. So do

individual editors. So, God help us, will a critique group. Many conflict. The truth is, you can't please all the people all the time. At some point, you have to come out of research and development mode, break ground and start digging. In the end, your book's Unique Selling Point is the Unique Author's Vision.

Jenny Haddon – Novelist

Write about the things that you know about. It doesn't matter if they are dull, mundane or excruciatingly boring (see *Diary of a Nobody*) and if you don't know anything at all find a subject that nobody has a clue about (tripe, Morris Dancing etc) and make it your own property. Plagiarism then ensures that no other author can touch the subject and you have eliminated competition. An unploughed furrow offers a healthy harvest and all you need now is a lot of luck.

Bill Tidy – Writer and cartoonist

You must read and read and read other writers. You must keep turning up at your own blank page with unfailing regularity. You must practise the craft, for the process is as important as the word count. You must write because you must.

Laura Wilkinson, Editor & Kim Rooney, Assistant Editor – hagsharlotsheroines.com

Just keep going. As Samuel Beckett said, "No matter. Try again. Fail again. Fail better".

Irene Yates – Author, educational books

I would say, you have to like your own company and you have to find it thrilling rather than terrifying never to know where the next penny's coming from.

Flic Everett – Writer and journalist

Write about what you want to find out about, not about what you already know. It's more fun and less boring that way.

Tracy Chevalier – Chair of The Society of Authors

Find your own unique voice.

Gaynor Davies – Fiction Editor, *Woman's Weekly*

Go for it. Work hard. Be prepared to learn. Have a plan. Read well. Accept it could be a hard road. Be determined.

Merric Davidson – Literary agent

Do you wannabe a writer or do you want to write? A lot of people would like to have written a novel, fewer people actually want to write one (it involves way too much typing for starters). If you really want to write you will. Giving up TV frees a huge amount of time.

Sarah Duncan – Novelist

Fire ahead but until you have a sizeable scrapbook of your published work, don't give up the day job. And use the internet. If you're a journalist, find forums that match your chosen subject and contribute, contribute. Start arguments online, post think pieces. If you're a novelist, create a blog – you can be anyone you want to be.

Marina O'Loughlin – Food writer

Just get on with it. No excuses.

Judy Astley – Novelist

Write first and foremost from the heart, for the love of it and not just for commercial success. If you are passionate about what you do, I think there's a far greater chance that your readers will be too. Go for it! Writing can be the source of enormous, almost-unrivalled satisfaction, but be equally aware of the flip-side and, unless doing it purely for pleasure, that means a fair share of rejection and dejection.

Fiona Walker – Novelist and journalist

If you're serious, then work hard – write as often as you can, even if you can't get much done at each sitting – and enjoy it. Then, even if you never get published, you'll have spent time doing something you enjoy. Look at it that way and you can't lose.

Kate Long – Novelist

Get on with it then.

Wendy Holden – Novelist

To say "I want" is negative. Say "I will be." Then it will happen.
Sue Houghton – Freelance writer

Wannabe a writer? Apart from the obvious advice – don't – I can only endorse all the other advice you've been given, and will be given in the future. Read, read, read, write what you want to write and keep going. Never mind about those strict headmistresses who say "You must write at least 2000 words a day" or "Always write at the same time to get your mind in training". Writers' minds aren't like that. Do it your way, but keep DOING it!"
Lesley Cookman – Author

I don't think you can want to be a writer. I think you either are or you're not.
Amanda Ross, Richard & Judy Book Club

Do it. Really do it.
Helen Lederer – Actress and author

Lay in a very large quantity of snacks and put on some extra-large tracksuit trousers. You are going to be welded to your chair for a very long time.
Mel Giedroyc – Writer and performer

And what do I say?

Good Luck!
And thank you
for reading

INDEX

Wannabe a Writer?

Novel-writing Competition

Sponsored by Writers' Holidays and the Teresa Chris Literary Agency Ltd

Closing Date 31st December 2007

Judging Panel includes:

Jane Wenham-Jones
Literary agent Teresa Chris
Best-selling novelist Mil Millington

Write the opening pages of a novel and win a five-day writing course at Writers' Holiday in Caerleon, Wales, worth over £380. Includes a one-to-one tutorial with Jane Wenham-Jones plus publication on the *Wannabe a Writer?* website and the chance to submit your full manuscript to a top literary agent.

Conditions of Entry

1. Entrants are invited to write the beginning of a novel in any style or genre (maximum 1000 words). Entries should be the original, unpublished work of the author.
2. Entries should be in English, typed and double-spaced on one side of the paper only.
3. The author's name should not appear on the manuscript; please attach an official entry form (no photocopies please).
4. Manuscripts should be secured with a staple or paperclip. Please include the title of the novel on each sheet.
5. One entry per person.
6. Manuscripts cannot be returned.
7. The judges' decision will be final and no correspondence can be entered into.

8. Entries which fail to conform to these conditions may be disqualified.
9. No cash alternative to the main prize will be offered.

Copyright remains with the author but permission will be requested to showcase extracts from the long and short-listed works on the *Wannabe a Writer?* website.

The long list will be posted on **www.wannabeawriter.com** by 28th February 2008, the short list announced on the website by 31st March and the final winner notified by 30th April 2008. The prize of a five-day writing course will be offered at Writers' Holiday in Caerleon in Wales in July 2008. For further details see **www.writersholiday.net.** The prize includes an hour's private tutorial with author Jane Wenham-Jones. (Travel to and from the course is not included.)
Short-listed authors will be invited to submit their full-length manuscript to top literary agent Teresa Chris.

Wannabe a Writer?

Novel-writing Competition

Entry Form

Name . . . .

Address . . . .

. . . .

. . . . Post code . . . .

Phone number . . . .

Email address . . . .

Title of Novel entered . . . .

Word count . . . .

Please read conditions of entry carefully.

Good Luck!

About the Judges

Jane Wenham-Jones is a novelist, freelance journalist and author of *Wannabe a Writer?* (Accent Press). Everything you need to know about her is in there. For the totally insatiable she also has a website. **www.janewenham-jones.com**

Teresa Chris has been the agent for bestselling authors and wannabes for many years. She sells her books internationally and in her 'stable' she numbers several successful graduates of writing groups and conferences Always on the lookout for another 'gem' she is happy to work with those showing real potential.

Mil Millington is the creator of the cult website **www.thingsmygirlfriendandIhavearguedabout.com** and the author of three best-selling novels, *Things My Girlfriend and I Have Argued About, A Certain Chemistry* and *Love and Other Near Death Experiences,* all published by Orion. He also writes for various newspapers and magazines and was named by the Guardian as one of the top five debut novelists of 2002.

We hope you enjoyed *Wannabe a Writer?*

If you have a comment or query or are simply missing us already, then please visit

www.wannabeawriter.co.uk

to get the news, give your views, chat with other writers and much, much more...

With best wishes from Jane Wenham-Jones and everyone at Accent Press Ltd

Hope to see you online very soon

and

Happy Writing!

Notes

Notes

Notes

Notes

Notes

Notes

Notes

Notes

Perfect Alibis

Jane Wenham-Jones

*"Throughly enjoyable and full of deft,
sparky humour"* – Jill Mansell

Stephanie – bored housewife and disillusioned mother – wants a job, and Madeleine's recruitment company appears to be the ideal place to go. Except that PA's isn't quite what it seems.

Far from providing companies with Personal Assistants, the agency offers Perfect Alibis to unfaithful women. And as Stephanie soon discovers, there are lots of them about!

Founder member Patsy is a serial philanderer and there could even be a dark side to her best friend Millie. For the well-heeled ladies of Edenhurst, PA's is a ticket to risk-free adultery.

When Stephanie's first love, Troy returns to town even she is tempted. But her life is soon in turmoil, and that's before the tabloids get involved....

ISBN 1905170858 / 9781905170852
£6.99

One Glass Is Never Enough

Jane Wenham-Jones

*"Delightfully sparkling, like champagne,
with the deep undertones of a fine claret."*

Three women, one bar and three different reasons for buying it. Single mother Sarah needs a home for her children; Claire's an ambitious business woman. For wealthy Gaynor, Greens Wine Bar is just one more amusement. Or is it?

On the surface, Gaynor has it all – money, looks, a beautiful home in the picturesque seaside town of Broadstairs, and Victor – her generous, successful husband. But while Sarah longs for love and Claire is making money, Gaynor wants answers. Why is Victor behaving strangely and who does he see on his frequent trips away? What's behind the threatening phone-calls? As the bar takes off, Gaynor's life starts to fall apart.

Into her turmoil comes Sam – strong and silent with a hidden past. Theirs is an unlikely friendship but then nobody is quite what they seem in this tale of love, loss and betrayal set against the middle-class dream of owning a wine bar. As Gaynor's confusion grows, events unfold that will change all of their lives forever...

ISBN 1905170106 / 9781905170104
£6.99